COMING OF AGE IN A GLOBALIZED WORLD: THE NEXT GENERATION

J. Michael Adams and Angelo Carfagna

Kumarian Press, Inc.

Coming of Age in a Globalized World: The Next Generation
Published 2006 in the United States of America by Kumarian Press, Inc.
1294 Blue Hills Avenue, Bloomfield, CT 06002 USA

Production and Interior Design by Rosanne Pignone, Pro Production
Index by Robert Swanson
Copyedited by Brian Slatterly
Proofread by Beth Richards

The text for *Coming of Age in a Globalized World: The Next Generation*
   is set in Times Roman 10.5/12.5.
Printed in the United States of America on acid-free paper by Thomson-Shore, Inc.
Text printed with vegetable oil-based ink.

The paper used in this publication meets the minimum requirements of the American National Standard for Information Sciences—Permanence of Paper for Printed Library Materials, ANSI Z39.48–1948.

Library of Congress Cataloging-in-Publication Data
Adams, J. Michael.
Coming of age in a globalized world : the next generation /
     J. Michael Adams and Angelo Carfagna.
          p. cm.
     Summary: "This book is a primer on the impact of globalization and the case for world citizenship through global education. The authors stress the importance of global education as they seek to reconcile the contrast between national bonds and global interests"—Provided by publisher.
     Includes bibliographical references and index.
     ISBN-13: 978-1-56549-212-7 (pbk. : alk. paper)
     1. World citizenship. 2. International education. 3. Education and globalization. 4. Globalization—Social aspects. I. Carfagna, Angelo. II. Title.
JZ1320.4.A33 2006
303.48'2—dc22
                                                            2005028064

14 13 12 11 10 09 08 07 06 05   10 9 8 7 6 5 4 3 2 1

From Michael

*My portion of this humble effort is dedicated
to my best friend and wife, Susan Adams.
She sustains me in periods of challenge,
celebrates with me in moments of success, and
inspires me whenever we are together.
From my view, she is a true world citizen.*

From Angelo

*This book belongs to the globe and to my tribe.
It is dedicated to all those who hope—and act—
for a better tomorrow. It also belongs to Sharon,
who has given me the opportunity to hope and to dream.
And it is inspired most of all by Cheyenne and Damien,
who make me smile. May their hopes always prevail.*

CONTENTS

LIST OF ACRONYMS

ACE	American Council on Education
AFS	American Field Service
ECOSOC	United Nations Economic and Social Council
FBI	Federal Bureau of Investigation
FDI	Foreign direct investment
G8	Group of Eight (leading industrial nations)
GATT	General Agreement on Tariffs and Trade
GDP	gross domestic product
GNP	gross national product
IAEA	International Atomic Energy Agency
ICBL	International Campaign to Ban Landmines
ICONS ˙	International Communication and Negotiation Simulations Project
iEARN	International Education and Resource Network
IMF	International Monetary Fund
MLA	Modern Language Association
NCSS	National Council for the Social Studies
NGO	nongovernmental organization
SAP	structural adjustment program
UNA-USA	United Nations Association of the United States
UNCTAD	United Nations Conference on Trade and Development
UNDP	United Nations Development Programme
UNESCO	United Nations Educational, Scientific, and Cultural Organization
UNHCR	United Nations High Commissioner for Refugees
UNICEF	United Nations Children's Fund
USAID	US Agency for International Development
WHO	World Health Organization
WTO	World Trade Organization

INTRODUCTION

Have you ever returned to the old neighborhood to be stunned by how much had changed in your absence? When you lived there day after day, everything seemed to stay the same. The truth probably is that change was occurring, but it escaped your attention. We often do not recognize change when we are surrounded by it.

At other times, change rises up and slaps you in the face. After September 11, 2001, most Americans believed that they woke up to a new era. There was justifiable anger, surprise, rage, and sadness. We also realized there was much about the world and other people that we simply did not understand.

Whether dramatically or methodically, each day brings something new. Our world steadily shrinks, new technologies suddenly appear, and the quantity of information routinely overwhelms us. How do we figure it all out? What do we need to know? What do we need to do?

Those are the ultimate questions posed in *Coming of Age in a Globalized World: The Next Generation*. By now, most have heard the term "globalization" and many are generally aware that the world is changing, yet few understand the meaning and significance of what is occurring. This book, designed for use in and out of the classroom, introduces and describes the complex issues relating to globalization. It reconciles the contrast between love of country and global interests, and the opportunities and dangers in a world without borders. It invites and empowers you to claim your rights and responsibilities as a world citizen.

The essence of the case made in the book is fairly straightforward. The impact and implications of globalization are profound.

Through technological advances, we are literally closer to each other than we have ever been before in the history of our species. We can move physically across borders in just minutes and hours, and connect to each other in cyberspace in nanoseconds. Such closeness brings tremendous rewards. Our networks of connections can quickly transmit great ideas and benefits, but they can also rapidly spread conflict, disease, and devastation. And while we are increasingly connected, we still do not know very much about each other.

If you are going to survive and succeed, you must understand the changes taking place in your neighborhood and world. You must be able to adapt to different environments and work with diverse people. Whether you are an artist or an accountant, a security specialist or a software programmer, the fabric of your profession increasingly is woven with the interests of those from afar.

Beyond professional concerns, there is a moral and humanitarian imperative. Global problems and international threats cannot be overcome in isolation. The need to understand globalization and to be able to respond and adapt is perhaps the most crucial challenge facing humanity. While its processes are inevitable, the direction and the shape of globalization remain in our control. The future depends on developing a sense of agency, accepting responsibility to address global problems, and acting as world citizens. The future depends on the next generation being able to collaborate across cultures and nations to forge global solutions.

The origin of this work derives from our experiences at Fairleigh Dickinson University, which in 2000 adopted a mission to prepare world citizens through global education. We hope that the book helps prepare you to become a world citizen as well.

Coming of Age in a Globalized World: The Next Generation would not be possible without the efforts and guidance of too many people to mention. We thank first of all the professors, mentors, scholars, and friends who helped shape our worldview. Our colleagues at Fairleigh Dickinson University have provided wonderful support and direction. Mark Campbell offered the essential metaphor with his story about diner placemats and connecting the dots. In our research, we were greatly assisted by the extremely helpful and unfailingly courteous professionals at the Fairleigh Dickinson libraries, especially Kathleen Stein Smith. We are deeply indebted to Steve McCurry, an extraordinary photographer, whose incredible portraits adorn the cover.

Last, and most of all, we thank our families and friends for listening and always being there.

Enjoy the journey!

—*J. Michael Adams*
—*Angelo Carfagna*

A publisher's note: While the authors refer to themselves as "we" throughout the work, there are several instances of personal stories introduced with the pronoun "I." In these cases, the "I" refers to Michael Adams.

1

MAKING CONNECTIONS

Mankind are then divided into those who are still what they were, and those who have changed: into the men of the present age, and the men of the past. To the former, the spirit of the age is a subject of exultation; to the latter, of terror.

—John Stuart Mill
The Spirit of the Age, 1831

I have steadily endeavoured to keep my mind free, so as to give up any hypothesis, however much beloved (and I cannot resist forming one on every subject), as soon as facts are shown to be opposed to it. Indeed I have had no choice but to act in this manner, for with the exception of the Coral Reefs, I cannot remember a single first-formed hypothesis which had not after a time to be given up or greatly modified.

—Charles Darwin
The Autobiography of Charles Darwin, 1887

Connecting the Dots

Remember those connect-the-dots puzzles? Often printed on paper placemats in diners or restaurants, their purpose is to entertain children until the meal arrives. The goal is to trace lines between a series of numbered dots. If done correctly, an image eventually emerges—a house, a horse, a flower. From what first appear to be unrelated, random points, the lines acquire visual meaning. Something real and recognizable is created, and children often gleefully respond, "I see it."

Connecting the dots, finding patterns and relationships between seemingly unrelated ideas or events, can also be a useful adult skill. The result is a new view, new opportunities, or a new approach. The adult response, equally gleeful, might be, "I see how all this fits together—I get it."

1

As a society, we are flooded with information. It can be overwhelming, but it is critically important to find meaning. Ignorance is not bliss; it is dangerous. Without understanding relationships and connections, we are forced only to react to isolated events. We can never make decisions or act in a way that anticipates or takes advantage of trends or events. We must each therefore develop the ability to connect the dots.

Our world is increasingly connected, and globalization is an incredibly powerful phenomenon. It is also a concept that is little understood, with even less awareness of its implications. We are often told that events and ideas at one location can influence and initiate events in other locations. But what does this really mean, and how should we respond?

And, where do you begin to seek understanding about globalization? Is it with the International Monetary Fund (IMF) and the World Bank, with the *Economist* and its pages about world politics and national economies, or is it in local events? How do you, as in the children's game, connect the dots and form new patterns and understandings?

One problem with connecting the dots as an adult is that the dots continually move and change. New ones appear and old ones dim. Information dots about our world are not like the stars in the night sky. Every evening the stars move across the sky, but the basic picture remains the same. We can see the same patterns night after night. But in the reality of our world, new events and ideas are constantly emerging. The moment you think you understand, something else happens. The events of September 11, 2001, are a prime example. Americans thought they understood their world and their place in it, but suddenly disaster struck, and a new image emerged.

How can you gain understanding when the playing field is constantly in motion? One answer is to momentarily freeze the dots, gain an understanding from that pattern, and then be prepared to adjust it when new information appears. That was exactly Darwin's message in the quote above: Form an initial hypothesis, but be prepared to change your position with new information.

In mathematics, this is called a "construct." From available information, one creates a model, a frozen moment of understanding against which new ideas and alternatives are tested. When new data are added, the model evolves and changes. New data can either confirm the model or completely change it. It is important, however, to have a foundation from which to measure and make decisions about new events, ideas, or information.

This book will help provide that foundation. It offers the opportunity for you to form an initial construct about globalization—a framework from which to respond to your world. It introduces and explores key information and ideas about globalization to help individuals understand the links between their lives and the rest of the world, bringing together historic and contemporary events, discussions from different individuals, and research that, initially, might appear unrelated. But that is the point. All of us must learn to see relationships between seemingly disjointed pieces of information.

Looking Back to See Ahead

We know that we are in the midst of a revolution. Newspapers and magazines have convinced us it is so, and we see sweeping changes in all dimensions of human existence. The driving forces of globalization are technological changes that begin with the power of digital computing. We are living in the age of the Internet, the laptop, mobile telephones, iPods, dramatic advances in genetic science, and a longer list of trivial and significant programs and gadgets. These advances enable us to extend our reach faster and further than ever before.

If we are in a revolution, are there any historic periods similar to today, from which we can learn and suggest what is to come?

At the end of the 1980s, Professor Paul David at the Stanford Institute for Economic Policy Research asked an important question: What can we learn from studying the historical experience of technologically driven transformations that affected many elements of culture, commerce and society—as the digital information technology revolution is expected to do?

He found a series of changes like those happening now in the period leading to the twentieth century, connected with the development of electricity supply systems and the use of electric power for lighting, transportation, and a growing range of industrial and domestic applications. David reviewed the literature of that period, the popular press, trade and scientific publications, writings on business and commerce, and even themes in novels and periodicals. What emerged was an interesting picture, not only of the changes that were taking place, but the reactions of those immersed in the revolution.

We do not wish to oversimplify Paul David's work. In our view, it is a landmark study, and has been widely cited. But it is worth trying to summarize three of its particularly powerful and compelling conclusions. They form part of the context, or environment, in which to view globalization.

■ Conclusion One:
Large Systems Inherently Resist Change

Large "techno-economic" systems are characterized by significant inertia. They do not readily adjust to incorporate new ideas, and in fact resist change, even when there are economic actors on the scene who are visionary advocates of innovation. This is so in large part because such systems typically have been built up from many complementary components. It is therefore necessary to alter, or scrap and replace, many things that are still working well, before the system can be reconfigured around the new technology and become commercially successful.

The processes of technical integration and organizational adaptation themselves are likely to be disruptive, requiring learning new ways of working. Instead of being accomplished overnight, the "revolution" may extend over two or more generations.

■ Conclusion Two:
The Real Transition Costs Are Initially Hidden

When major transformations are first getting under way, they usually become quickly identified with some new artifact that embodies the core innovation—the hardware of the new technology, such as "the electric dynamo," or "the computer." Understandably, individuals and organizations often suppose that by acquiring the hardware, they will enjoy the benefits of "joining the revolution." Yet that is only the simplest and most quickly accomplished part of the transition. Learning how to exploit the new technology effectively for particular purposes is a far more complicated and costly process.

Thus, today, a firm introducing new digital information technologies into its core business activities will find that the cost of purchasing the necessary computer equipment and software actually represents only 10 percent of the total costs it will incur to make a successful transition. Forty percent will be spent in training and recruiting an upgraded workforce, and the remaining 50 percent will be incurred in reconfiguring the organization to effectively use the new tools.

■ **Conclusion Three:**
   Change Grows with Irresistible Momentum

By the same token, once change gets under way concurrently in a number of critical areas, the incentives for adaptation in other, lagging areas and enterprises become much stronger. This happens either because new opportunities for incremental change have larger and more immediate payoffs, or because the laggards become exposed to competitive pressure from the leaders.

Thus, the transformation acquires increasing momentum, and its impact upon the economy and society eventually become readily discernible—but later than most people expect, and well after skeptics have declared "the revolution" to be an illusion or a scam (David 1990).

* * *

Paul David's work is an important first dot of information for your construct. He suggests that there are historic precedents from which to anticipate the future. We should not be surprised that large systems resist change. So do we, as individuals.

As John Steinbeck wrote in *Travels with Charley in Search of America* (1962), "It is the nature of a man as he grows older . . . to protest against change, particularly change for the better." But change is hard for young and old alike. Even a character who seemingly epitomizes youthful restlessness, like Holden Caulfield in J. D. Salinger's *The Catcher in the Rye* (1951), wishes to sometimes stop the motion around him: "Certain things they should stay the way they are. You ought to be able to stick them in one of those big glass cases and just leave them alone. I know that's impossible, but it's too bad anyway."

Holden's anxiety is understandable. Change brings the unknown, which is uncomfortable and even fearful. We are creatures of habit and fiercely resist change, especially in the face of major, rapidly developing movements. But we need to confront our fears and adjust to new realities. And we must shape our institutions and the systems in which we operate to reflect these new realities. We cannot ignore globalization and the obviously-developing world community. Our creative prowess threatens to race ahead of our sense of understanding. That has probably always been the case. That is why David observes that the full impact of a revolution takes two or more generations.

Even when we acknowledge change, we often only do so at a superficial level. As David explains in his second point, buying the new toys of the revolution is not the same as adjusting a mindset or viewpoint. And it is that mindset, that attitude, that will ultimately determine whether globalization produces positive or negative outcomes.

Finally, David's conclusion about the power of increasing momentum emphasizes what globalization realists have been saying all along: There is no turning back.

A New Reality

Globalization is altering nearly every dimension of our lives. But we are failing to keep pace. Sure, we see lots of dots—new technology, more international connections, lots of hype, new products, new modes of business. But we sometimes feel secure remaining in the old mindset. We sometimes miss the big picture while playing with the new gadgets of the modern age. Some recall earlier, simpler lives with longing, and believe they can resist or ignore what is happening.

Early in the Industrial Revolution, a group of individuals believed exactly that. They were called Luddites, named after their inspirational hero, Ned Ludd. New technologies were revolutionizing England's textile industry. New tools, such as the spinning jenny and flying shuttle, were rapidly replacing workers' jobs. Far from ignoring change, Luddites used violence to try to turn back the clock. They set about to systematically destroy the new tools that were changing the form and character of industry, believing that they could prevent change and maintain the old way of life. They were exactly wrong. The Luddite movement was swept away by a tidal wave of manufacturing innovation and new ways of doing business.

Corporations around the world have bought into the hardware of the new digital technology, using it to lower costs and increase profits. But many individuals and corporations have yet to understand that another wave of change in behavior, organization, and attitudes is happening. Paul David's unstoppable momentum of change is under way.

We need to reconfigure our way of thinking to adapt to globalization. And we all need to make the adjustment—not just CEOs of multinational firms, politicians, or international traders, but all of us. The need becomes apparent when the power of globalization is studied. Moving with unprecedented force, globalization can bring tremendous benefits, but it also can cause untold havoc. The dangers are real and the threats are seemingly everywhere. And because so much is truly interconnected in our world, we may not have the luxury of multiple generations to adapt to globalization.

By understanding what is happening, by connecting the dots, you become empowered to not only react to the changes taking place, but to actually direct them. If you understand, then you can influence the forces of globalization to improve individual lives and our world.

The goal is for you to "get it" about globalization. But in saying that, we understand that individuals may see different patterns in the same points of information. That is okay. It is natural for people from different backgrounds with different roles to see globalizing forces differently.

Points of View

Your point of view shapes your world and your place in it, and it can be anything from an opinion on a particular issue, to a perspective that reflects your cultural, economic, or social background, to your overall attitude about life. Growing up on the plains of central Illinois, I thought I knew where the world ended. I could see it seven miles away at the horizon. And I thought I knew my place in that world. Education changed that. My upbringing, however, defined my first point of view.

Your attitudes and assumptions can expand or influence how you view life, and how you react to it. Consider these starkly different points of view. Some will recall Voltaire's *Candide* (1759), with the memorable Dr. Pangloss. Pangloss was an incurable optimist, believing that "all is for the best," and this is "the best of all possible worlds." Candide adopted that point of view, which led him to accept a wild assortment of tragic and outrageous events with quiet resignation.

Then there is the point of view endorsed by Machiavelli in *The Prince* (1513). His fundamental message was that the ends justify the means. Machiavelli believed, with ample evidence, that those who did what was morally right and acted virtuously would, more often than not, bring about their own ruin. Such ruthlessness has its advocates today, but it is a view that leaves little room for embracing humanity.

History and literature are full of points of view across a spectrum of possibilities, each of which has influenced and guided individual reactions. In direct contrast to Machiavelli, Gandhi believed that if the right means were used, the ends would take care of themselves. Different points of view; different reactions to the world.

Your point of view is most strongly influenced by those closest to you—your parents, your friends, and your teachers. That seems obvious and natural. But should the development of a point of view stop there? How many of us consider that our point of view should also be affected by a peasant farmer in Peru, or a little girl working in a sweatshop in China?

Technology has shrunk our world. Developing a point of view without an appreciation of those distant and different from us is sure to result in a very limited perspective of both ourselves and our world. And that is a prelude to failure, even tragedy. To cooperate with others and learn from them, we must take the time to understand their viewpoints and their perspectives.

You might have read accounts, diaries, or journals of early American explorers and pioneers journeying through lands occupied by Native Americans. While there are countless descriptions of these "strange primitives," you would be hard-pressed to find anything even resembling consideration for or contemplation of their point of view. The outcome of violence and devastation was preordained by the Europeans' inability to put themselves in the place of the inhabitants.

The same problem is apparent today. When your point of view is limited, and when you refuse to consider an alternative, the future is foretold.

Your Viewpoint Determines What You See (And What You Don't)

Sounds obvious, right? But consider that what you see and what you don't see define how you solve a problem and what solutions are available to you. Limited view, limited options, limited future. This applies on a personal as well as a global scale. Much hangs in the balance. It is a very big deal.

The position or attitude from which you consider an individual, idea, or event shapes and forms what you perceive as reality. The key is to understand the personal, societal, and cultural biases that influence your perception.

In *Reframing Organizations,* the noted authors Lee Bolman and Terrence Deal introduced the idea of "frames," or ways of viewing organizations.

> All of the work on organizational learning converges around the basic idea that our ability to make sense out of a complicated and ambiguous world depends very much on the frames or mental models that we bring to the task. (Bolman and Deal 1997, 28)

Individual upbringing, experiences, associates, and education influence how we "see." Among their many insightful observations, Bolman and Deal offer that in Japan, there are four major religions, each with its own beliefs and assumptions:

Buddhism	Confucianism
Shintoism	Taoism

Though the religions are very different in their history, traditions, and basic tenets, many Japanese feel no need to choose only one. They use them all, taking advantage of the strengths of each for suitable purposes or occasions (Bolman and Deal 1997, 34).

This is a fascinating, radical concept from our Western point of view. In the Judeo-Christian tradition, we are taught a monolithic view of the universe and the world. There is only one God. There is only one truth. As Janet McIntyre-Mills has observed, "Linear thinking and 'either or thinking' continue to be the mainstays of Western thinking and problem-solving" (McIntyre-Mills 2000, 44).

We are trained to look for and expect one answer to any specific issue, problem, or question. The concept of simultaneous "truths" is confounding. From an Asian point of view, however, there is no contradiction.

The Indian religion known as Jainism, originating some six centuries before Christianity, is another more multidimensional approach. The Jains subscribe to the "Doctrine of Maybe." Something may be true, false, both true and false, and indescribable all at the same time. There are few absolutes.

Perhaps Westerners could gain from an increased ability to accept multifaceted explanations and adopt different points of view, depending upon the need or subject.

Bolman and Deal further suggested that all contemporary theories of management and organization fall into one of four basic views.

- In the *structural frame,* formal structures and organizational systems are the key to development, and people are peripheral to the process.
- In the *human resources frame,* people are viewed as vital resources who determine whether a company is successful.
- In the *political frame,* organizations are political arenas in which individuals and groups fight for power.
- In the *symbolic frame,* symbols express an organization's culture, and problems are solved by offering inspiration and meaning.

The view or "frame" one uses influences how one sees and reacts to a particular problem or situation. Any given frame is neither right nor wrong. Each simply allows an individual to translate what they see into meaning, and therefore make a decision or move to action.

Problems occur when people become trapped in their frames and are unable to consider other ways to view problems and devise solutions—or, worse, when they fail to even recognize the frames they use. People who view their company (or their world) as one big family and people who view their company as a political jungle will inevitably not share everything in common, but can they live and work together peacefully? It depends on how well they understand each other's point of view, and how tolerant they are. In the same way, people who uncritically pay homage to globalization will never be able to work with those who see it as the source of all evil.

Often when we credit someone for "thinking outside of the box," we are acknowledging that we too often limit ourselves to bounded frames and limited points of view. Going beyond the usual borders to envision things differently opens up a whole new world. As McIntyre-Mills has argued,

> It is essential to think in terms of the *interconnectedness* of social problems and achieve the intellectual dexterity to see the connections and avoid thinking in terms of categories or boxes. At least this will enable us to see what we can do to address the bigger picture. (McIntyre-Mills 2000, 102)

The idea that your viewpoint determines the scope of your vision—and, in fact, the extent of your reach—is critically important. Your frame influences what stands and actions you take. Alter the frame, and your future is changed.

All of your previous life forms a framework for viewing the world. You must, however, be able to adjust and view issues from different frames—even be able to see a problem through the eyes of someone with a completely different background. Without that ability, world problems will never be solved, because we each think our viewpoint and solution are "right."

My thesis advisor, Jacob Stern, told a story about taking a group of Midwestern farmers to a developing country on a project for the US Agency for International Development (USAID). The goal was to assist local farmers to improve food production. In one village, the American "experts" found terrace farms. Local farmers cut a flat area into the hillside, proceeded up the hill a bit, and cut another flat area, forming steps. They would then plant in the horizontal spaces.

The Americans immediately told the locals they were doing it wrong. "You must practice contour farming, plowing with the outline of the hill. Do away with those plateaus," they said. The villagers did exactly that and planted seeds. During the next major rainstorm, the entire surface of the hillside slid down into the valley.

Sometimes our viewpoint results in arrogance, reflected by the belief that our way is the only "right" way. In reality, there might be many different "right" ways.

Developing a Global Point of View

The dean of a leading art and design school would often ask prospective students why they thought they wanted to be designers. The most common answer was, "Because I am very good at drawing."

Wrong answer. Anyone can learn to draw. The foundation of a great design education—indeed, any type of education—is not technique, but forming and expressing a point of view.

Great artists and designers have a point of view. They see the world from particular perspectives, and interpret what they see in new, creative ways. They use their abilities to draw not to copy their world, but to interpret it through particular lenses.

Like many artists, Picasso began in realism. He painted pictures of objects, seeking exact duplication of reality through his craft. His early work is interesting, but not great. Only as he developed a point of view of the world and the relationship of his work to it did Picasso become a world-class artist.

In education, a point of view comes from "connecting the dots." It comes through exploration and immersion in ideas from different times, cultures, and experiences. In an era of globalization, what is needed to fulfill the promise of tomorrow, to even have a tomorrow, is a global education.

Education thus far has done a poor job of helping us to understand and direct the forces of globalization. But a global education encourages you to connect the dots of your contemporary world, with attention to the global as well as the local. Failing to develop your own viewpoint, or developing a construct in isolation, leaves you myopic and mystified. We need to understand the links between people and events in a globalized world. Understanding how to connect the dots, combined with the skill to continually adapt and adjust multiple views, positions you as a world citizen. And once those connections are made mentally, then the real connections—the personal bonds between peoples and across cultures—can blossom.

The purpose of this book is to help you understand globalization and develop a point of view. Connecting the dots will encourage a global outlook that appreciates and respects other perspectives throughout the world. Such an outlook will enable and compel you to work alongside others from different backgrounds to improve our world.

As we learn how to respond to the changes around us, we should look to a global education as the foundation from which to develop global views, attitudes, and outlooks. A global education enables us to measure our roles and our duties aboard this flying sphere.

Of course, one of the unavoidable realities on a planet filled with six billion other humans is that there are bound to be conflicting views. Globalization magnifies these clashes and brings the good and bad directly in our sights on a daily basis.

In this era, to celebrate what is good, to confront what is bad, and to overcome whatever challenges await, a new type of citizen must emerge. This citizen must be able to balance the local identities that provide cultural distinctiveness and emotional sustenance with the global connections that make apparent our shared humanity and fate. In short, the citizen for tomorrow—the citizen of the next generation—must be a world citizen, aware of commitments that stretch beyond borders and needs that know no boundaries.

Active world citizens are able not only to make connections among pieces of information; they are able to cross boundaries and connect with people from different backgrounds who have different worldviews. These connections are the only way to effectively respond to international challenges and crises. They are the best hope for a future marked by peace and tolerance, rather than violence and prejudice.

If we understand what globalization entails, learn to develop global viewpoints, and embrace our role as world citizens, the future is truly in our own hands. Globalization will continue and there is much to discuss, but the real story is how globalization affects individuals, and how we as individuals understand the changes and act within this new environment. The real story is how we change and what we do. And no matter how forcefully the current of globalization flows, there are ways that, united across borders, we can sail peacefully and with prosperity.

This book hopes to set a course for that adventure.

References

Bolman, Lee G., and Terrence E. Deal. 1997. *Reframing Organizations: Artistry, Choice, and Leadership*. Second edition. San Francisco: Jossey-Bass.

David, Paul A. 1990. The Dynamo and the Computer: An Historical Perspective on the Productivity Paradox. *American Economic Review* 80, no. 2: 355–361.

McIntyre-Mills, Janet J. 2000. *Global Citizenship and Social Movements: Creating Transcultural Webs of Meaning for the New Millennium*. Amsterdam: Harwood Academic Publishers.

2

IT'S A NEW WORLD!
SO, WHAT ELSE IS NEW?

Two thousand years after Christ's obscure birth in a dusty town in Judea, the world's six billion people . . . rode their turning blue planet across time's invisible line today and, by common consent, looked into the dawn of a new millennium. What they saw first was a party. It was garish, glittering and global, and millions, setting religious considerations and personal concerns aside, joined in the festivities to celebrate the conjunction of a new year, a new century and a new thousand-year cycle of history.

—*New York Times*
January 1, 2000

Are We the First?

Humans are fascinated with the digits zero and one.

We each celebrate one birthday every year. For most individuals, it represents a brief opportunity for a party, with a candle-adorned cake and gifts. There are landmark years, however, that attract special attention: thirty, forty, and fifty, for instance. For many people, their thirtieth, fortieth, and fiftieth birthdays are moments of woe and loss. Why are there not the same sensations at birthdays twenty-nine, thirty-nine, and forty-nine? Does anyone really notice a physical or intellectual change between forty-nine and fifty? Of course not.

So, why the emotional response? Because we are fascinated by zeros. Irrational and insane, but true.

But our real obsession is with the number one. We like being first. We believe being first means being unique. The first to fly across the Atlantic, the first to climb Mount Everest, the first in our neighborhood to own the latest technological marvel—we like being

15

unique. Annual sales of *The Guinness Book of World Records* document the inexplicable human fascination with being the first, the biggest, or the fastest.

In a similar manner, we often cherish that our conditions, situations, or challenges are unique, even if they are bad: "Ain't nobody seen the troubles I've seen." We like to believe that we are the first to pass through a particular environment or experience. It makes us feel special. The reality, however, is that new emotions, experiences, or sensations are probably quite rare. After all, modern humans have been around for well over a hundred thousand years. That is sufficient time for many replications.

And then we had January 1, 2000. All of our fascinations aligned. The arrival of the new millennium inspired a worldwide celebration. Imagine, three zeros in a row and the first day of a new thousand-year cycle (well, technically the first day of the last year of a thousand-year cycle, but let's not quibble over that one). Our world, our societies, had made it to another landmark. The event created a worldwide sensation that we were in a revolutionary and unique period in the history of humanity. Triple nulls, a once-in-a-millennial occasion.

Our age is indeed unique, and our world is certainly revolutionary, but not because of the movement of the clock, a new page on the calendar, or the convergence of three zeros. Rather, it is about efficiency, effectiveness, and the speed of channels of communication, commerce, and ideas.

New Year's Eve 2000 was absolutely the first global celebration. We watched on television as different countries, cultures, and peoples celebrated the rotation of our earth around the sun as the clock ticked to midnight, local time.

This same global communication system has helped produce a mass consciousness that we are entering a new era—the era of globalization. Frank Lechner and John Boli, editors of *The Globalization Reader,* observed that "underlying the various nuances of the term [globalization] . . . is a shared awareness that the world itself is changing" (Lechner and Boli 2000, 1).

With this shared awareness—illustrated by the unmistakable realization on that New Year's Eve that we were all citizens of the world—has come a global sentiment that we are sailing into uncharted waters, at the mercy of the powerful tide of globalization.

This sentiment has validity and raises many questions about how we should prepare and respond to this changing world. But if we are to educate ourselves to face a new world with an understanding of all that is different today, we must first humbly appreciate the fact that we are not the first to explore such frontiers.

There is nothing magical about three zeros in a row.

Maybe We're Not Unique

In 1935, the American philosopher and educator John Dewey wrote, "Transformations in the family, the church, the school, in science and art, in economic and political relations, are occurring so swiftly that imagination is baffled in attempt to lay hold of them" (Dewey 1935, 56).

The statement could easily be from any current newspaper column. It is clear that we do not have to go far back in history to see that others felt equally adrift in a whirlpool of change.

We are not as unique as we think. As the Greek philosopher Heraclitus wrote some twenty-five centuries ago, "Nothing is permanent except change." It is trite but true: Change is the only constant.

It is less common, however, for entire cultures and societies to recognize that they are part of a significant alteration in human relations, as we seem to recognize today, at least on a general level. Most often, societies have simply gone from day to day, and it is only with the perspective of history that we can trace pivotal movements or critical moments.

Historians have helped us to chronicle the history of humanity by labeling certain eras. The Middle Ages, the Renaissance, and the Enlightenment, for example, are terms invented by historians to describe periods of great change. During these times, however, while some may have been cognizant of history's motion, most were probably unaware of how their world was changing.

There have been notable exceptions, however. In particular, during times of war and crisis, savvy individuals appreciated that the pendulum of history was about to swing one way or another.

"The war to end all wars" in 1914 brought perhaps the first mass sensation of global transition. Linked with new and terrible technologies of conflict—tools that killed human beings with alarming effectiveness—everyone knew that the world was different. Similarly, the climactic events of World War II undoubtedly convinced many that their lives would never be the same. World War II was much more of a global battle than World War I, but in both cases, it was telling that the epic dramas were labeled as "world wars." Humanity recognized that it was coming together and acting on a global stage.

Change Always Wins

Wars are dramatic evidence of change in both individual lives and countries affected by conflict. Violence, however, is not the only harbinger of change. Many positive events and innovations formed the foundation for alterations in the condition and character of human existence.

One of the most significant examples is the development of print communications. In the thirteenth century, the Western world was introduced to paper money and playing cards from China. The technique and technology were block printing. Chinese characters were carved into a wooden block, ink was added, and the words were transferred to paper. The process was tedious and expensive.

In the middle of the fifteenth century, a revolution began with the development of movable type. Johann (Gansfleisch) Gutenberg, in Mainz, Germany, is credited with the invention. The mirror image of individual letters rather than entire words was cast on a small block. The letters moved easily and could be placed together to form words. The words were then formed into lines of type, which made up the pages. By reusing and rearranging pieces of type, an endless assortment of texts could be printed.

Within a half-century of Gutenberg's 1455 Bible, the use of movable type produced revolutionary changes. It became much cheaper to produce books. Intellectual interests were broadened as more people had access to information. Society was transformed (McKay, Hill, and Buckler 1983, 437).

Federico of Montefeltro, Duke of Urbino, was a brilliant and cultured political leader, general, and humanist. He came to power in 1444 and ruled until his death in 1482, presiding over a prosperous and culturally rich court that is often acknowledged as one of the most magnificent of the Italian Renaissance. One of the focal points for this enlightened leader was his library, which was filled with classical works and books devoted to religion, philosophy, medicine, mathematics, music, and other fields. Federico passionately searched everywhere for fine manuscripts to add to his growing collection, with a decided preference for handwritten volumes with artistic bindings that he felt were aesthetically superior to anything that could be done with the new printing technology. In fact, it is said that he would not even look at a printed book.

The result was that, by the time of Federico's death, his library was filled with nine hundred beautifully produced volumes that drew the attention of scholars throughout Europe. Not bad, but consider what the library could have become if he embraced the new print technology. Ignoring or discounting an innovation does not make it go away.

It is impossible to oppose world-sweeping revolutions of technology and change, although, like the Duke, many certainly were prejudiced against print at the end of the fifteenth century. They recognized that profound change was under way, but refused to adapt. For his part, the Duke of Urbino would have been better served if he had embraced and influenced the printing press. His impact could have been profound. Few today recall his library, which was rendered comparatively small by the development of the printing press and eventually absorbed into the Vatican's collection.

In his efforts to resist change, Federico could be labeled a Luddite. They exist in every era of change. The print revolution in general certainly had its share of detractors, as globalization does today. All revolutions do. But Luddites never seem to grasp that it is ultimately futile to resist powerful forces of change.

Author James Burke accurately described the revolutionary change enacted by print technology:

> The coming of the book must have seemed as if it would turn the world upside down in the way it spread and, above all, democratized knowledge. Provided you could pay and read, what was on the shelves in the new bookshops was yours for the taking. The speed with which printing presses and their operators fanned out across Europe is extraordinary. From the single Mainz press of 1457, it took only 23 years to establish presses in 110 towns: 50 in Italy, 30 in Germany, nine in France, eight in Spain, eight in Holland, four in England, and so on. (Burke 1978, 105)

The process of learning was enormously enhanced by this development. Previously, books were the exclusive property of the elite, particularly the clergy. But now students could buy their own books, and information was readily accessible to vastly greater numbers than ever before. Between 1450 and 1517, seven new universities were established in Spain, three in France, and nine in Germany; six new colleges were established at Oxford in England (McKay, Hill, and Buckler 1983, 439).

Printing also meant that ideas critical of the establishment could be disseminated much easier than before. For example, the publication of Erasmus's *The Praise of Folly* (1509) helped launch the Reformation, while after 1517, the printing press contributed to the spread of Martin Luther's views. The printed word eventually influenced every part of human society.

It can be argued that the printing press brought the world closer together and ushered in an earlier era of globalization. And it is also commonly understood that many discerned the significance of the changes. Were there other times when people recognized a seismic shift in social, economic, and political relations?

Globalization, Act I

Toward the end of the nineteenth century, another nonviolent wave of change occurred, paralleling our modern-day onslaught of globalization. Like today, these changes resulted in greater economic connections and fewer barriers to travel and trade. Also like today, this era was primarily fueled by technological advances in transportation and communication. Historians call it the Industrial Revolution.

Refinement and broad utilization of the railroad, the telegraph, the telephone, and the steamship brought people and ideas closer together. Huge quantities of goods could be shipped farther, faster, and cheaper than at any time in human history. The immediate result was to alter and disrupt local economies.

Some labeled this the "first globalization." Writing in the *New York Times,* David Feldman notes,

> In many ways, the first globalization was more profound and transforming than our contemporary experience. The technological forces that altered the American landscape from rural-agricultural to urban-industrial also bound together international markets for raw materials, agricultural products and manufactured goods. (Feldman 2002)

Labor became transient to an extent never before seen. In fact, the number of workers moving across countries was greater than today. There were no passports and few restrictions on immigration, which led to one massive migration after another. As Feldman (2002) writes, "The transportation revolution facilitated the mass movement of people from low-wage regions of Europe to high-wage lands in the Americas and Australia." From 1878 to 1914, approximately sixty million people sailed from Europe to North America and Australia (Yergin and Stanislaw 2002, 385).

Not only could people travel cheaper and faster, they could keep better track of overseas investments. As the *New York Times* reported, economics professor Jeffrey Williamson said the volume of trade "was comparable to what one observes now . . . The barriers to trade were much lower than they were until very recently" (Stille 2001).

Exports as a percentage of world gross domestic product (GDP) rose from 5 percent in 1870 to 8.7 percent by 1913 (Taylor 2002). As economist Michael Bordo said, the level of economic integration was in some ways greater than today. "Before World War I, half of British savings were invested overseas, far more than the US or any European country now does. Levels in Germany, France, Belgium and the Netherlands weren't far off" (Stille 2001). Indeed, "at its peak, the capital outflow from Britain reached 9 percent of GNP [gross national product], and was almost as high in France, Germany and the Netherlands" (Masson 2001, 3).

At the time, many realized great changes were under way in the world. Yet the experiment in trade liberalization crashed to a halt with an act of terrorism in 1914—the assassination of Archduke Ferdinand of Austria—and the outbreak of World War I. There is much reason to believe that increased trade competition stimulated the growth of nationalism, which aggravated tensions between nations. In addition, as the *New York Times* noted, "there was a growing backlash to early globalization starting in the early twentieth century that led to high tariffs, barriers to trade and immigration, all of which contributed to the Great Depression" (Stille 2001). Economic and cultural nationalists condemned the flow of immigrants and sought to halt the tide.

The global economy was disrupted, trade barriers were increased, and the movement of goods dwindled. "World trade, which had been growing 33 percent per decade since 1800, abruptly slowed to a growth of 0.9 percent annually in the years after World War I" (Yergin and Stanislaw 2002, 386).

This first period of globalization planted the seeds of its own destruction, and some warn we could follow the same path if we are not very careful. Describing this period, but in words that eerily resemble what many feel is happening today, the *New York Times* observed,

> It is one of the paradoxes of globalization that the changes it brought helped stimulate the growth of national politics that ended it. In other words, the wild fluctuations in prices, employment and wage levels that came with being part of an international system created a demand for a social safety net as well as demands for protection and a halt to immigration. (Stille 2001)

Similarly, today the stubborn force of nationalism seeks to derail or at least diminish the flow of globalization.

Defining Globalization

We are not the first to see massive change taking place. And we are not even the first group to become aware of a developing global society.

In 1943, Wendell Willkie, the Republican presidential nominee who was defeated by Franklin D. Roosevelt in 1940, wrote the best-selling book *One World,* which helped produce a rising international-ist outlook and emphasized that "the world has become small and completely interdependent" (Greider 1997, 16).

The fact that historical parallels exist does not imply that we should be complacent about our current revolution. We downplay the importance of the changes taking place around us at our own peril. The point of looking back is to remind us to be cautious about exaggerating the novelty of this period, and mindful of how others have fared during periods of great change.

Though if we are not experiencing an altogether new phenomenon, what is it about today's globalization that captures the imagination of so many and escalates the fears of so many others? As Dewey further observed, "Flux does not have to be created. But it does have to be directed" (Dewey 1935, 56). To do that will require not only a general awareness of our globalized world, but an in-depth understanding of the elements that make globalization so powerful. As argued in chapter 1, we must connect the dots.

So much has been said about globalization that any attempt to describe it could be seen as a trivial or redundant exercise. The word itself, which was first used in 1962, has been described by the *Economist* as "the most abused word of the 21st century" (Chanda 2002). It has come to mean all things for many people and can be used to glorify and demonize. But the term must be explored and clarified.

Today's groundbreaking developments in communication and transportation technologies have irrevocably altered our world. With new technology has come the spread of information, production, finance, and trade, all linking together millions from every corner of the globe. Finances, goods, services, and human destinies are connected in ways never before imagined. Through the marvels of technology, we have new neighbors far and near. Our hopes and our fates are tied together.

The IMF has described globalization as "the growing economic interdependence of countries worldwide through the increasing volume and variety of cross-border transactions in goods and services and of international capital flows, and also through the more rapid and widespread diffusion of technology" (Wolf 1997). Not bad, but globalization involves much more than money and economic relations. More detail is needed before we can begin to understand.

Many point out that globalization first and foremost involves "a stretching of social, political and economic activities across frontiers such that events, decisions and activities in one region of the world can come to have significance for individuals and communities in distant regions of the globe" (Held, et al. 1999, 15). On a general basis, scholars agree that globalization is basically about overcoming the boundaries of time and space. As Gerard Delanty simply puts it, "space matters less" (Delanty 2000, 82).

We like the clear summary of globalization provided by Jim Garrison, president of the State of the World Forum. He wrote,

> Globalization is the Copernican revolution of our day. It is making the world truly round because it is bringing all of humanity into a single ecosystem of embedded, overlapping networks. Borders, boundaries, delineations, and walls of any kind are slowly giving way to the compelling force of integration and interdependence. (Garrison 2004, 38)

At its essence, globalization represents interaction and integration on a worldwide scale. It is all about connections, as Lechner and Boli argue.

> After World War II, the infrastructure for communication and transportation improved dramatically, connecting groups, institutions, and countries in new ways. More people can travel, or migrate, more easily to distant parts of the globe; satellite broadcasts bring world events to an increasingly global audience; the Internet begins to knit together world-spanning interest groups of educated users.
>
> Such links are the raw material of globalization. They are molded into new organizational forms as regional institutions go global or new ones take shape on the world stage. Increasing international trade and investment bring more countries into the global capitalist system; democracy gains strength as a global model for organizing nation-states; numerous international organizations take on new responsibilities in addressing issues of common concern.
>
> These institutions, in turn, are crystallizing into a comprehensive world society. The world is becoming a single place, in which different institutions function as parts of one system and distant peoples share a common understanding of living together on one planet. This world society has a culture; it instills in many people a budding consciousness of living in a world society. To links and institutions we therefore add culture and consciousness. Globalization is the process that fitfully brings these elements of world society together. (Lechner and Boli 2000, 1)

There is a great deal to absorb in that passage. Much of it has been the focus of serious contemplation, some of it raises more questions and concerns, but little of it is subject to dispute. Globalization is a fact of life. And it relates to all of those processes that are producing an increasingly interwoven world society. Its effects are easily discernible, and globalization has spawned equally passionate fans and foes.

Supporters point to immeasurable benefits: rapid increases in financial growth and production, the growth of democracy and humanitarian movements, increased access to education, the spread of modern conveniences, rising living standards, and the increasing availability of the fruits of human progress. But others refer to those left behind, the exploitation of workers, the abuse of the environment, and the threats to local culture. The interconnections that globalization brings carry both conflict and commonality. And the impact is indeed substantial and long-lasting. Despite the trendy nature of the concept and the forces opposed to it, globalization is not a fad that can be brushed aside. And it certainly is not a thing, but a process of increasing and irrevocable integration and connection.

There are those who would rather ignore the whole subject of globalization, or have trouble connecting this seemingly abstract notion to their day-to-day lives. But any slice of daily life can bring globalization sharply into focus. Take this passage from Scott Sernau, speaking to a hypothetical observer who is unable to connect the dots about globalization.

> You're just getting over the flu (from Hong Kong), and all you want to do is slip into silk (from China) pajamas (India) and a heavy cotton robe (Native America), take your cold medication (made in Puerto Rico by a German conglomerate from derivatives of two Native American healing herbs), have a cup of tea (from India by way of a British-American multinational venture), and turn on C-SPAN for some satellite-relayed mindless diversion: shots of European royalty cavorting in the Caribbean while trying to avoid paparazzi (an Italian word for these Italian, French, and American photographers) outside their French-built, Japanese-financed, Afro-Caribbean-staffed hotel. For better or worse, the world is at your doorstep. History is repeating itself in your living room; for that matter, in your body. Like some physicist's model of a vortex in space-time, nothing is distant, and history and geography converge in your own experience. You may be simply unaware of how often. Remote now only refers to the buttons you hold in your hand; it no longer applies to any aspect of human experience. (Sernau 2000, 23)

Although the word globalization had not yet caught on, Martin Luther King, Jr. described the connections and the sense of interdependence that today are often characterized as globalization. He wrote,

> All men are interdependent. Every nation is an heir of a vast treasury of ideas and labor to which both the living and the dead of all nations have contributed. Whether we realize it or not, each of us lives eternally "in the red." We are everlasting

debtors to known and unknown men and women. When we arise in the morning, we go into the bathroom where we reach for a sponge which is provided for us by a Pacific islander. We reach for soap that is created for us by a European. Then at the table we drink coffee which is provided for us by a South American, or tea by a Chinese or cocoa by a West African. Before we leave for our jobs we are already beholden to more than half of the world.

In a real sense, all life is interrelated. The agony of the poor impoverishes the rich; the betterment of the poor enriches the rich. We are inevitably our brother's keeper because we are our brother's brother. Whatever affects one directly affects all indirectly. (King 1967, 181)

The Difference This Time

So globalization is all around us. But again we ask, is this really such a novel development? It does seem obvious that globalization can be considered part of a longer historical movement towards greater integration of world society. Scott Sernau writes that globalization has long been driven by three Cs: commerce, control, and curiosity. In other words, globalization is one part economics, one part politics, and one part culture (Sernau 2000, 19–20). And these elements have been part of human civilization since the beginning.

It is true that we have been moving toward a single world community throughout human history. Primitive hunters and gatherers lived in isolated groups that only rarely came into contact with relatively close neighbors. As agricultural communities developed, so too did trade and military conflicts that brought larger regions together. The process moved slowly, though. Classic civilizations and empires, like the contemporary Roman Empire and Han dynasties, basically lived in separate worlds. But the process began to gain speed, and by the early sixteenth century, the age of exploration and increasing trade began to produce the first significant signs of a global community (Reischauer 1973, 20–25).

The engines of global integration began heating up about five hundred years ago. Wayne Ellwood explains, "Globalization is a new word which describes an old process: the integration of the global economy that began in earnest with the launch of the European colonial era five centuries ago" (Ellwood 2001, 12). Indeed, when the transatlantic trade routes were opened up, not just products, but food, animals, diseases, and ideas crossed the oceans, in a massive wave of cultural migration and cross-cultural integration. Ellwood adds,

> The entanglement of diverse cultures and economies . . . has been spreading for centuries and the world has been shrinking as a result. In that sense, it [globalization] is an old story. Peppers, maize and potatoes, once found only in Latin America, are now common foods in India, Africa and Europe. Spices originally from Indonesia thrive in the Caribbean. The descendants of African slaves, first brought to work the land of the "new world," have become Americans, Jamaicans, Canadians, Brazilians and Guyanese. (Ellwood 2001, 8)

Despite these historical processes of integration, and while dynamics fundamental to globalization were at work in previous periods, we suggest that there is still something unique and compelling about the current era. Consider another definition of globalization, this one by *New York Times* columnist Thomas Friedman. In his bestselling book *The Lexus and the Olive Tree,* he defines globalization as the

> inexorable integration of markets, nation-states and technologies to a degree never witnessed before—in a way that is enabling individuals, corporations and nation-states to reach around the world farther, faster, deeper and cheaper than ever before, and in a way that is enabling the world to reach into individuals, corporations and nation-states farther, faster, deeper, cheaper than ever before. (Friedman 1999, 9)

The key part of that definition is the emphasis on how much faster things are happening today. As we have seen, it is not the particular process of integration that marks this era; rather, as Friedman observes, the "defining measurement of the globalization system is speed—speed of commerce, travel, communication and innovation" (Friedman 1999, 10).

Of course, this round of globalization has its own unique technologies, ranging from satellite communications to the Internet. These certainly have been significant in bringing about extensive changes, altering lifestyles and society in profound ways. Still, it is not the changes themselves or the underlying processes integrating us and altering our daily lives that are so different, but the pace of the changes and the speed of their impact. It may be debatable whether we are experiencing the most radical transformations in human history—in economic, cultural, and political realms—but it is far less controversial that we are literally and figuratively covering more ground in less time than ever before.

Ellwood, after recognizing the historical context, notes that the "old story" of globalization "has developed a new twist sparked by the rapid rate of technological change over the last 25 years. The micro-electronics revolution has irrevocably changed the essence of human contact on Earth. Distances are shrinking and information is spreading faster than ever before" (Ellwood 2001, 8–9).

New tools and technologies catch on much faster than before. In the United States, it took forty years for radio to develop an audience of fifty million listeners. Personal computers were being used by that same number of people in only fifteen years. Just four years after the Internet was available, fifty million people were surfing it (Giddens 2000, 30).

Because of the communications revolution, the changes are more conspicuous. News events flash before our eyes seconds after they happen, while the buzz is never far from our notice. We know how fast our world is changing, even if our perspectives could use some broadening. As pointed out by Crispin Tickell, an onlooker from outer space would find more change on the surface of the Earth "in the last two hundred years than in the preceding two thousand, and more change in the last twenty years than in the preceding two hundred" (Tickell 2002).

Looking at the broad overview of humanity's integration, former Harvard professor Edwin Reischauer wrote,

> It took many millenniums for mankind to move from the almost completely self-contained and isolated tiny groupings of pale-olithic times to the limited indirect trade and culture contacts of the great classic empires. In the next millennium, man moved through the periods of contact by means of the nomadic peoples and early oceanic commerce to the great breakthrough of an incipient "one world" around 1500. It took less than four centuries from then to the next breakthrough of apparent world unity through Western domination in the second half of the nineteenth century. The next phase of World War I, the League

of Nations, and the world depression was a mere matter of decades. And the new phase since World War II is moving even faster. (Reischauer 1973, 32–33)

Commercial Connections

The transformations have been most stunning in the area of commerce, and they have been revolutionary. As Daniel Yergin and Joseph Stanislaw observe,

> The hallmark of this new globality is the mobile economy. Capital sweeps across countries at electron speed; manufacturing and the generation of services move flexibly among countries and are networked across borders; markets are supplied from a continually shifting set of sources . . . Borders—fundamental to the exercise of national power—are eroded as markets are integrated. (Yergin and Stanislaw 2002, 406)

Total world trade, according to Yergin and Stanislaw, grew in the 1980s at a rate of 4.5 percent annually. But in the 1990s, the rate rose to 6.8 percent annually and the value of world trade doubled to almost $8 trillion (Yergin and Stanislaw 2002, 393).

Since World War II, global trade has increased 1,000 percent (Donnelly 2003). At the same time, international trade has grown from 7 percent to 21 percent of total world income (Gilpin 2000, 20).

Another measure of globalization, writes Timothy Taylor, is the share of economic production destined for sale in other countries.

> In the U.S. economy, exports of goods and services were 4.9 percent of GDP in 1965 but 10.8 percent of GDP in 2000. From a global perspective, exports rose from 12 percent of GDP in 1965 to 22 percent of GDP in 2000. In round numbers, international trade of goods and services has doubled in about four decades. (Taylor 2002, 25)

. Another economic indication of globalization is the fact that toward the end of the last century, "U.S. ownership of foreign assets increased sharply, while foreign ownership of assets in the United States increased even more" (Caplow, Hicks, and Wattenberg 2001, 262). From 1980 to 1999, the value of foreign assets owned by Americans went up sixfold. During that same period, US investment abroad rose from $5,406 per American to $26,286 per American. In

the meantime, the value of assets in the United States owned by foreigners rose more than eightfold (Caplow, Hicks, and Wattenberg
2001, 262). Foreign direct investment (FDI) rose to more than $1.3
trillion in 2000 (Micklethwait and Wooldridge 2003).

More money is flying in and out of countries, and faster than
ever before. In 1986, traders moved an average of $190 billion daily
through global markets; by 2001, that number had skyrocketed to an
estimated $1.2 trillion per day (Yergin and Stanislaw 2002, 394).
Even with a global economic slump in the first years of the new century, the reduced amount of capital crossing borders was still significantly higher than it was just a few years before.

Massive Mobility
Along with the rapid movement of financial capital, but not quite as
strong, has come the migration of people across greater distances.
According to the United Nations, at least 185 million people live in
countries other than where they were born, compared to just 70 million three decades ago (Crossette 2002).

No doubt such migration is sparked in part by the ability to easily travel to distant lands and communicate with people thousands of
miles away. When such technologies first became available, only the
wealthy could afford them. Not any more. Look at the increase in air
travel: From 1970 to 2000, the number of international air travelers
nearly doubled, from 75 million to 142 million (Yergin and Stanislaw
2002, 405). And more of us are not only flying to each other, but
talking more to each other, thanks to the communications revolution.
In 1930, it cost about $300 to make a three-minute call from the
United States to the United Kingdom. In 1976, it cost about $8. By
2000, that same call could cost as little as 36 cents (Yergin and Stanislaw 2002, 405). In 1969, a call from Hong Kong to Chicago cost
nearly $10 per minute, but by 2001, you could make that call for as
little as $1.20 per minute (Watson 2004, 147).

Such falls in price helped boost the number of trans-border
calls from 200 million in 1980 to 5.2 billion in 1999 (Yergin and
Stanislaw 2002, 405). Now, we have cellular phones that link us
around the globe. And of course we have the Internet, the king of
instant and relatively cheap communication. So if we are unable to
actually travel, many of us can instantly cross borders in cyberspace.

Thanks to improvements in transportation and communication,
companies cross borders even faster than people do. The mass impact

of these giant firms is unprecedented, as they assemble and market their products over vast divides.

> Along with the surge in trade, one indicator of the rapidity of change is the transformation of more and more firms into multinationals that provide the world market with goods and services that are conceived, produced, and assembled in several countries. The criterion of "national origin" has given way to "local content," which in turn is becoming harder and harder to pin down. The spread of fast, reliable information and communications technology pushes companies to draw on people and resources the world over. (Yergin and Stanislaw 2002, 406)

But racing across borders and hurtling forward at breakneck speed, while thrilling, can be fraught with peril. Globalization is uniting the world in many respects, but it is also disrupting and radically restructuring industries, relationships, and lifestyles. It is also flying ahead of our ability to assess what is happening or learn about our new world.

To borrow from Friedman, "Global integration has raced ahead of education. Thanks to globalization, we all definitely know 'of' one another more than ever, but we still don't know that much 'about' one another" (Friedman 1999, 127). Integral to the definition of globalization is a mass consciousness of our interdependence, an awareness widely promoted in nearly every medium. But too often, that awareness is on a general level at best. Education must catch up.

What happens in a world changing so fast that we cannot keep up? What happens when there is no time to learn about another advance or weigh its consequences? Some are thoughtfully asking these questions, but many are watching complacently while the world changes all around them. Others, frightened by what they do not and do understand, lash out at the forces and consequences of globalization. Major protests in Seattle, Washington, Prague, Genoa, and other places have seen unlikely allies come together to decry what is often described as globalization run amok.

Cultural Consequences

Many see globalization as Westernization, Americanization, or even worse, a homogenizing force that will render local cultures obsolete. It is an understandable sentiment, considering the strength and influence of the United States and American companies in the post-Cold War era: "Disney movies are children's fodder the world over. Barbie dolls, fast-food restaurants, hip-hop music and corporate-driven American-style youth culture attract millions of new converts" throughout the world (Ellwood 2001, 9).

The emerging global culture certainly is strongly influenced by the United States. From *Baywatch* to Britney Spears, from McDonald's to Michael Jackson, from designer jeans to destructive arms, American exports have dazzled the world and disrupted the fabric of traditional lifestyles and cultures with unprecedented speed and scope. The trend has spawned new terms such as Coca-Colonization and the Marilyn Monroe Doctrine. Critics and fans alike argue about the degree of danger, but agree on one thing: there is no turning back.

At the same time that many are running to buy American products, they also often have negative opinions of the United States because of its dominance. It is hard to miss the point. After all, McDonald's—with more than thirty thousand restaurants in 119 countries—serves nearly fifty million people worldwide each day. Ronald McDonald is the second-most recognizable figure in the world to children, trailing only Santa Claus. Coca-Cola serves one billion people worldwide daily, and Hollywood generates 85 percent of the most watched films in the world. All of this does not even mention American leadership in finance, weaponry, and education (Hunter and Yates 2002, 324). Whether it is in the form of economic power or military might, such dominance breeds fear, resentment, hostility, and very little sympathy. That is not hard to comprehend. We ourselves relate more to the underdogs. We root for David over Goliath, and enjoy seeing the top team upset.

But focusing here on culture, the issue is not simply a case of American products flooding the world in a one-way direction. Globalization should—and often does—work in multiple ways. Throughout the world, many local cultures have assimilated Western influences within the framework of their culture (called localization, hybridization, or sometimes, glocalization). There is the "Confucian merchant" in China, the businessperson who combines modern business techniques with traditional Chinese culture; or the software engineers in Bangalore who garland their computers in Hindu ceremonies; or the synthesis of Christianity and traditional religions in Africa; or the hamburger sitting alongside Wiener schnitzels on the Hungarian lunch table; or South African hair styles that result in young white male environmentalists with dreadlocks while black soccer players dye their hair blond (Berger 2002, 10–11; Kovács 2002, 166; Bernstein 2002, 221).

Even locals who target American products emulate and sometimes incorporate something from their rivals. Take the Middle Eastern soft drink Mecca-Cola, which uses a familiar red and white label, while at the same time seeking to brand itself as the anti-Coca-Cola.

Philippe Legrain praises the benefits of what he calls the "cross-fertilization" of cultures. He describes a "rich feast of cultural mixing that belies fears about Americanized uniformity." For example, he says, "Algerians in Paris practice Thai boxing; Asian rappers in London snack on Turkish pizza, Salman Rushdie delights readers everywhere with his Anglo-Indian tales" (Legrain 2003).

Again, such integration is far from a historical novelty. Throughout history, even when cultures have clashed violently and one side has been seemingly overwhelmed, assimilation has taken place on both sides. There are many examples of syncretism—the blending of elements of two cultures to create something new. Take, for instance, the early Native Americans of the Great Plains, who adopted horses and guns from the Europeans into their traditional lifestyle. The Europeans also brought domesticated animals such as pigs, oxen, and chicken that influenced native cultures.

In turn, the settlers adopted Native American medicines, words, names, symbols, and, perhaps most notably, food. The cuisine of the settlers in America, and indeed that of Europe and the rest of the world, was significantly shaped by Native American staples such as corn, sweet potatoes, tomatoes, beans, and peanuts. Almost half of all major crops now grown in the world originally came from the Americas. The American hot pepper (capsicum) rapidly spread first to Europe and then to Africa, Asia, and the Middle East, enlivening cuisines and altering farming practices. The sweet potato helped sustain Chinese farmers and contributed greatly to Cantonese culture (Loewen 1995, 68; Coatsworth 2004, 44; Watson 2004, 153–54).

Even today, among the most pervasive Western cultural exports, such as popular music, there exists a distinctive traditional element—in this case, African-American musical forms—that has been blended with modern styles. Moreover, many American cultural exports are themselves hybrid results of cultural integration.

Examples of cultural integration are common today. In addition, many American firms tailor their products distinctly to local audiences. MTV is the world's most widely distributed television network, with more than four hundred million subscribers in 164 countries and territories. Its international growth has been spectacular, beginning with MTV Europe in 1987 and expanding throughout the globe, reaching Africa in 2005. It has been astutely aware of local differences. As the vice president of MTV once stated, "Many of the younger ends of our audience don't even know that MTV is an American company because they've only known it as being locally Taiwanese or locally German, or locally Argentine or whatever" (Hunter and Yates 2002, 342). MTV Indonesia includes a call to prayer for its many Muslim viewers, MTV Japan emphasizes technology-oriented programming, and MTV Italy has cooking shows.

Many other companies pride themselves on working with people from the community to fit in with local tastes. In India, McDonald's has opened restaurants with burgers made from lamb, and offers numerous vegetarian alternatives. In Germany, you can have beer with your Big Mac, and in France, you can have wine while enjoying local fare like Danone fruit yogurts and the French soft drink Orangina. In Egypt, the fast-food giant introduced the McFalafel. Similarly, KFC has long served rice with its meals in Indonesia, and its food there is prepared according to Islamic dietary laws. In Chile, it sells avocado sandwiches. In Mexico, the three favorite toppings on Domino's pizzas are jalapeño peppers, ham, and pineapple. To satisfy local tastes, Nestlé offers two hundred varieties of its popular instant coffee Nescafé, including much stronger blends for Russian coffee drinkers, while its popular Kit Kat bar in Japan features flavors like lemon cheesecake.

Even the paragon of globalized commerce, the shopping mall, has developed local alterations. The Philippines' Megamall features a church for Catholic masses, while a mall in Saudi Arabia bans men so women can shop without being veiled (Salcedo 2003, 1097).

In addition, many countries besides the United States export their culture and influence. From French wines to Chinese restaurants to Italian fashions to Latin American music, the world often proves to be a cultural melting pot. Japanese management techniques are emulated the world over; Pokemon, a Japanese card game, caused a frenzy in American schools; and Japanese anime has generated tremendous followings, particular in the United States. New Age practices from India, such as yoga and meditation, are popular in the West, while Opus Dei, the influential international Catholic organization, began in Spain and is especially dominant in Latin America (Berger 2002, 12; Srinivas 2002, 90).

Bollywood, India's colorful and prolific film industry, has rapidly risen in popularity and influence in many areas of the globe, particularly the United States and the United Kingdom. Indeed, international influences are perhaps most obviously visible on American television and cinema. Smash television hits such as *Survivor, Big Brother,* and *Mighty Morphin Power Rangers* were adaptations of successful programs abroad. Popular movies *Shall We Dance, The Ring,* and *The Grudge* were remakes of Japanese movies, and *Vanilla Sky* was originally a Spanish science fiction film. Other blockbusters, such as *The Matrix* and its sequels, heavily featured elements of Japanese pop culture (Jenkins 2004, 119, 132). While this is not altogether a new trend—Western classics like *The Magnificent Seven* and *A Fistful of Dollars* were also based on Asian works—the proliferation of international influences is greater than ever before, and major studios are gobbling up the rights to films from places such as South Korea, Japan, and Hong Kong.

Hybrid cultures are emerging. Globalization is much more than a two-way street; it is a vast series of highways, thoroughfares, and side roads. Still, critics have ample reasons to be concerned. The power of Western and particularly American exports can indeed endanger the vitality of local cultures. As Benjamin Barber notes, "One McDonald's in Tiananmen Square may enhance diversity in China . . . But the market corporations of McWorld aspire not just to penetrate but also to permeate markets, and their ultimate objective is monopoly." He adds, "With a Starbucks on every corner in traditional coffeehouse Vienna, the city loses its distinctive Viennese coffeehouse culture" (Barber 2003).

We must be careful and consider how American dominance in the cultural realm can affect local populations. Too often, national and transnational forces have trampled over local cultures. But we need not be overly pessimistic either. Local cultures can continue to endure, even slightly modified by outside influences. As Harvard professor James Watson rightly states, "The *appearance* of homogeneity is the most salient, and ultimately the most deceptive, feature of globalization." He adds that "people everywhere have an unquenchable desire to partake of the fruits of globalization while celebrating the inherent uniqueness of their own local cultures" (Watson 2004, 169).

Worrisome Gaps

In addition to concerns about homogenization, globalization has been criticized for causing economic problems. Despite the wealth that has been generated by globalization and the movement of capital, economic integration has risks and consequences. Increasing international capital flows have been linked to several destructive financial crises, including the damage done to the success stories of globalization, the "tiger" economies of Thailand, Taiwan, Singapore, Malaysia, and South Korea.

The economic downside of globalization was highlighted in a 1999 United Nations Development Programme (UNDP) report, which noted,

> When the market goes too far in dominating social and political outcomes, the opportunities and rewards of globalization spread unequally and inequitably—concentrating power and wealth in a select group of people, nations and corporations, marginalizing the others. (Ellwood 2001, 97–98)

UNDP described a "grotesque and dangerous polarization" between those enjoying the fruits of globalization and those left hanging on the vine. The rapid advance of globalization has also coincided with a widening income gap in both rich and poor countries: "In 1960, the fifth of the world's people who live in the richest countries had 30 times more income than the fifth living in the poorest countries. By 1997, the income gap had more than doubled to 74:1" (Ellwood 2001, 98).

Today, the richest 20 percent of the world's population possess three-quarters of global income, while the poorest 40 percent have just 5 percent of world income and the poorest 20 percent have just 1.5 percent. (United Nations Development Programme 2005, 36). According to the 2005 UNDP's Human Development Report, "In 1990, the average American was 38 times richer than the average Tanzanian. Today the average American is 61 times richer" (UNDP 2005, 37).

Upon accepting the Nobel Peace Prize in 2002, former US President Jimmy Carter said that "the most serious and universal problem is a growing chasm between the richest and poorest people on earth. . . . And the separation is increasing every year. Not only between nations, but within them" (Carter 2002).

There are, though, many economists who argue that globalization has been unfairly blamed for this gap. They point to the fact that many of the more globalized countries are less unequal than less globalized ones. They also contend that those nations most plugged into the global economy—those that are the most open and globalized—grow the fastest, and that "the rising tide indeed seemed to lift all boats" (Wright 2000).

> This theory helps explain why East and Southeast Asia, with their embrace of global markets, have massively reduced poverty, while sub-Saharan Africa, featuring more statist economies and an unappetizing political environment for foreign investment, has been less successful. (Wright 2000)

There is evidence on this side. In general, says David Dollar of the World Bank, "developing countries that have increased their participation in trade and attracted foreign investment have seen accelerated growth and poverty reduction" (Dollar 2003, 27). According to the World Bank, in the 1990s, the twenty-four most-globalized developing nations, those with the highest ratio of trade to national income, saw their GDP rise by an annual average of 5 percent, while less-globalized developing countries saw their GDP drop annually by an average of 1 percent (Micklethwait and Wooldridge 2003; Dollar 2003, 27). A link between trade openness and per-capita income growth has also been shown in individual countries, including South Korea, China, India, and Mexico (Masson 2001, 7; Bhagwati 2004). Such trends help explain why attitudes about global integration are surprisingly more enthusiastic in developing countries than wealthier nations (Dollar 2003, 26). Of course, openness to world trade must be accompanied by other positive elements, such as quality services and a secure environment.

Globalization has often sparked massive growth, but other factors have played roles in each country's development or lack thereof. Many believe that several Asian countries prospered because they combined liberal economic policies with some measures of protection for their fledgling domestic industries. And despite the openness of many Latin American countries, their growth has not been great. In fact, growth was slower in Latin America in the 1990s than it was during the 1960s, when trade protectionism was in vogue.

But even granting the income-generating potential of the globalized economy, it is less apparent that the gains have been well distributed. While poverty has been reduced in some areas, the number of poor is still staggering. As UN Secretary-General Kofi Annan has commented, "Try to imagine what globalization can possibly mean to the half of humanity that has never made or received a telephone call" (Annan 2001). Billions are not reaping any benefits from globalization.

The global playing field produces giant winners and many losers. The number of people who live on less than $1 each day is an enormous 1.1 billion (World Bank 2005). And 2.5 billion people, about 40 percent of the world's population, live on less than $2 a day (UNDP 2005, 4).

Furthermore, more than 1.4 billion have no direct access to clean drinking water, 0.9 billion are illiterate, and 0.8 billion suffer from hunger or malnutrition (Camdessus 2001). And 33 percent of all children under five suffer from malnutrition, with about thirty thousand dying from preventable diseases every twenty-four hours (Garrison 2004, 41).

As a 1998 United Nations report observed, "Economic growth alone will not carry us all ever upward. In the global currents, rising tides do not raise all boats, they swamp some and drown others who are stranded on the beach" (Sernau 2000, 77). The disparities are evident everywhere. The richest countries in the world, containing only 20 percent of the planet's population, are responsible for 80 percent of total consumption, while the poorest 20 percent on the globe consume just 1.3 percent of the world's resources (Hinrichsen 2002, 18).

We want to emphasize that while we believe that globalization is not the sole cause of such disparities, we must do a better job of narrowing these gaps, or the backlash, the anger and resentment, will explode and threaten the many positive aspects of globalization. If globalization even partly contributes to more homogenization, environmental devastation, and greater income disparities, the consequences will be felt by all. Closing such gaps is not just a moral imperative, but a necessary antidote to growing social conflict and potential natural disasters.

Nowhere is the danger more evident than in environmental concerns. Globalization has all too often contributed to severe environmental damage. This includes the deterioration of land and the accumulation of wastes; the pollution of salt and fresh water (at least 60 percent of world fisheries are fully exploited or overfished, and up to three billion people could be facing severe water shortages by 2050); increasing rates of extinction (one in four mammal species face a high risk of extinction in the near future); and the changing composition of the atmosphere, including the depletion of the ozone layer and the rise in greenhouse gases, which is predicted to lead to warmer temperatures and higher sea levels (Tickell 2002). There is much we do not understand about how we are affecting the environment. But in many areas, the danger is clear, and even in those areas generating some controversy, the potential for disaster is worth some alteration in our behavior.

The environment and environmental challenges perhaps best illustrate the degree of connections on planet Earth. Popular scientist Carl Sagan described very well the threads that bind our fates:

> In North America, we breathe oxygen generated in the Brazilian rain forest. Acid rain from polluting industries in the American Midwest destroys Canadian forests. Radioactivity from a Ukrainian nuclear accident compromises the economy and culture of Lapland. The burning of coal in China warms Argentina. Chlorofluorocarbons released from an air conditioner in Newfoundland help cause skin cancer in New Zealand. Diseases rapidly spread to the farthest reaches of the planet and require a global medical effort to be eradicated. And, of course, nuclear war and asteroid impact imperil everyone. Like it or not, we humans are bound up with our fellows, and with the other plants and animals all over the world. Our lives are intertwined. (Sagan 1997, 80)

There is obvious danger in being so interdependent. Sagan touched on the spread of diseases. With increased air travel, trade, and tourism, so too come increased chances of infectious diseases spreading like wildfires. Look how quickly and to how many countries SARS (severe acute respiratory syndrome) could spread. During the outbreak of 2003, more than eight thousand people in thirty countries were infected in just three months.

As professor of virology Richard Tedder commented, "What SARS has done is rekindle the concept of the global village. Somebody's problem on a peninsula in South East Asia is Toronto's problem a few days later" (BBC News Online 2003). Similarly, World Health Organization (WHO) Director-General Gro Harlem Brundtland warned that new illnesses would continue to emerge and that countries must work together to stop their spread: "There will no longer be any islands of safety in the world. There are no impenetrable walls between the healthy, well-fed and well-functioning world and the sick, undernourished and poor world" (Reuters 2003).

Still, despite the drawbacks and challenges, there is great reason to be optimistic about globalization. There is much to celebrate in the global exchange of people, products, and ideas. As Wayne Ellwood, no cheerleader for globalization and the global economy, writes, "In many ways it [globalization] is a positive process containing the seeds of a better future for all the world's people. Globalization cannot help but be a positive force for change if we come to recognize the common thread of humanity that ties us together" (Ellwood 2001, 9).

Global Gains

Consider what globalization has done. Only a century ago, the vast and overwhelming majority of the planet's citizens were born and died in the same local region, without (or rarely) making contact with those from different areas. Technology now rapidly carries us across the planet and enables us to communicate regularly with those halfway around the world. Our family, friends, and colleagues, no matter where they live, can be reached in seconds.

Our increasing contact with others sometimes confronts us with serious challenges, but it also leads to tremendous satisfaction, widespread benefits, and new ways of thinking. It also starkly reveals our common interests and shared fates. Often, technology and that realization can combine to form a greater, global form of civil society. And despite the economic inequalities, there is no disputing that millions who are not in the upper strata have still seen their fortunes rise. Many people in developed nations today live in conditions better than those that monarchs and princes enjoyed not too long ago. And while the gap between the richest 10 percent and the poorest 10 percent has increased, the gap between the richest one-third of humanity and the poorest one-third has in fact narrowed (Singer 2002).

At the same time, improved health standards and the spread of knowledge in preventing and curing illness has led to dramatic increases in life spans and greatly reduced infant mortality rates: a decline of forty to fifty per thousand in developing countries from 1970 to 1999 (Masson 2001, 5). Education has been greatly improved in many developing countries, shown markedly by great decreases in adult illiteracy rates. The IMF's Paul Masson can say with significant evidence that "advances in living standards, health and education have occurred because flows of goods, capital and information have allowed poorer countries to use modern technology in local production and public services" (Masson 2001, 6).

Democracy is more widespread than ever before and, in many areas, global standards have been forged by an international community sensitized to our mutual needs. Collective agreements, advances in international law, and the spread of multinational coalitions are producing significant gains and accelerating the development of a global society. States and citizens have worked together to prohibit land mines and chemical weapons, restrict the testing and deployment of nuclear weapons, forge environmental pacts, and establish an international criminal court.

Since the Rio conference on the environment in 1992, a number of international gatherings have focused on major issues such as climate change, biodiversity, population, women and children, racism, HIV/AIDS, social and sustainable development, and human rights. While discussions and negotiations have not all been fruitful, the rise of these types of forums, along with the tremendous growth of nongovernmental organizations (NGOs) and international citizens groups, heralds a new era in international cooperation.

Ultimately, all of these developments can be termed as aspects of globalization, which simply comes down to the processes that bring us together as members of the same species sharing the same planetary address; the processes that expose us to a great variety of influences, ideas, and cultures; and the processes that increase our levels of interdependence. Today, those processes are working at a feverish rate, sometimes faster than we can handle. But we have to adjust because there is no turning back the clock to the days of societies and communities living in perpetual isolation. We are the world and the world is us. Or, to refer to a phrase that applies to water pollution, we all live downstream now.

It is more than symbolic that the terms for the key technologies of our age, the Internet and the World Wide Web, directly underline the interconnected and global nature of our modern reality (Sernau 2000, 20). We are rapidly moving toward each other. Of course, those same technologies that link us together and help us reach out to one another can also disrupt traditional forms of socialization and breed alienation and isolation. But the process of dehumanization cannot take place without our consent.

Globalization is an undeniable reality, but how we respond is entirely up to us. Despite its speed and strength, the forces of globalization are still within our control. We must learn to tilt the scales toward the parts of globalization that empower us, and away from the parts that can alienate and dehumanize us. We must manage globalization and accentuate its positive aspects while reducing its potential for harm. Hanging in the balance is the future of our entire planet, because globalization has unprecedented powers to unify and the unmatched capacity to overwhelm everything in its path.

A World Cup Half Full

Despite its struggle for acceptance in the United States, football, or soccer as it is known here, is easily the world's most popular sport. It may be the single largest global phenomenon. And every four years, nations hold their collective breath while their representatives "on the pitch" compete for national glory in arguably the globe's greatest tournament: the World Cup. An incredible two billion people watched the 2002 final between Germany and Brazil. In some cases, athletes play for much more than bragging rights. Other political and cultural considerations add a magnitude to the competition completely out of proportion to the actual significance of the event.

The same forces that have encouraged cross-border movements and facilitated the global marketplace have enabled players and coaches to span the globe. Players and owners travel without regard to borders, searching for lucrative opportunities and winning sides. Club teams, even from soccer havens like Italy, Spain, and the United Kingdom, are often dominated by foreign stars. The biggest squads, like Manchester United or Real Madrid, are in effect multinational conglomerates marketing themselves throughout the world, and their stars are celebrities worldwide. This same sporting trend is evident in the Olympics, for which many athletes switch countries.

While the processes of globalization have been unfolding for years in soccer, their manifestations were vividly displayed during the 2002 World Cup. For one prominent example, look at one of the surprise teams of the tournament, Senegal, which opened the tournament with a win over France, its former colonial master. Almost all of the Senegalese players competed in France, while all of the French stars played in the United Kingdom, Italy, and Spain. The same was true for many squads, as stars who honed their skills elsewhere, foreigners, and immigrants represented nations they might not even call home. The Brazilians who led their team to the ultimate triumph mostly played overseas, and one of Germany's leading players hailed from Switzerland and barely spoke German.

Coaches, too, paid no mind to national borders. The Senegal team was coached by, what else, a Frenchman. The upstart Koreans were coached by a Dutchman, the Paraguay side was led by an Italian, and even the proud English were led for the first time by a coach from across the channel, the Swede Sven Goran Eriksson. And the trendsetter in coaching abroad, Bora Multinovic, this time applied his skills on behalf of the Chinese. This pattern has continued. In the 2004 European Championships, both finalists were coached by foreigners: Portugal by a Brazilian and Greece by a German.

The bottom line is that it is becoming harder to latch onto the symbolic elements of nationalism when players and coaches move around at will. When traditional powers AC Milan and Liverpool faced off in the 2005 Champions League final, one might have expected a clash between Italian and English footballers. Actually, AC Milan fielded only four Italian starters and had representatives from four other countries in the starting lineup. Liverpool, though, easily bested them in diversity by starting players from nine countries, with only two English stars in the lineup. In total, the two teams featured players from nineteen countries.

Another aspect of the globalization of soccer is that styles traditionally confined to certain regions have been imported and blended together. While some regional forms remain pronounced, and teams like Brazil probably will always play like Brazilians, the growing amalgamation of talent and styles may mean that the distance has narrowed between the traditional powers and other nations.

The hope is that globalization can work in the same way in other realms of society, bringing cultures together, narrowing gaps, and improving the lives of millions. Yet despite the promising signs illustrated by the globalization of soccer and the World Cup, one would not have to look very far to see how intolerance and nationalist prejudices remain strong. In the midst of the global sporting celebration, you could find alarming tendencies on the Internet message boards for fans of the national teams. Despite guidelines for some degree of civility, the rampant ethnic slurs and racist aspersions on the sites remind us that national loyalties are fiercely held, and many confuse nationalist pride with nationalist superiority. Menacing mobs gather, fans scream racial epithets, and hooligans threaten violence at nearly all major tournaments. For those who think it is primarily European fans who foment violence, witness the frenzy of Chinese nationalism and anti-Japanese fervor that almost led to major rioting at the Japan-China 2004 Asian Cup final, after which the winning Japanese side had to leave Beijing ahead of schedule and under heavy police escort. The same troublesome trends occur regularly at club levels, as local rivalries are often inflicted with ruthless, tribal sentiments and unrelenting hostility. Sadly, many still refuse to recognize our common humanity, let alone consider the possibility of world citizenship.

This is not disappointing just from a moral perspective; it is destructive from a practical standpoint, because the excesses of nationalism and the politics of the nation-state in isolation will make any attempt at dealing with global problems futile or even tragic. Much work remains for those who believe in the promise of our globalized world.

So, We're Not the First

We like to believe we live in unique times. This belief is both true and false. There is something new about our era, particularly our technological advances. But the processes that propel radical change have all occurred before in one way or another. What is different, and what characterizes today's globalization more than anything, is the speed of development, the rapid rate of the changes. As globalization integrates peoples, cultures, and nations, the need to keep pace, respond, and learn more about what is happening, what is new, and what is not—in short, to learn more about each other—becomes imperative for our survival. Globalization has led to tremendous achievements, but we must understand the problems and the challenges, and humanely direct the process.

References

Annan, Kofi A. 2001. News release. In Address to World Economic Forum, Secretary-General Says Globalization Must Work for All. January 29, http://www.un.org/news/press/docs/2001/sgsm7692.doc.htm (accessed September 14, 2005).

Bhagwati, Jagdish. 2004. *In Defense of Globalization*. New York: Oxford University Press.

Barber, Benjamin R. 2003. Brave New McWorld. Review of *Creative Destruction: How Globalization is Changing the World's Cultures*, by Tyler Cowen. *Los Angeles Times*, February 2.

BBC News Online. 2003. How the 'Global Village' Faced SARS. *BBC News Online*, May 2, 2001. http://news.bbc.co.uk/go/pr/fr/-/2/hi/health/2991725. stm (accessed September 14, 2005).

Berger, Peter L. 2002. The Cultural Dynamics of Globalization. In *Many Globalizations: Cultural Diversity in the Contemporary World,* edited by P.L. Berger and S.P. Huntington, 1–16. New York: Oxford University Press.

Berger, Peter L., and Samuel P. Huntington, eds. 2002. *Many Globalizations: Cultural Diversity in the Contemporary World.* New York: Oxford University Press.

Bernstein, Ann. 2002. Globalization, Culture, and Development: Can South Africa Be More Than an Offshoot of the West? In *Many Globalizations: Cultural Diversity in The Contemporary World,* edited by P.L. Berger and S.P. Huntington, 185–249. New York: Oxford University Press.

Burke, James. 1978. *Connections.* Boston: Little, Brown & Company.

Camdessus, Michel. 2001. The IMF at the Beginning of the Twenty-First Century: Can We Establish a Humanized Globalization? *Global Governance* 7 no. 4 (October–December): 363–370.

Caplow, Theodore, Louis Hicks, and Ben J. Wattenberg. 2001. *The First Measured Century: An Illustrated Guide to Trends in America, 1900–2000.* Washington, D.C.: The AEI Press.

Carter, James E. 2002. Nobel Peace Prize acceptance speech. December 10. http://archives.cnn.com/2002/WORLD/europe/12/10/carter.transcript (accessed September 14, 2005).

Chanda, Nayan. 2002. Coming Together: Globalization Means Reconnecting the Human Community. *YaleGlobal Online*, November 19. http://yale global.yale.edu/about/essay.jsp (accessed September 14, 2005).

Coatsworth, John H. 2004. Globalization, Growth, and Welfare in History. In *Globalization: Culture and Education in the New Millennium,* edited by M.M. Suárez-Orozco and D.B. Qin-Hilliard, 38–55. Berkeley: University of California Press.

Crossette, Barbara. 2002. U.N. Coaxes Out the Wheres and Whys of Global Immigration. *New York Times,* July 7.

Delanty, Gerard. 2000. *Citizenship in a Global Age: Society, Culture, Politics.* Philadelphia: Open University Press.

Dewey, John. 1935. *Liberalism and Social Action.* New York: Capricorn Books.

Dollar, David. 2003. Globalization and Poor Nations: Opportunities and Risks. *Phi Kappa Phi Forum* 83, no. 4 (Fall): 26–29.

Donnelly, John. 2003. CIA Had Idea of Contagion, and of Governments' Reactions. *Boston Globe,* April 27.

Ellwood, Wayne. 2001. *The No-Nonsense Guide to Globalization.* Oxford: New Internationalist Publications.

Feldman, David. 2002. Global Economy's Deep Roots. *New York Times,* May 14.

Friedman, Thomas L. 1999. *The Lexus and the Olive Tree*. New York: Anchor Books.

Garrison, Jim. 2004. *America As Empire: Global Leader or Rogue Power?* San Francisco: Berrett-Koehler Publishers.

Giddens, Anthony. 2000. *Runaway World: How Globalization Is Reshaping Our Lives*. New York: Routledge.

Gilpin, Robert. 2000. *The Challenge of Global Capitalism: The World Economy in the 21st Century*. Princeton: Princeton University Press.

Greider, William. 1997. *One World, Ready or Not: The Manic Logic of Global Capitalism*. New York: Touchstone.

Held, David, Anthony McGrew, David Goldblatt, and Jonathan Perraton. 1999. *Global Transformations: Politics, Economics and Culture*. Stanford: Stanford University Press.

Hinrichsen, Don. 2002. Measuring Footprints: A Tale of Two Families. *National Wildlife* (August–September): 18–19.

Hunter, James Davison, and Joshua Yates. 2002. In the Vanguard of Globalization: The World of American Globalizers. In *Many Globalizations: Cultural Diversity in the Contemporary World,* edited by P.L. Berger and S.P. Huntington, 323–357. New York: Oxford University Press.

Jenkins, Henry. 2004. Pop Cosmopolitanism: Mapping Cultural Flows in an Age of Media Convergence. In *Globalization: Culture and Education in the New Millennium,* edited by M.M. Suárez-Orozco and D.B. Qin-Hilliard, 114–140. Berkeley: University of California Press.

King, Jr., Martin Luther. 1967. *Where Do We Go From Here: Chaos or Community?* New York: Harper & Row.

Kovács, János Mátyás. 2002. Rival Temptations and Passive Resistance: Cultural Globalization in Hungary. In *Many Globalizations: Cultural Diversity in the Contemporary World,* edited by P.L. Berger and S.P. Huntington, 146–182. New York: Oxford University Press.

Lechner, Frank J., and John Boli, eds. 2000. *The Globalization Reader.* Malden, MA: Blackwell Publishers.

Legrain, Philippe. 2003. Cultural Globalization Is Not Americanization. *The Chronicle of Higher Education,* May 9: B7–B10.

Loewen, James W. 1995. *Lies My Teacher Told Me: Everything Your American History Textbook Got Wrong*. New York: Touchstone.

Masson, Paul. 2001. Globalization: Facts and Figures. IMF Policy Discussion Paper, October.

McFadden, Robert D. 2000. A Glittering Party for Times Square: Gleeful Embrace of a New Year Links the Globe's Midnights. *New York Times,* January 1.

McKay, John P., Bennett D. Hill, and John Buckler. 1983. *A History Of Western Society, Volume B: From the Renaissance to 1815.* Second edition. Boston: Houghton Mifflin Company.

Micklethwait, John, and Adrian Wooldridge. 2003. Rebuilding the Alliance to Rebuild Globalization. *New York Times,* April 13.

Reischauer, Edwin O. 1973. *Toward the 21st Century: Education for a Changing World.* New York: Alfred A. Knopf.

Reuters Online. 2003. WHO Chief Says Need for Openness Key SARS Lesson. July 11. http://reuters.com/newsArticle.jhtml?type=healthNews& storyID=3073723 (accessed July 11, 2003).

Sagan, Carl. 1997. *Billions and Billions: Thoughts on Life and Death at the Brink of the Millennium.* New York: Ballantine Books.

Salcedo, Rodrigo. 2003. When the Global Meets the Local at the Mall. *American Behavioral Scientist* 46, no. 8 (April): 1084–1103.

Saul, John Ralston. 2004. The Collapse of Globalism. *Harper's Magazine* 308 (March): 33–44.

Sernau, Scott. 2000. *Bound: Living in the Globalized World.* Bloomfield, CT: Kumarian Press.

Singer, Peter. 2002. Speaking on One World: The Ethics of Globalization. Lecture hosted by Carnegie Council on Ethics and International Affairs, New York City, October 29.

Srinivas, Tulasi. 2002. A Tryst with Destiny: The Indian Case of Cultural Globalization. In *Many Globalizations: Cultural Diversity in the Contemporary World,* edited by P.L. Berger and S.P. Huntington, 89–116. New York: Oxford University Press.

Stille, Alexander. 2001. Globalization Now, A Sequel of Sorts. *New York Times,* August 11.

Suárez-Orozco, Marcelo M., and Desirée Baolian Qin-Hilliard, eds. 2004. *Globalization: Culture and Education in the New Millennium.* Berkeley: University of California Press.

Taylor, Timothy. 2002. The Truth about Globalization. *The Public Interest* no. 147 (Spring): 24–44.

Tickell, Crispin. 2002. Human Responsibility in the Global Environment. *Asian Affairs* 33 (June): 206–215.

United Nations Development Programme. 2005. *Human Development Report.* http://hdr.undp.org/reports/global/2005/ (accessed October 13, 2005).

Urbino in the age of Federico Di Montefeltro, http://www.uniurb.it/Uborse/ worken.htm (accessed October 7, 2002).

Watson, James L. 2004. Globalization in Asia: Anthropological Perspectives. In *Globalization: Culture and Education in the New Millennium,* edited by M.M. Suárez-Orozco and D.B. Qin-Hilliard, 141–172. Berkeley: University of California Press.

Wolf, Martin. 1997. Why This Hatred of the Market? In *The Globalization Reader,* edited by F.J. Lechner and J. Boli, 9–11. Malden, MA: Blackwell Publishers.

World Bank. 2005. News release. Launch of World Development Indicators 2005 Report. April 17. http://www.worldbank.org (accessed April 21, 2005).

Wright, Robert. 2000. Will Globalization Make You Happy? *Foreign Policy* no. 120 (September-October): 54–64.

Yergin, Daniel, and Joseph Stanislaw. 2002. *The Commanding Heights: The Battle for the World Economy.* New York: Touchstone.

3

MY COUNTRY:
RIGHT, WRONG, OR IRRELEVANT?

Our Country! In her intercourse with foreign nations, may she
always be in the right; but our country, right or wrong!
—Stephen Decatur, 1816

And say not thou, 'My country right or wrong'
Nor shed thy blood for an unhallowed cause.
—John Quincy Adams, c. 1847

A Nation is Born

It started in familiar fashion. Colonial rulers imposed their will,
extracting resources and exercising arbitrary power over local citizens. The natives were often abused, and grew increasingly dis-
contented. Local leaders emerged who tapped into the desire for self-
determination. Their voices shouted for freedom. Resistance met
with hostility, and violence broke out. The people stood firm, struggled valiantly, and earned respect and admiration far and wide. Eventually, they broke free from colonial bonds and claimed their
independence.

The story could be that of the United States, Algeria, India, or
any of a number of places. In this case, the story was that of East
Timor, which on May 20, 2002, became an independent and sovereign
country. Twenty-seven years after Portugal relinquished its colony and
Indonesia invaded, its aspirations for independence prevailed.

A triumphant celebration ensued. As the BBC described it, "All
over town [Dili, the capital] children in their Sunday clothes nestle
close to their parents, waving small paper flags in the red, yellow and
black triangle and star design of this new state" (Markus 2002). One

activist told the news agency, "It's wonderful, like a dream in the middle of the day."

Supported by the United Nations and applauded by much of the world, East Timor became the first new nation formed in the twenty-first century. Yet its birth may be remembered as a concluding chap-ter in a remarkable growth of nations.

At the end of World War II, there were just 74 nations in the world. But propelled by local independence movements and the dismantling of colonialism, the second half of the twentieth century was marked by nations forming with celebrations not unlike what occurred in Dili. In Africa alone, 25 nations were formed between 1960 and 1964. By 1995, the number of independent nations had grown to 192 (Garrison 2004, 178).

National aspirations have fueled tremendous movements and given rise to hopes and dreams. The security and comfort offered by nationhood has sustained peoples everywhere. We all want to belong to an independent nation. While the expansion of nations today cannot possibly match the last century, nations will continue to form and evolve. They are neither permanent nor static concepts. Think of the United States' own shifts in geographic dimensions. A little more than one hundred fifty years ago, our nation did not extend to the Pacific Ocean. Borders will continue to be drawn and redrawn. But what does independence and nationhood mean in an era when global forces interject in the most significant operations of daily life?

Can a nation steer its own course amidst the tides of globalization? Or is it relegated to little more than coloring its flag and composing its anthem? Have globalization, multinational firms, and international bodies like the IMF, the World Bank, and the World Trade Organization (WTO) destroyed national autonomy? Can a country still decide its own fate? If not, where should citizens look for protection? How should we adapt?

What is a Nation?

What defines a nation? In 1933, the Seventh International Conference of American States was held in Uruguay. Called the Montevideo Convention on the Rights and Duties of States, a formal declaration set out the parameters of statehood. The definition identified four qualifications:

a. A permanent population

b. A defined territory

c. A government and

d. The capacity to enter into relations with other states

Others suggest broadening the definition to include common historical memories, a mass public culture, a common identity, and a common economy.

Some use the terms "nation" and "nation-state" interchangeably. Scholars Fred Dallmayr and José Rosales make a clear distinction between the two. According to them, a nation is defined as a group of people who see themselves as a community united by common historic experiences or shared ethnic origins (Dallmayr and Rosales 2001, xvi).

A nation-state is a legal structure. The state refers to the governing institutions, the nation to the people who share a sense of identity based on history, culture, or language.

The historic foundation of the sovereign nation-state is commonly traced to the treaties following the Peace of Westphalia in 1648. The settlements ended the Thirty Years' War in Europe, but more importantly, established a community of sovereign states that recognized and guaranteed each other's independence. This meant that for the first time, the territorial nation-state was officially declared the highest form of political authority.

Although there were nations before 1648, people defined themselves more by local and religious loyalties than as citizens of a particular country. After Westphalia, the Holy Roman Empire no longer had dominion over the Christian world, and the concept of the nation-state was firmly established.

National Sovereignty or a Worldwide Empire?

The perception of nation-states as autonomous, distinct, and the ultimate civil authority is entrenched in our minds. But is that view accurate and appropriate in a globalized world? How much sovereignty or autonomy can an East Timor or even the United States have as technological innovations render territorial and geographical barriers less important for transportation, communication, and commerce?

As Jean-Marie Guéhenno, former French ambassador to the European Union, now United Nations under-secretary-general for peacekeeping operations, wrote,

> . . . we have passed from a network of navigable waterways and railroads to an infrastructure of air transport and telecommunications that has profoundly upset the notion of space. . . . The essential is not to master a territory but to have access to a network. (Guéhenno 1995, 8)

Geography is not completely unimportant, but it is becoming less significant. Nowhere is that more evident than in the concept of what is called the global economy. When most people speak of globalization, they are only talking about the links between dollars, pesos, marks, and yen. Capital and goods have spread farther and faster than people have, and the economic links among nations are deeper than the intercultural connections within nations. As the global economy expands, the interests of nations are often superseded by the governing rules of the global market.

Former US Secretary of Labor Robert Reich argues, "As almost every factor of production—money, technology, factories, and equipment—moves effortlessly across borders, the very idea of an American economy is becoming meaningless" (Reich 1991, 8).

He says that in the future, "there will be no *national* products or technologies, no national corporations, no national industries. There will no longer be national economies, at least as we have come to understand that concept" (Reich 1991, 3).

One of the more interesting and influential recent books is *Empire,* written by Duke literature professor Michael Hardt and the Italian radical writer Antonio Negri. Hardt and Negri portray an emerging empire that has evolved beyond the power bases historically defined by nationalist expansions and colonialism. This empire, they write, is characterized by a system of diffuse national and supranational networks. These networks have no center of power. They are links created by individuals and organizations with shared desires and goals acting in close alignment.

The authors say that the dominance of these supranational networks of power, capital, and assembly and production has overshadowed the role of the nation. They suggest further that the nation itself has contributed to this process, functioning as a major participant in the organization and function of global capitalism. They write,

As the world market today is realized ever more completely, it tends to deconstruct the boundaries of the nation-state. In a previous period, nation-states were the primary actors . . . but to the world market they appear increasingly as mere obstacles. (Hardt and Negri 2000, 150)

Hardt and Negri suggest that this world market

has consisted first of all in the monetary deconstruction of national markets, the dissolution of national and/or regional regimes of monetary regulation, and the subordination of those markets to the needs of financial powers. (Hardt and Negri 2000, 346)

It is the same message articulated by Thomas Friedman and both fans and foes of globalization. Financial policies and other regulations cannot be imposed on a national basis, but must adapt to international realities.

Production, like power, has been decentralized. The assembly line has been replaced by flexible networks that cover the world. Knowledge and work can be instantaneously shared everywhere. This has created what Friedman describes as a "global playing field," in which individuals and companies have greater opportunities for innovation and collaboration. This is evident in the creation of products and services we use every day. For just one example, take a journey with us as we piece together your Dell notebook. As Friedman describes,

The Intel microprocessor came from an Intel factory either in the Philippines, Costa Rica, Malaysia, or China. The memory came from a Korean-owned factory in Korea, a Taiwanese-owned factory in Taiwan, a German-owned factory in Germany, or a Japanese-owned factory in Japan. . . . The keyboard came from either a Japanese-owned company in Tianjin, China, a Taiwanese-owned factory in Shenzen, China, or a Taiwanese-owned factory in Suzhou, China. . . . The wireless card came from either an American-owned factory in China or Malaysia, or a Taiwanese-owned factory in Taiwan or China. . . . The hard-disk drive was made by an American-owned factory in Singapore, a Japanese-owned company in Thailand, or a Japanese-owned factory in the Philippines. . . . The power cord was made by a British-owned company with factories in China, Malaysia, and India. The removable memory stick was made by either an Israeli-owned company in Israel or an American-owned company with a factory in Malaysia. (Friedman 2005, 416–417)

Everything was coordinated so the right pieces arrived at the assembly point at just the right time. The world market and this global supply chain have irrevocably tied countries together.

The future of a nation is tied more closely to this global production process and the movement of capital than to the individual wishes of citizens. This message was well summarized in graffiti written in Poland, "We wanted democracy, but we ended up with the bond market" (Held et al. 1999, 232).

There is a sense that the global economic picture is too complex for the average citizen to understand. Many feel that it is better to let the experts sort it out and figure out what is best for us. Just as troubling is the tendency to condemn certain groups and people. Many would like to believe there is a global plot to take over the world through control of financial resources.

Humans like intrigue. We like to imagine that somewhere, there is a small, secret group of villains seeking global domination. We like to demonize and focus on the bad guys, like the evil organization SPECTRE in James Bond films.

It is an easy image to conjure up. Authors and screenwriters know our fascination with the guys in the black hats. From Iago to Lex Luthor, Inspector Javert to Darth Vader, cowboys with black hats to the Klingons, we like to direct our wrath against clear-cut villains. We like having an unmistakable enemy to be allied against—a despicable foe with no redeeming qualities. The battles over globalization are no different.

When things do not go well, we especially like to cast blame. But who are the bad guys? Who are the villains in our globalized world? They used to be almost exclusively despotic regimes, but lately the focus has shifted.

Spanning the Globe

Are corporations now the bad guys? Their influence and interests span the globe, and they have drawn the anger of protestors. Companies such as Coca-Cola, Pepsi, Wal-Mart, Mars, General Electric, Microsoft, Wrigley, General Motors, Exxon Mobil, Nike, and McDonald's have all come under fire.

Firms that operate beyond an individual nation's borders are called multinational or transnational corporations. Multinational means that the organization does business and has operations in more than one country. Transnational means that its operations transcend or are beyond the scope of national boundaries. How much power do these global businesses really have?

We recently visited the world headquarters of Coca-Cola in Atlanta, Georgia. On previous visits, we simply drove up to the front door. No longer. You must now drive two blocks away to a large parking lot, then move through a canopy, where your car is inspected. Guards check under your car with mirrors, open the trunk, and ask where you have been. What are they looking for? Bombs or contraband cans of Pepsi? Only after you pass inspection can you park your car. Finally, you wait for a shuttle bus, which takes you to the headquarters' entrance.

Why has Coca-Cola implemented such extreme security measures? The attacks of September 11 are the obvious public justification. But even within the context of terrorism, why would Coca-Cola be a potential target? Is it an American icon? Yes, but it is just flavored water.

A story here might provide some clue as to why a company such as Coca-Cola is both so loved and also so feared. It comes from a senior administrator for the public relations firm Porter Novelli.

> A friend of mine told me a story very soon after the genocide in Rwanda. He was there as a military representative accompanying an NGO tour of the area. The situation was awful. There was also no infrastructure to get to the people in need. And so there were United Nations convoys that just couldn't get through. This delegation literally sat there on the road for hours going nowhere. By the time they finally reached their destination, they discovered that Coke had already been there for two weeks distributing what they needed. . . . It shows you just how powerful the global market is and this brand in particular. . . . I suppose if Microsoft needs to be there, they'll be there too. (Hunter and Yates 2002, 323)

Why would a company such as Mars, or even Hershey, be on the list of multinational forces envied and hated? What does chocolate have to do with the global picture? The competition for chocolate sales illustrates how multinational trading battles overlap with political conflicts involving nation-states.

The Chocolate Wars

On July 17, 1990, former Iraqi President Saddam Hussein delivered his "Revolution Day" speech, filled with fiery rhetoric and loaded with attacks on Kuwait. The same day, a corporate attorney working for the Mars chocolate company received a personal translation of Hussein's comments. It came from "the intelligence unit at Mars Electronics, a division of the company that, among other things, gathers information on political activities around the world that might affect Mars operations" (Brenner 1999, 5).

The Mars organization closely monitored such developments because the Persian Gulf region represented $40 million in annual sales, with strong distribution of M&M's, Snickers, Milky Ways, Starburst Fruit Chews, and Uncle Ben's rice. Saudi Arabia accounted for 50 percent of that market, and Kuwait 25 percent.

When Iraqi troops invaded Kuwait, the crisis had fully emerged. All channels into the region were blocked by the US Navy. Communications into and out of Kuwait were nearly impossible.

By August 8, 1990, though, when Iraq "annexed" Kuwait, a Mars team was already in the war zone. A Mars SWAT team had been flown in from London and set up a "crisis management center" in a conference room at the King James Hotel in Riyadh, Saudi Arabia, which was the headquarters for every major media organization, including CNN. The team's mission, as directed by headquarters, was to protect the Mars franchise and increase sales.

In just a few days, the team developed a two-pronged campaign, code-named "SuperSavers." The first element was a program of special rebates, coupons, and price breaks, linked with personal visits by Mars delegates to distributors and shopkeepers.

The second was a presentation to the generals at the US Army Command center, which was in charge of managing the flow of hundreds of warships to the Persian Gulf. The core appeal was that "Snickers bars are just as necessary as weaponry."

> . . . none of the countries participating in Operation Desert Shield, as the initial maneuvers came to be known, had time to establish supply lines before sending troops to the region. Mars was the only company to operate an air-conditioned distribution warehouse and control an enormous fleet of refrigerated supply trucks, a boon to the troops who were being scattered throughout the 400,000 square miles of Saudi Desert. Overnight, Mars

received permission to continue shipping its products . . . (Brenner 1999, 7–8)

The Snickers battle was won. Mars not only saved its operation, but actually increased volume and market share. More importantly, it prevented the real enemy—Hershey—from being anywhere in the region. Using a similarly aggressive strategy, Mars later made a spectacular expansion into Russia following the dissolution of the Soviet Union, in what became known as the "Snickerization" of Russia (Brenner 1999, 284).

"Business Without Borders"
This is a critical point in understanding the global mosaic: Multinational firms have incredible power both to influence governments and to work outside of their jurisdiction. They are looking for the most profitable places to make and sell their products. They do not believe they are constrained by boundaries, and it is this mentality, more than any particular fact or figure, that defines the global economy.

As a Microsoft ad campaign proudly declared in 2004 and 2005, "We see business without borders." The flexibility and mobility of these multinationals make them poised to move and act faster at the global level, without the constraints that states usually face.

Their size and power command attention. According to the Institute for Policy Studies, in 2002, fifty-two of the world's one hundred largest economies were multinational corporations. General Motors was larger than Saudi Arabia. Toyota's sales revenue was comparable to the total GDP of Greece and Finland. General Electric was larger than Portugal and Ireland, while IBM was larger than Colombia (Institute for Policy Studies 2005).

Many countries could only look with admiration at the enormous wealth generated by the number one Fortune 500 firm, Wal-Mart, which earned $245 billion in revenue in 2002. That was more than the economies of all but thirty nations (Weiner 2003). Wal-Mart's global expansion is the envy of all major transnational firms. In 1990, it operated only in the United States, but in less than a decade, it expanded into Mexico, the United Kingdom, Canada, Germany, China, Brazil, South Korea, and Argentina. By 2003, it was the largest retailer in Canada and the largest private employer in Mexico, controlling close to 30 percent of all supermarket food sales (Weiner 2003). But a cashier at a Wal-Mart in Mexico makes about

$1.50 an hour, compared to $9 an hour in the United States. And some condemn the homogenizing effect such a conglomerate's products have on commerce and culture. A Wal-Mart in Mexico is very similar to a Wal-Mart in America. But for better or worse, its power is unmistakable.

Wal-Mart is not alone in its global reach. According to the United Nations Conference on Trade and Development (UNCTAD), in the early 1990s, there were 37,000 international companies with 175,000 foreign subsidiaries. By 2003, there were 64,000 international firms with 870,000 subsidiaries (*Economist* 2004a).

Amnesty International noted the decline in the power of nations compared with multinationals.

> . . . the top 200 multi-national corporations have more economic power than the poorest four-fifths of humanity . . . Through this sheer size, economic dominance and mobility, the multi-nationals can set the agenda for development, sway political decisions and have a major impact on the reality of human rights for very many people. (Amnesty International 1998, 188)

About six hundred multinational firms control approximately one-quarter of the world's economy and 80 percent of world trade (Burbules and Torres 2000, 6). Some of the heads of multinationals personally possess more wealth than many nations. Bill Gates's net worth at one point exceeded the gross national product (GNP) of all Central America nations combined (Sernau 2000, 72).

Who Wins the Race to the Bottom?

C.F. Hathaway shirts are an American tradition. Founded in 1837, the company supplied clothes for Union soldiers in the Civil War. It once initiated a popular advertising campaign featuring a man with an eye patch. But in 2002, after 165 years of making shirts in Maine, the company closed its doors and moved production overseas. President Donald Sappington explained simply that the company could not compete when production costs were so much lower in other countries. Hathaway is not alone among apparel and shoe companies that have left the country. In fact, it was the last major shirt factory left in the United States (*New York Times* 2002).

Fruit of the Loom is America's largest manufacturer of screen print T-shirts. From 1995 to 1997, the company closed down nearly all of its US operations and relocated overseas, and "by 1998, over 95 percent of its goods were being sewn in Central America, Mexico, or the Caribbean" (Benjamin-Gomez, 2002, 170).

In the mid-nineteenth century, a Bavarian immigrant named Levi Strauss began producing jeans that would become an American tradition. US factories have stitched and sewn more than 3.5 billion pairs of the red-tag jeans. As much as any piece of clothing, Levi's blue jeans scream American pop culture and have been worn with flair by American icons such as Bruce Springsteen and James Dean. But in the 1990s, faced with brutal competition, more and more Levi's factories began closing. On January 8, 2004, the last of the Levi's manufacturing plants in America shut down. Today, the bulk of the company's jeans are manufactured by suppliers in fifty foreign countries, including those in Asia and the Caribbean, where labor is considerably cheaper.

As the *New York Times* described, Levi's was "another casualty of the shrinking homegrown apparel industry that since 1995 has halved its domestic work force in favor of cheaper foreign labor" (Blumenthal 2003). One woman whose job at Levi's was relocated overseas said, "I make $12 an hour. The people who'll be doing the work, they get paid $12 a week" (*Hackensack Record* 2003).

This trend is not limited to the apparel or textile industry. We have seen it occurring with automakers, electronics firms, and others. From manufacturing to white-collar services such as data processing and writing computer software, the globalization of production— commonly referred to as offshore outsourcing—has expanded into nearly every realm of business. The gains for companies are clear: more growth, new resources, opportunities for innovation and efficiency, and, perhaps above all, lower costs. A computer programmer in India makes about $8,000 a year, while one in the United States is paid about $70,000 (Morley 2004). A highly skilled machinist in the United States makes about $3,000 to $4,000 each month, while a factory worker in China earns about $150 per month, on average (Friedman 2005, 124). Companies, consumers, and some workers enjoy numerous gains, but many others are left behind.

To attract capital, nations must create a favorable environment for profit. Nations compete to attract multinational investment by selling low-cost labor and offering tax breaks and freedom from burdensome regulations, and companies run to where they can make the greatest profits. These practices are routinely condemned and often referred to as a race to the bottom.

It was not too long ago when US companies threatened to move to Mexico to escape the high wages needed to pay American workers and stringent environmental regulations. Mexico offered a reprieve on both counts and defined the race to the bottom. No longer. Now, China is most commonly described as the best deal for production. Labor costs in Mexico in 2003 rose to a whopping $1.20 per hour. Still sounds like a bargain, right? Not when you consider the same rate in China was 48 cents (M. Stevenson 2003). So factories packed their bags and moved from Mexico to China, where workers produce such items as statuettes of Mexico's patron saint, the Virgin of Guadalupe.

We have all read stories of exploited workers toiling in oppressive conditions to manufacture sneakers and soccer balls. No multinational firm goes into a country with the intent to harm its workers. When the competition heats up, however, and when worker-friendly regulations are scarce, abuses are often a consequence. In these instances it can be great to be a multinational seeking a profit, but not so great to be a worker looking to make a living. Some economists point out that even the low wages of multinationals offer workers greater opportunities than they would have otherwise, and provide a base for future earnings. And of course the multinational giants heavily promote their contributions to progress other than the jobs provided, such as the rising amount of foreign investment that usually accompanies their arrival.

There is a joke often repeated in business schools that the only thing worse than being exploited by transnational corporations is not being exploited by them. There may be an element of truth in that. As one Mexican citizen said when discussing the increased presence of Wal-Mart, his country's biggest private job generator,

> That's globalization, and Mexico has to play the game, right? Maybe some of the profit leaves Mexico, but Mexico gets back some foreign investment, right? That's how things work. It doesn't matter to me if I'm buying from a multinational company, as long as they give me what I want. (Weiner 2003)

Countries must attract foreign firms and investments. They cannot afford to be left out of the game. Such investment is absolutely critical, especially for developing countries, and not just because it brings money. As management and economics professor Lester Thurow points out, "Global companies possess markets, technology, and scarce management or engineering skills that developing countries must have if they are to participate in the global economy" (Thurow 2003, 198). He adds, "Because countries need corporations more than corporations need countries . . . the relative bargaining power of governments and multinational corporations is shifting in favor of corporations" (Thurow 2003, 282).

Many giant firms no longer pay any taxes to governments. In fact, some governments now pay the multinationals to come to them. Israel, for example, paid Intel $600 million in grants, financing, and tax rebates (Thurow 2003, 282). Incentives are also offered within nations. In the United States, Alabama and South Carolina have paid large bills to attract automakers, while New Jersey offered tax breaks to keep Verizon from moving.

As economic growth levels declined in the early part of this decade, countries desperately tried to make themselves attractive to corporations and investors. In 2002, seventy governments passed a record number of 248 investment-friendly legal and regulatory changes (*Foreign Policy* 2004).

The Real Axis of Evil?

Multinational firms with their power to influence governments and economies have been increasingly resented and attacked. But three organizations have emerged as particularly conspicuous targets on the global landscape:

- The IMF
- The World Bank
- The WTO

In the words of the president of the International Forum on Globalization, the three form an "unholy trinity" or "iron triangle" that "couldn't have done a more harmful job on people and the planet if they set out with these goals in mind" (Hunter and Yates 2002, 328).

Are these supranational organizations the real "axis of evil?" Are they the bad guys? Most individuals have little or no knowledge of their backgrounds or purposes. How can you connect the dots and make an informed judgment without that understanding?

Understanding the IMF and the World Bank
At the conclusion of World War II, the IMF and the World Bank were created to bring some semblance of order and stability to the global economy, while encouraging international trade. Both are specialized agencies within the United Nations system, with 184 member countries.

The IMF is charged with promoting international monetary cooperation and exchange rate stability. It offers economic policy advice, technical assistance, and, perhaps most importantly, emergency loans for countries in financial trouble. In effect, the IMF often serves as a lender of last resort. Funds are provided through the contributions of member nations. Trillions have been lent. All of this is good.

Whether because of corrupt local leadership, ineffective project management, unreasonable loan requirements, or simply poor historic judgment, however, many countries have ended up dedicating significant portions of their budgets to debt payments.

The World Bank was formed to encourage international investments and help ravaged countries rebuild after World War II. Initially, it provided loans for projects in Europe. Its focus, however, soon turned to the developing nations of the Third World, with loans, grants, and technical assistance to help countries build their infrastructure and improve health, education, and other services. In 1948, it made its first loan to the Third World—$16 million to Chile for power-plant and agricultural machinery. The World Bank has also financed the construction of hydroelectric plants, highway systems, and other major projects. All of this is also good.

The World Bank's investments in infrastructure have been judged fundamental to economic growth. The Bank stepped in not only because the recipient countries could not afford the cost themselves, but also because they could not attract private capital to the projects.

Like any other large bank, the World Bank raises money by selling bonds to investors. The bank also receives financing from donor nations, including the United States, its highest contributor. It then lends the money out to the public sectors of countries at rates below those commercially available, and typically allows longer times for repayment. In an average year, the World Bank lends roughly $20 billion to the governments of developing countries (World Bank 2005).

Despite the trillions of dollars it has provided for development-related projects, "even the bank's supporters say it has not done enough" (R. Stevenson 2002). Some World Bank-sponsored projects damaged the environment and were fraught with mismanagement. Such problems have led to a shift in focus. In 1980, 21 percent of bank lending went to power projects. In 2002, only 7 percent did. At the same time, the percentage of funding dedicated to social services has risen.

Understanding the World Trade Organization (WTO)
The WTO was established in 1995, replacing the loosely structured treaty known as the General Agreement on Tariffs and Trade (GATT). The GATT took effect in 1948, establishing a set of rules to encourage trade and help build the foundation of the global economy. The WTO inherited the GATT's principles and substantially expanded upon them. It created a stronger dispute resolution mechanism and has greater authority to impose punishments. Looking strictly at the dramatic rise in world trade since 1948, there is no question that the GATT and WTO have been hugely effective.

The WTO has 149 member states, which abide by an agreement twenty-six thousand pages long (Ellwood 2001, 32). The agreements have been negotiated and signed by members and ratified by their governments. In effect, the WTO acts as an international arbiter. It has the authority to attack many kinds of protectionist measures that infringe upon free trade, whether it is in the form of government subsidies, health rules that serve only as import barriers, or trade preferences. It can also impose a variety of penalties and trade sanctions.

The WTO is a forum in which poor countries can seek justice and defend their rights. On some occasions, its negotiations have ended in failure, but it has at other times solved lingering disputes, such as the recent battle over access to generic medicines. Poor nations vigorously complained that they needed to import generic versions of expensive drugs to combat epidemics like AIDS, malaria, and tuberculosis. But the United States protested that such measures ran counter to trade laws protecting patent rights. The WTO brokered a solution in 2003 that allowed generic versions to be imported as long as the case was a public emergency. Supachai Panitchpakdi, then-director general of the WTO, said the agreement "proves once and for all that the organization can handle humanitarian as well as trade concerns" (Becker 2003). Perhaps, but critics of that deal believed the hurdles would prove too daunting for poor nations to import the needed drugs.

The aims of the IMF, World Bank, and WTO appear to be fundamentally about improving both the stability of countries and the quality of the lives of millions of people around the world. So why is there such controversy?

Striking Back

It is an understatement to say that the three organizations receive criticism. Their rules for trade and economic policies have come under fierce attack, for both their perceived bias against developing countries and their limitations on national sovereignty. The protests first entered the international spotlight in what was known as the "Battle of Seattle." In late 1999, tens of thousands of protestors disrupted the Seattle meeting of the WTO, causing the talks to collapse. It particularly struck observers that the protests featured a motley coalition of environmentalists, consumer groups, autoworkers, steelworkers, and other unlikely allies. From Seattle, protests have spread throughout the world, and international institutions now meet with the expectation of drawing demonstrations and media attention.

While activists are commonly labeled anti-trade or antiglobalization, the vast majority actually protest current rules and practices. Rather than being anti-globalization, their movements are themselves global. Most seek a kinder, gentler globalization, one that spreads economic benefits to more people and protects the environment. Journalist and activist Naomi Klein strongly objects to the term anti-globalization: "The way I see it, I am part of a network of movements that is fighting not against globalization but for deeper and more responsive democracies, locally, nationally and internationally. This network is as global as capitalism itself" (Klein 2002, 77).

Many among the protestors agree that international trade can create jobs, raise standards of living, and bring people closer together. It has inspired new energies while opening societies to new ideas, prosperity, and hope.

Throughout history, increased trade and mobile capital have brought great progress to many parts of the world. Tremendous wealth has been generated. Advanced nations found new markets for their products, while developing countries enjoyed greater economic development, new employment opportunities, and higher living standards. The exchange of people and ideas created great opportunities for both developed and developing nations. Economic development helped clear the way for advancing civil liberties and political liberalization. In many cases, gains from trade have exceeded losses, and in general, the concepts of open access and fair trade are positive values worth supporting.

But opening up a country to free trade can also severely undermine the local economy. Alongside gains associated with trade have come cultural clashes and military conflicts that generate hostility to this day. Controversies over colonial legacies are still fresh. Did the British East India Company prove to be a positive influence on the history of India? Not when you consider the cruel management, exploitative practices, and plunder of many cities, such as Bengal. Did Columbus's trade mission bring prosperity? For some, yes; but for the natives already living in the New World, the answer is obvious.

The costs and benefits of the history of trade, economic integration, and exploitation can certainly be debated, and have been the subject of many writings. For our purpose of connecting the dots, what is undeniable is that economic links are bringing people and countries together. Again, it is an old process, but the incredible speed of integration and the extent of the links are new.

In 1997, a local financial crisis in Thailand quickly became regional in its devastation and global in its impact. Within two years, Malaysia's economy shrank by 25 percent, South Korea's by 45 percent, and Indonesia's by 80 percent (Brecher, Costello, and Smith 2000, 8). Because of so many integrated links, economic aftershocks reverberated in Russia and Brazil. The same banks that held Thai baht also held Brazilian reales.

> A few small, localized financial difficulties had set off a chain reaction of failures that swept across national boundaries, creating a huge currency devaluation and stock market crashes from Asia to South America. It eventually caused the single biggest point loss ever of the Dow Jones Industrial Average . . . (Barabási 2003, 210–211)

Such networked crises are ammunition for those who condemn the connections of globalization. Critics also feel that citizens have little or no role to play in the decision-making process, and much work is not subject to public review. That position is reinforced by the fact that WTO, IMF, and World Bank officials are not elected and thus not directly accountable to the public.

Protesters see unrestricted, external organizations intruding on national sovereignty. As the Sierra Club's director for international programs put it,

> The reason we were in Seattle protesting the WTO is because these trade agreements fundamentally challenge environmental laws not only in this country, but in any country that restricts trade. We have a problem with that—and so do environmentalists in other countries. (Hunter and Yates 2002, 328)

Joseph Stiglitz is a Nobel Prize–winning economist, the former chairman of the Council of Economic Advisers to President Bill Clinton, and a former senior vice president at the World Bank. He knows a thing or two about the economics of globalization. Stiglitz has attacked the inequities created by globalization, arguing that trade policies have caused great suffering and protest. But, he says, perhaps the number one "discontent" is that prevailing economic policies force nations to take a backseat in decision-making. He describes, for instance, how the International Monetary Fund

> undermines the democratic process, because it dictates policies. When [South] Korea needed money, it was told, "Only if you open up your markets faster than had been agreed and only if you have a central bank independent and focused exclusively on inflation." In the United States, the Federal Reserve Board focuses on inflation, employment and growth. And yet the IMF gave Korea no choice. It's not only that I think it's bad economic policy, but I think those are the kinds of things that countries should decide for themselves. (Stiglitz 2002)

Structural adjustment programs (SAPs) have been of particular concern. In exchange for needed loans, the IMF and World Bank often require that countries enact wholesale structural changes in their governments and economies. This means opening up nations' markets to outside investment, emphasizing the reduction of budget deficits, and often, significantly reducing public sector and social services, such as education and health care. IMF supporters claim such emphases have greatly reduced poverty in countries like China and India.

> The idea is that such tough medicine—or "shock treatment" as it's sometimes called—will revitalize moribund economies burdened with the dead weight of flabby, corrupt public sectors. This approach will free up entrepreneurial energies that will, in time, bring prosperity to all. . . . [Those who lose their state jobs and pensions] and who have seen food and electricity prices go through the roof after government price regulations are abolished—will eventually find good jobs in the private sector, while foreign investors will be handsomely paid. (Hackensack Record 2001)

Unfortunately, history has not always validated the theory. Promised benefits often have not materialized, and SAPs in some instances have led to more hardships.

Thurow noted, "Historically, the IMF has been very good at restoring financial stability (its primary job) but horrible at restoring domestic prosperity (its secondary job)" (Thurow 2003, 231). In many countries, debts have soared, leading to increased burdens on national budgets, while SAPs often have not been successful in improving economic performance. According to Nancy Alexander, "SAPs exacerbated the gap in per capita income (gross national product [GNP]) between the countries with the richest fifth of the world's people and those with the poorest fifth" (Alexander 2001, 319). But the pressure to conform to IMF prescriptions is enormous because other creditors and donors often follow the IMF's lead.

As Ellwood notes, the conditions of these programs have "diverted government revenues away from things like education and healthcare, towards debt repayment and the promotion of exports. This gave the World Bank and IMF a degree of control that even the most despotic of colonial regimes rarely achieved" (Ellwood 2001, 49).

Another common critique of the IMF and other global financial organizations is that they fail to account for local cultures and varying conditions that require flexibility and diversity. Robert Solow, a professor emeritus of economics, points out that IMF and World Bank programs "tend to have an awful lot in common, whether they're aimed at Turkey or Thailand" (Massing 2002). Thurow observed, "With some justification the IMF is accused of being a doctor with one set of medicines (fiscal austerity, high interest rates, freer capital markets, and privatization of state-owned industry) that are administered whatever the disease" (Thurow 2003, 231).

But in a world so diverse, one size does not fit all.

Who is in Control?

In the summer of 2002, the IMF approved a much-needed $30 billion loan to Brazil. That approval, however, came with strict conditions for the government. Most of the money would be delivered a year after the agreement was signed, and only if the government met certain budgetary goals. That the IMF aid came with strings demanding increased fiscal austerity was nothing new, but the timing of the agreement was interesting: The deal was culminated during the final stages of Brazil's elections. The dictates of the world financial order and the limitations on domestic leaders and democratic processes were thrust into the spotlight.

In that election, the two leading opposition candidates hailed from the left of the government's candidate, and both were running on platforms that involved significant government spending for social welfare programs. Their promises were impossible to keep if the IMF's budgetary surpluses were to be met.

But with so much money at stake, both candidates ended up endorsing the deal, albeit reluctantly. One was quoted stating the obvious: "This limits the capacity for social investment we plan to make" (Rohter 2002). And indeed, the pledges to support the IMF did reduce the funds available for social programs. In fact, not long after being elected president, Luiz Inácio Lula da Silva began following many of the policies he had long criticized. This included ordering a multibillion-dollar increase in the budget surplus, which left little for the ambitious social programs he had promised. In the process, he angered many longtime followers, though less than a year after he was elected, Lula da Silva was described by *New York Times* writer Larry Rohter as the "darling" of the IMF and Wall Street investors (Rohter 2003).

Whether the IMF's conditions lead to eventual prosperity for Brazil is ultimately beside the point. The core issue is that the international financial community, ruling without popular consensus, influenced which policies could and could not be enacted by a democratically elected government. The desires of the local government and the people were overruled by the dictates of the market.

Let us look more closely at perhaps the most powerful organization in the financial community, the WTO. It can impose trade sanctions on member countries if it believes human rights laws or environmental and public health policies are unfair impediments to trade. This, in effect, allows an international group to challenge and overrule a nation's policies.

One example involves a WTO decision on the European Union's preferential treatment in importing bananas from former European colonies in Africa, the Caribbean, and the Pacific. The European governments believed it was a matter of sovereign foreign policy in relation to former colonies, but the United States protested, and the WTO ruled against the preferential treatment.

Another WTO decision overruled the European Union's refusal to import hormone-fed beef from the United States. The WTO ruled in favor of the United States, arguing that the Europeans had not produced sufficient evidence of health hazards from the beef, and that the ban therefore was an illegal trade barrier.

These two examples show how the policies of even a powerful confederation of nations, the European Union, can be overruled. Of course, it is important to add that the WTO cannot overturn a country's law; it can only authorize countries to retaliate with trade restrictions and tariffs. But the effect is usually the same.

It is also instructive that even the most dominant nation in the world is subject to severe punishment under the WTO. In 2003, the WTO ruled that steel tariffs imposed by the United States violated global trading rules. The United States protested the decision, but a WTO appeals panel ruled that the tariffs were illegal and that the European Union could impose sanctions on American imports worth $2.2 billion if the import duties were not removed. The United States ended up removing the tariffs. In another important ruling, in 2004, the WTO again ruled against the United States, determining that American cotton subsidies violated international trade rules.

Also in 2004, the European Union, following a WTO decision, imposed tariffs on $4 billion of American exports. The penalty—the largest sanction ever approved by the WTO—was incurred because of tax breaks the United States had given to American corporations. Congress passed a bill later that year eliminating the subsidies, and in early 2005, Europe lifted the trade sanctions. These decisions show again that no matter how strong they are, individual countries still have to play by the global rules.

The Golden Straitjacket

The operations and actions of the IMF, World Bank, and WTO are complex, powerful, and far-reaching. But we must understand that these institutions are just a part of globalization. Like multinational firms, they are products of globalization, not the causes of it. The processes they manage, whether perceived as beneficial or malignant, have been under way for some time and would continue even if these groups were abolished: "International financial capital was putting desperate squeezes on debtor countries well before the IMF stepped in to manage and rationalize the process" (Brecher, Costello, and Smith 2000, 35).

Indeed, the basic dynamics of the global economy would remain the same even without these organizations. These dynamics include:

- "Global competition to lower labor, environmental and social costs"
- "The power of highly mobile capital"
- "The bargaining power of corporations"
- The power concentrated in links between multinational giants and supranational institutions such as the WTO and IMF (Brecher, Costello, and Smith 2000, 35–36)

The confining nature of the economic conditions imposed by the world economic market is well depicted by Thomas Friedman's metaphor of the golden straitjacket. The conditions include:

- Making the private sector drive economic growth
- Shrinking state government and privatizing state-owned industries
- Keeping a low rate of inflation and price stability
- Maintaining a balanced budget
- Cutting tariffs on imports
- Removing restrictions on foreign investment
- Deregulating the economy, among other things (Friedman 1999, 105)

The potential benefits of participating in the global economy are so great—and the risks of not participating so grave—that countries must accept the constraints. But this golden straitjacket then narrows the political and economic policy choices of nation-states.

> Once your country puts it [the golden straitjacket] on, its political choices get reduced to Pepsi or Coke . . . Governments . . . that deviate too far from the core rules will see their investors stampede away, interest rates rise and stock market valuations fall. (Friedman 1999, 106)

While these policies benefit global finance, they are not always successful for the local economy. Making a country profitable for investment is not the same as making it a great place to live and raise a family. Public investment in quality of life areas is not always viewed favorably by multinationals looking for a workforce, or bond traders looking for quick growth. Education, health, and pension benefits, clean air regulations, or workplace safety are not always attractive priorities. What Friedman calls the electronic herd of investors wants to see stability and favorable conditions for profit.

Governments seemingly have no real choice. They must play by the rules of global finance or be left out of the game altogether. A nation's options are limited if it wishes to prosper in the global economy.

If companies and countries are driven by economic motives to win the race to the bottom, to whom can citizens look for protection? Can nation-states adequately balance protecting their citizens and the need for economic growth?

Will Nationalists Rebound?

Some have already written an obituary for powerful nation-states, or at least declared them to be in critical condition. Kingwell suggests that national sovereignty "seems to be a patient on life support" (Kingwell 2000, 6). As early as 1995, Kenichi Ohmae wrote that the nation-state

> has begun to crumble . . . in terms of real flows of economic activity, nation states have *already* lost their role as meaningful units of participation in the global economy of today's borderless world. . . . In terms of the global economy, nation states have become little more than bit actors. (Ohmae 1995, 207)

And Yergin and Stanislaw write,

> While the publics vote only every few years, the markets vote
> every minute. And it is private capital . . . that is being courted
> and lured by what used to be called the third world. But this
> financial integration comes with a price. . . . National govern-
> ments, whether in developed or developing countries, must in-
> creasingly heed the market's vote—as harsh as it sometimes can
> be. (Yergin and Stanislaw 2002, 394)

As commerce continues to globalize, the declining influence of
the nation-state will become more apparent. But it is clear that the
forces of nationalism remain strong. It is also clear that many owe a
great deal to the nation-state and will defend it against the onslaught.

As with East Timor, the formation of nations captures our attention. Well-established countries, particularly those that were once
colonies, continue to jubilantly celebrate their independence and nationhood. In 1976, the American bicentennial was marked by an overwhelming display of patriotism, with fireworks constantly soaring
and American flags streaming everywhere. Each year, the country's
birthday is a festive occasion that marks its ascension to nationhood,
an ascension that inspired numerous movements against colonial
empires.

After the era of imperialism, the concept of an independent
nation-state brought fulfillment and renewed notions of self-identity
to people who had struggled under colonial rule. Nationalism played
the defining role in overcoming foreign domination and defeating
colonialism.

Yet the forces of nationalism have brought with them at
times a collective conceit—a national ego that renders a group apart
from others simply on the basis of geography and the accident of
birthplace.

As William Greider notes,

> Every nation, especially the wealthier ones, promotes its own
> version of national arrogance, a natural self-centeredness that is
> very difficult to set aside. But global commerce undermines—
> and perhaps will someday destroy—the ancient nativist stereo-
> types by which different peoples are ranked and rank them-
> selves. (Grieder 1997, 470)

This sense of a national ego or arrogance is a strong force that can be found, to some degree, in every country in the world. However, it is based on an artificial creation and a false notion that the nation-state can control its own destiny.

There is nothing sacred or preordained about the nation-state. Some say that if the flames of nationalistic rituals were not stoked from time to time, the nation-state might not have lasted nearly this long. Thus, writes Bryan Turner,

> the communal basis of citizenship has to be constantly renewed within the collective memory by nostalgic festivals, public ceremonies of national struggle, and effervescent collective experience. National culture has all the characteristics of a patriarchal civil religion. (Turner 2001, 211)

But the forces of globalization are stronger than national cultures, national constructions, and national egos. Thurow uses a compelling metaphor to express the new role of the nation-state.

> In the 20th century, governments came to think of themselves as economic air traffic controllers controlling the flows of their economies. With globalization this power is disappearing for governments large and small. Governments are still important in the knowledge-based economy, but instead of being air traffic controllers of economic events within their borders, governments are increasingly having to become airport builders constructing runways to attract global economic activity to locate within their borders. (Thurow 2003, 286–287)

Beyond the global economy, other changes stemming from globalization force nation-states to look beyond their shores. Nations working on their own are simply too weak to overcome problems that do not know borders. Alone, no single country can solve global warming and environmental degradation, or the spread of disease and terrorism.

In 2003, WHO issued a global alert for the first time in its history. It created a global SARS network, recognizing that only through international collaboration and collective problem solving could such a challenge be met. When SARS was declared successfully contained, a large share of the credit was given to a powerful network of cooperation.

Professor of global health Ilona Kickbusch observed how in the field of health care, as in so many others, divisions between domestic and global policies "do not work any more." She added, "Just as many of the determinants of health are now beyond the control of nation-states conversely the action or inaction of a sovereign nation-state can endanger the health of the global community." Countries must "pool both sovereignty and resources based on a new mindset" and work within an international framework. "No state can go it alone" (Kickbusch 2003).

None of this means that the irrelevance of the nation-state is inevitable; just that its power is reduced and often subordinate to transnational forces. But the nation-state is not ready to wither away. In many areas, it still holds all the cards. Political forces ingrained for centuries are not easily cast aside. Core electoral constituencies still matter. People still find enormous comfort and confidence looking to national leaders and embracing national ideals. And those individuals treated most harshly by globalization will increasingly look to states to cushion the blow.

Within the overall framework of the globalized economy, nations still have options. States remain powerful actors, capable of dealing with a host of issues and acting in very efficient and different ways. While weakened, national regulations still apply, and borders and local policies still influence international transactions and determine where goods and services flow.

The issue is not whether the nation-state and national patriotism will survive in our time. They will. The main point is that in a global, interrelated world economy, the influence of national governments is declining.

National Interests in a Global Context

Let us be absolutely clear. Nations will continue to play significant roles. And they will continue to compete and concern themselves with strategic advantages. But the state must now share the stage with other actors.

Nations must somehow express national interests within a global context, understanding that their powers are limited and that multinational cooperation is the most effective way to address global problems. For countries as powerful as the United States, that humility does not and will not come easily, but it is necessary.

In the United States, it also becomes essential to understand the widespread resentment against our nation. Many see the IMF, World Bank, and WTO as instruments of American aims and desires.

Among other things, critics point out that the president of the World Bank is always an American citizen chosen by the US government (the managing director of the IMF has always been a European), and that the United States enjoys about 17 percent of the voting power in the IMF and the World Bank. The voting privileges are based on each state's contributions, and the United States has sufficient votes to veto the 85 percent special majority needed for significant decisions (Woods 2003, 74).

It is true that the United States has often acted in favor of multinational firms and their trading desires, and that the United States has used its power and influence to generate wealth for US firms and citizens. But it is also true that criticism of the United States is often used to deflect the focus from local mismanagement. In either event, and often unfairly, the result is the same: The United States is blamed when people suffer.

The United States must take the lead in ensuring that bodies such as the IMF and WTO treat people fairly by advocating for basic standards of health and welfare. The United States also needs to balance its leadership with a willingness to work with the international community. By embracing collective pursuits and initiating partnerships, even when it has the power to go it alone, the United States can show that it has the enlightened understanding needed to prosper in the twenty-first century.

For individual citizens, the challenge is even greater. A global consciousness is needed to understand the world of today. When finance dictates the rules that we live by, and when it is free to ignore borders, what does it mean to be a citizen of a particular nation? This is not a comfortable question for many. In fact, if people had a choice, most would rather continue thinking of themselves as belonging to a place—to the United States, Japan, Germany.

But as Greider argues,

> The deepest social meaning of the global industrial revolution is that people no longer have free choice in this matter of identity. Ready or not, they are already of the world. As producers or consumers, as workers or merchants or investors, they are now bound to distant others through the complex strands of commerce

and finance reorganizing the globe as a unified marketplace. The prosperity of South Carolina or Scotland is deeply linked to Stuttgart's or Kuala Lumpur's. The true social values of Californians or Swedes will be determined by what is tolerated in the factories of Thailand or Bangladesh. The energies and brutalities of China will influence community anxieties in Seattle or Toulouse or Nagoya. (Grieder 1997, 333)

A global society is emerging, and we can be pioneers.

Protecting Our Own

There is a common sentiment, expressed heatedly at times, demanding that citizens of a nation buy from within that nation. The intent is to increase the success of domestic businesses and improve the overall nation's prosperity. We all have heard the patriotic rallying cry, "buy American!" And many of us have felt a bit of guilt as we drive our Japanese automobiles through town. The advocates of that position mean well and perhaps truly believe that protection is a black-and-white issue that divides us from them. In an earlier era, they may even have had the laws of economics on their side.

However, the reality is that most companies and corporations today are interconnected in ways that defy clear positions. An American company may be based in the United States, employ domestic workers, and reinvest profits in the American economy. But it is increasingly likely that a company based in the United States may only have its headquarters here and manufacture many of its products overseas. Or, an overseas company may have operations here that in fact employ more American workers than the typical American company does.

As tensions rose during the UN debates over Iraq and patriotism spread across the land, a number of anti-French movements emerged because of France's opposition to the United States. There were loud calls to boycott French products, and in South Carolina, the state house passed a resolution for a boycott, 90 to 9. Yet something happened before the state senate could consider the measure. It seems that one of the biggest losers in the boycott would have been the French firm Group Michelin SA. As it turns out, many of the Michelin tires sold in the United States are in fact made in South Carolina factories. So the boycott movement was stopped dead in its tire tracks. Michelin's response was instructive: "A boycott of Michelin products in the U.S. wouldn't be a boycott of French products. It would be a boycott against American products, made in 17 U.S. factories, located in seven states" (Simpson 2003).

South Carolina Commerce Secretary Bob Faith was quoted as saying, "The global economy is so interconnected today, you'd be shooting yourself in the foot. You might be putting your neighbor out of work" (Simpson 2003). According to the US Department of Commerce, by the year 2000, foreign firms "employed 6.4 million U.S. workers with a payroll of some $330 billion" (Simpson 2003).

So "buy American" might mean "buying French" or "buying Japanese" or "buying German." And in other cases, "buy American" might not significantly benefit the American economy.

Americans should be concerned about the American economy and the effects their actions have on their country's prosperity. But they also need to understand how their country's economy is interwoven with that of the rest of the world, and how financial interests spring like branches of a tree from one continent to another and back again. In the words of Shashi Tharoor, a senior UN official,

> American jobs depend not only on local firms and factories, but also on faraway markets, grants of licenses and access from foreign governments, international trade rules that ensure the free movement of goods and persons, and international financial institutions that ensure stability.

That is part of the reason why, he adds, there are "few unilateralists in the American business community" (Tharoor 2003).

Citizens must recognize that their productive impact lies in forging alliances across frontiers and working on behalf of all people. The state cannot be counted on for everything, and individuals must work with institutions and others outside their nation.

As globalization has enabled companies to work collaboratively and branch out around the globe, so too can it help citizen groups actively confront the real sources of power and make effective contributions toward a better future. The good news about globalization is that while it has made the powerful global economy possible, it also has provided the tools for individuals to reach across borders and channel their common aspirations into meaningful dialogue and expression. The more the negative aspects of globalization threaten local communities and human citizens, the more those communities and citizens spawn movements that fight back and create opportunities for democratic expression.

What Change Do You Wish to See?

With the sheer scope of the corporate-driven global economy and the power of the World Bank, IMF, and WTO, what can any individual do? As Mahatma Gandhi said, "You must be the change you wish to see in the world."

Arising from the same forces of globalization—but playing catch-up to the global economy—is the spread of global citizens' groups and international associations brought together by common political and civil interests, needs, and desires.

History professor Craig Calhoun writes that it is not uncommon for the actions of individual movements to lag behind the mobilization of private capital. He says that one way to look at history is "as a race in which popular forces and solidarities are always running behind. It is a race to achieve social integration, to structure the connections among people and organize the world. Capital is out in front" (Calhoun 2002, 107).

But capital's lead may be shrinking.

The Rise of NGOs

An NGO is a group of citizens who come together to support a particular issue or address a problem. The rapid emergence of international NGOs is changing the political, economic, and cultural landscape. These associations of citizens are passionately fighting for social causes on a global scale.

Margaret Keck and Kathryn Sikkink describe these forces as "transnational advocacy networks." These forces help build links among citizens, states, and international organizations, and "multiply the channels of access to the international system" (Keck and Sikkink 1998, 1).

Advocacy networks are not new. Keck and Sikkink point to some prominently successful examples from history, including the international campaigns to abolish slavery and increase women's rights, as well as human rights efforts and environmental networks. Such campaigns have been able to pressure states and businesses to bring about significant change.

The number of these networks has risen dramatically in recent years. According to the *Yearbook of International Organizations,* in 1954, there were 1,008 international NGOs. By 2000, that number rose to 17,364 (Muldoon 2004, 144). In 1948, the United Nations "listed 41 consultative groups that were formally accredited to cooperate and consult with the UN Economic and Social Council (ECOSOC); in 1998, there were more than 1,500" (Simmons 1998).

There are many examples of these groups working internationally. Major organizations like Greenpeace and Amnesty International are well known, but empowered by technology, much smaller groups routinely forge links across borders.

These advocacy networks represent a startling new force arising in the midst of a world long dominated by nations and markets. They have radically changed the global dynamic, and contributed greatly to the expansion of awareness and action beyond the nation-state. An article in *Foreign Affairs* called "Power Shift," by Jessica Mathews, summed up the change:

> The end of the Cold War has brought no mere adjustment among states but a novel redistribution of power among states, markets, and civil society. National governments are not simply losing autonomy in a globalizing economy. They are sharing powers—including political, social, and security roles at the core of sovereignty—with businesses, with international organizations, and with a multitude of citizens groups, known as non-governmental organizations (NGOs). The steady concentration of power in the hands of states that began in 1648 with the Peace of Westphalia is over, at least for a while. . . . International standards of conduct are gradually beginning to override claims of national or regional singularity. Even the most powerful states find the marketplace and international public opinion compelling them more often to follow a particular course. (Mathews 1997)

Another journal, *Foreign Policy,* in 1998, described the rise of NGOs well.

> Until recently, NGOs clustered in developed and democratic nations; now groups sprout out from Lima to Beijing. They are changing societal norms, challenging national governments, and

linking up with counterparts in powerful transnational alliances. And they are muscling their way into areas of high politics, such as arms control, banking, and trade, that were previously dominated by the state. (Simmons 1998)

In *Multitude,* their sequel to *Empire,* Hardt and Negri describe the vast potential of the growing network of citizens and movements to effect change. They assert that the same forces that made the empire of commercial networks possible have created great opportunities for democratic expression. The multitude, which they describe as "the living alternative that grows within Empire," features diverse people and groups focused on multiple causes and subjects, who converge in a common web or network. "What the multitude produces is not just goods or services; the multitude also and most importantly produces cooperation, communication, forms of life, and social relationships" (Hardt and Negri 2004, 339).

Writers across the landscape of ideas and opinions agree about the vast potential for individuals to act in concert to shape globalization, using the tools that have made globalization possible. We can all have a global reach.

A particularly powerful example is the work of the International Campaign to Ban Landmines (ICBL). Just five years after its founding in 1992, it was responsible for an international treaty prohibiting the use of antipersonnel landmines. The group's founder, Jody Williams, received the 1997 Nobel Peace Prize. The ICBL has been heralded for its use of technology, particularly e-mail, to build awareness and mobilize activists.

As Williams explains, working with activists in the developing world

forced us all to look at the speed, efficiency and cost-effectiveness of e-mail. My own bills dropped from around $400–$500 a month for telephone/fax bill to $20 for e-mail! . . . Electronic mail has permitted the ICBL to carry out its priority of frequent and timely internal communication to a greater degree than ever before. (ICBL 2002)

Empowered by New Tools

The capabilities of global communication technologies—particularly the Internet—have created opportunities to both effect change and cause havoc. Information can be instantly and cheaply relayed, and there is little that governments can do to control it. New partnerships and coalitions can be formed and expanded both within nations and across oceans. Examples appear everywhere.

- The Zapatista rebellion in Chiapas, Mexico, has relied heavily on the Internet to communicate its message and mobilize support. The movement became both local and global as it advocated indigenous rights in Mexico and criticized the operations of the global economy.
- Activists outraged by the 1984 Union Carbide gas leak that killed thousands in India established a Web site that not only has the background to the story, but also maintains current action alerts about recent developments in the case, and provides links among activists from India to Long Island, New York. Other Web sites have targeted particular companies alleged to have acted illegally or irresponsibly.
- In 1998, students in Indonesia used e-mail to coordinate protests against the Suharto dictatorship. In 2005, hundreds of thousands of protestors in Lebanon, urging the withdrawal of Syrian troops, were drawn together by e-mails.
- In 2002 and 2003, spurred by technology, anti-Iraq war protests spread faster and farther than perhaps any movement in history. Millions could log onto a number of Web sites to find out about global campaigns, sign antiwar statements and petitions online, receive e-mail alerts, and forward notes to elected officials.

Technology has helped change the nature of grassroots movements, lessening the need for flamboyant leaders and centralized operations that are usually essential to rapidly deploying people. As the *New York Times* reported, "the Internet has become more than a mere organizing tool; it has changed protests in a more fundamental way, by allowing mobilization to emerge from free-wheeling amorphous groups, rather than top-down hierarchical ones" (Lee 2003).

Cell phone text-messaging also has been used effectively in many movements, including the demonstrations in Lebanon and the 2004 antigovernment protests in Spain following the Madrid bombings. In 2001, the same technology helped oust Philippine leader Joseph Estrada on charges of corruption, as text messages spread the news about rallies and encouraged people to protest (Lee 2003). Text messages exchanged among China's mobile phone users helped expose the SARS epidemic in 2003, even as government authorities denied there was a problem.

Whether it is generating support for a cause or responding to a need, the Internet and new communications technologies are now indispensable. When a devastating earthquake sent tsunamis crashing into southern Asia in 2004, blogs and Internet bulletin boards provided some of the earliest accounts of the destruction, and were used to search for survivors and missing persons.

At the same time, technology has been used for less benign purposes. When Chechen rebels held hundreds of people hostage in a theater in Moscow in 2002, a pro-rebel Web site communicated details about the hostage-takers and their demands. In 2004, that Web site relayed news about attacks outside a Moscow subway station and at a school in the southern city of Beslan. While some view the rebels as fighting for independence and others see them as terrorists, the point remains the same: The Internet is a powerful tool that can spread information and inspiration—as well as fear and hate—worldwide in seconds.

In another notorious example, al-Qaeda threats have appeared on Web sites and were quickly disseminated throughout the world. The September 11, 2001 hijackers used the Internet to coordinate their movements and buy airline tickets, while Osama bin Laden regularly uses satellite television to disseminate messages. And we have become familiar with the gruesome sight of beheadings broadcast on the Internet.

Regardless of evil or humanitarian intent, new technologies are changing the dynamics of power and protests. The trend of NGOs linking online and targeting a government or corporation has been called an "NGO swarm" in a RAND study. The swarm, says RAND, "has no central leadership or command structure; it is multi-headed, impossible to decapitate. And it can sting a victim to death" (Brecher, Costello, and Smith 2000, 83).

Using new communication tools to spread resistance is not a new phenomenon. As mentioned in chapter 2, rebels challenging the Roman Catholic Church used the printing press to cultivate the Reformation. Later, cheap local presses helped revolutionaries like Thomas Paine communicate their ideas. But today, we have much more powerful tools to spread information.

Some governments are fighting back and attempting to censor the new technologies. They wish to stop the flow of information over the Web. Internet offenses can land users in jail in some countries. But despite these attempts to suppress information, the genie cannot be put back in the bottle.

The Internet certainly dominates, but we cannot ignore how important advances in broadcasting have been. The whole world watches when countries and companies act. Anyone with a digital recorder can portray suffering and misery from the most remote regions of the globe. Oppressive and ruthless acts and policies result more and more often in national and international scandals, boycotts, and sanctions. That global spotlight is an important determinant in shaping behavior. As Sernau and others have observed, these new technologies played a critical role in the demise of authoritarian regimes in Eastern Europe.

> Satellite television leaped over iron curtains and media censors with reports from around the world, and most importantly, in neighboring regions. . . . The flow of information was so vast with so many sources, that it could not be fully censored or contained. (Sernau 2000, 155)

Power of the Multitude

The swarm is poised to mobilize at a minute's notice. To be sure, it can be ruthless and counterproductive. Many NGOs are far from democratic or accountable, and some large ones have adopted brutal business practices. And many are only concerned with a narrow slice of interests. Working in isolation, they could guarantee not a stronger civil society, but a more fragmented world.

Author and activist Nicanor Perlas reminds us, though, that while a bee swarm can sting its enemies, it also is a pollinator, spreading new ideas in fertile soils around the world. International citizens' groups can be undemocratic and divisive, but they also can be very representative and unified, and can productively embrace the creative task "of shaping a better world" (Perlas 2000, 273).

Acting beyond the realm of states, citizens can influence governments, shape market realities, and help determine global labor and environmental standards. They can not only shine a global spotlight on miscreants who seek to circumvent such standards, but help to adopt new standards and expectations. That is the power of globalization. But it takes a new mindset, one that is willing to look beyond the nation-state.

Joshua Karliner poses the challenge well.

> The old 1960s slogan "Think globally, act locally" is no longer
> sufficient as a guiding maxim. Rather, civil society . . . must
> confront the essential paradox and challenge of the 21st century
> by developing ways of thinking and acting both locally and
> globally at the same time. (Karliner 1997)

Karliner cites a document titled "From Global Pillage to Global
Village," drawn up by a collection of seventy US-based grassroots
groups, which optimistically proclaims,

> The unregulated internationalization of capital is now being fol-
> lowed by the internationalization of peoples' movements and
> organizations. Building peoples' international organizations and
> solidarity will be our revolution from within: a civil society
> without borders. This internationalism or "globalization from
> below" will be the foundation for a participatory and sustainable
> global village. (Karliner 1997)

Perlas, who is a leading activist in the Philippines, describes the
emerging global civil society as a third force with the "elemental
strength to contest the monopoly of the two other powers (economics
and politics) over the fate of the Earth" (Perlas 2000, xx).

Friedman is similarly optimistic.

> In the future, globalization is going to be increasingly driven by
> the *individuals* who understand the flat world, adapt themselves
> quickly to its processes and technologies, and start to march for-
> ward—without any treaties or advice from the IMF. They will
> be every color of the rainbow and from every corner of the
> world. (Friedman 2005, 183)

But citizens must capitalize on available opportunities. To com-
plain about diminishing national autonomy does no good. And while
it is natural to want to blame somebody, pointing the finger at a particular group of perceived villains ignores the underlying processes
at work and does nothing to improve the situation.

Individual citizens across boundaries and cultures must realize
their common humanity, accept responsibility for their own fate,
understand the obstacles in their path, and work together to address

common problems. In other words, we must actively direct the processes of globalization. This ultimately can be the greatest source of our individual identity, working on behalf of all in need—both inside and outside our national borders.

The power to circulate, to reach beyond borders, brings sharply into focus the need to look beyond the local and adopt the global. As Hardt and Negri write, "the mobile multitude must achieve a global citizenship" (Hardt and Negri 2000, 361). We must think in terms of a human community and universal needs, rather than an exclusive national identity and particular desires.

Working within the parameters of the nation-state is simply no longer sufficient to address our national or global challenges. Blind allegiance to "my country right or wrong" will lead to disaster. John Quincy Adams, our sixth president, believed that we must possess an ethical foundation that cherishes our country, enjoys the freedom to disagree with a government policy or action, and understands that we are part of a greater whole. The good news is that, as the twentieth century advanced, the sense that we were part of an international community increased.

A survey taken of high school students in 1924 and 1999 showed a significant contrast. In both years, students were asked if they agreed that every good citizen should act according to the maxim, "My country, right or wrong." The percentage of those agreeing declined.

	Males	Females
1924	54%	66%
1999	47%	43% (Caplow, Hicks, and Wattenberg 2001, 211)

That still leaves, though, almost half who rigidly cling to national bonds.

In the words of Guéhenno, having lost the security of geographical boundaries, it is necessary to "rediscover what creates the bonds between humans that constitute a community" (Guéhenno 1995, 139). It is not one-dimensional notions of national identity. Today, we are "capable of building all sorts of 'virtual communities' that will liberate us from the constraints of geography, and from the traditional political structures that have for so long framed our actions" (Guéhenno 1995, 141).

You must be the change you wish to see in the world. There is no other way. Blaming villains will not get the job done. There is no ultimate power plotting an evil course. We hold the keys to the empire. We can and should still look to nation-states to help safeguard rights and meet social needs. They remain relevant. But increasingly, it is up to us to define the parameters under which we live. You do not have to be a politician or CEO to forge links across boundaries and make a difference. We must seize the opportunities globalization offers. Otherwise, we leave ourselves vulnerable to the random and sometimes ruthless forces of the global economy.

A Global Community Arises

The nation-state has been the dominant player on the global stage for centuries. Propelled by the speed of globalization today, however, new forces from within and without are diminishing its strength. Countries no longer control their own destinies. Economic institutions, in the form of giant multinationals and supranational organizations, are the most obvious rivals, imposing their dominance and dictating policies and regulations, often at odds with nation-states and many citizens. But citizens, too, have access to new means to alter their world, with or without the cooperation of the nation-state. There are other ways to garner an identity and to imagine a community outside of one's country. Ultimately, only by looking beyond the near horizon of nationality and only through the continued development of a global civil society can we combat the ills of today and answer the challenges of the twenty-first century. The promise of globalization makes such a civil society possible. The perils of globalization make it absolutely essential.

References

Alexander, Nancy C. 2001. Paying for Education: How the World Bank and International Monetary Fund Influence Education in Developing Countries. Special issue, Global Issues in Education, *Peabody Journal of Education* 76, no. 3 & 4: 285–338.

Amnesty International. 1998. AI on Human Rights and Labor Rights. In *The Globalization Reader,* edited by F.J. Lechner and J. Boli, 187–190. Malden, MA: Blackwell Publishers.

Barabási, Albert-László. 2003. *Linked: How Everything Is Connected to Everything Else and What It Means for Business, Science, and Everyday Life.* New York: Plume.

Becker, Elizabeth. 2003. Poor Nations Can Purchase Cheap Drugs Under Accord. *New York Times,* August 31.

Becker, Elizabeth. 2004. Trade Group to Cut Farm Subsidies for Rich Nations. *New York Times,* August 1.

Benjamin-Gomez, Arlen. 2002. T-Shirts for Justice. In *Rethinking Globalization: Teaching for Justice in an Unjust World,* edited by B. Bigelow and B. Peterson, 170. Milwaukee: Rethinking Schools Press.

Berger, Peter L., and Samuel P. Huntington, eds. 2002. *Many Globalizations: Cultural Diversity in the Contemporary World.* New York: Oxford University Press.

Bigelow, Bill, and Bob Peterson, eds. 2002. *Rethinking Globalization: Teaching for Justice in an Unjust World.* Milwaukee: Rethinking Schools Press.

Blumenthal, Ralph. 2003. As Levi's Work Is Exported, Stress Stays Home. *New York Times,* October 19.

Brecher, Jeremy, Tim Costello, and Brendan Smith. 2000. *Globalization From Below: The Power of Solidarity.* Cambridge, MA: South End Press.

Brenner, Joël Glenn. 1999. *The Emperors of Chocolate: Inside the Secret World of Hershey and Mars.* New York: Random House.

Burbules, Nicholas C., and Carlos Alberto Torres, eds. 2000. *Globalization and Education: Critical Perspectives.* New York: Routledge.

Calhoun, Craig. 2002. The Class Consciousness of Frequent Travellers: Towards a Critique of Actually Existing Cosmopolitanism. In *Conceiving Cosmopolitanism: Theory, Context, and Practice,* edited by S. Vertovec and R. Cohen, 86–109. New York: Oxford University Press.

Caplow, Theodore, Louis Hicks, and Ben J. Wattenberg. 2001. *The First Measured Century: An Illustrated Guide to Trends in America, 1900–2000.* Washington, D.C.: The AEI Press.

Carnoy, Martin. 2000. Globalization and Educational Reform. In *Globalization and Education: Integration and Contestation Across Cultures,* edited by N.P. Stromquist and K. Monkman, 43–61. Lanham, MD: Rowman & Littlefield Publishers.

Dallmayr, Fred, and José M. Rosales, eds. 2001. *Beyond Nationalism? Sovereignty and Citizenship.* Lanham, MD: Lexington Books.

De Jonquieres, Guy. 2002. Companies 'Bigger Than Many Nations.' *Financial Times,* August 13.

Detomasi, David. 2002. International Institutions and the Case for Corporate Governance: Toward a Distributive Governance Framework? *Global Governance* 8 no. 4 (October-December): 421–442.

Economist. 2004a. A Taxing Battle: Governments Around the World Are Scrabbling for Scarce Corporate Resources. *Economist,* January 31.

———. 2004b. Transatlantic Tiff. *Economist,* March 6.

Ellwood, Wayne. 2001. *The No-Nonsense Guide to Globalization.* Oxford: New Internationalist Publications.

Foreign Policy/A.T. Kearney. 2004. *2004 Globalization Index.* Washington, D.C.: *Foreign Policy.*

Friedman, Thomas L. 1999. *The Lexus and the Olive Tree*. New York: Anchor Books.

———. 2005. *The World Is Flat: A Brief History of the Twenty-First Century*. New York: Farrar, Straus and Giroux.

Garrison, Jim. 2004. *America as Empire: Global Leader or Rogue Power?* San Francisco: Berrett-Koehler Publishers.

Guéhenno, Jean-Marie. 1995. *The End of the Nation-State*. Trans. Victoria Elliott. Minneapolis: University of Minnesota Press.

Grieder, William. 1997. *One World, Ready or Not: The Manic Logic of Global Capitalism*. New York: Touchstone.

Hackensack Record. 2001. Editorial. Reviewing the IMF: A Cause of Anti-American Feeling. *Hackensack (NJ) Record,* December 28.

———. 2003. Last Two Levi's Plants in U.S. Fading into History. *Hackensack (NJ) Record,* December 17.

Hardt, Michael, and Antonio Negri. 2000. *Empire*. Cambridge, MA: Harvard University Press.

———. 2004. *Multitude: War and Democracy in the Age of Empire*. New York: The Penguin Press.

Held, David, Anthony McGrew, David Goldblatt, and Jonathan Perraton. 1999. *Global Transformations: Politics, Economics and Culture*. Stanford: Stanford University Press.

Henderson, Hazel. 2000. Transnational Corporations and Global Citizenship. *American Behavioral Scientist* 43, no. 8 (May): 1231–1261.

Hunter, James Davison, and Joshua Yates. 2002. In the Vanguard of Globalization: The World of American Globalizers. In *Many Globalizations: Cultural Diversity in the Contemporary World,* edited by P.L. Berger and S.P. Huntington, 323–357. New York: Oxford University Press.

Institute for Policy Studies. 2005. Corporate vs Country Economic Clout. http://www.ips-dc.org/index.htm (accessed April 1, 2005).

International Campaign to Ban Landmines (ICBL). 2002. http://www.icbl. org (accessed August 30, 2002).

Karliner, Joshua. 1997. Building Grassroots Globalization. *CorpWatch,* December 1, http://www.corpwatch.org/article.php?id=396 (accessed September 14, 2005).

Kaufman, Michael T. 2002. Nationhood: Putting Out More Flags. *New York Times,* May 19.

Keck, Margaret E., and Kathryn Sikkink. 1998. *Activists Beyond Borders: Advocacy Networks in International Politics*. Ithaca, NY: Cornell University Press.

Kickbusch, Ilona. 2003. SARS: Wake-Up Call for a Strong Global Health Policy. *YaleGlobal Online,* April 25. http://yaleglobal.yale.edu/display. article?id=1476 (accessed September 14, 2005).

Kingwell, Mark. 2000. *The World We Want: Restoring Citizenship in a Fractured Age*. Lanham, MD: Rowman & Littlefield Publishers.

Klein, Naomi. 2002. *Fences and Windows: Dispatches from the Front Lines of the Globalization Debate*. New York: Picador.

Lechner, Frank J., and John Boli, eds. 2000. *The Globalization Reader*. Malden, MA: Blackwell Publishers.

Lee, Jennifer. 2003. How Protestors Mobilized So Many and So Nimbly. *New York Times*, February 23.

Markus, Francis. 2002. Heady Days in East Timor. BBC News, May 19. http://news.bbc.co.uk/1/hi/world/asia-pacific/1997324.stm (accessed September 14, 2005).

Massing, Michael. 2002. Challenging the Growth Gurus: A Bitter Feud Is Heating Up Over Development Policy. *New York Times*, October 19.

Mathews, Jessica T. 1997. Power Shift. *Foreign Affairs* 76, no. 1 (January-February): 50–66.

Morley, Hugh R. 2004. Offshore Storm: A Growing Threat to the Middle Class. *Hackensack (NJ) Record*, October 17.

Muldoon, Jr., James P. 2004. *The Architecture of Global Governance: An Introduction to the Study of International Organizations*. Boulder, CO: Westview Press.

New York Times. 2002. Hathaway Closes Maine Factory, Last Major U.S. Shirt Plant. *New York Times*, October 20.

Ohmae, Kenichi. 1995. The End of the Nation-State. Excerpt. In *The Globalization Reader*, edited by F.J. Lechner and J. Boli, 207–211. Malden, MA: Blackwell Publishers.

Packer, George. 2003. Smart-Mobbing the War: Eli Pariser and Other Young Antiwar Organizers Are the First To Be Using Wired Technologies as Weapons. *New York Times Magazine*, March 9.

Perlas, Nicanor. 2000. *Shaping Globalization: Civil Society, Cultural Power and Threefolding*. Saratoga Springs, NY: The Center for Alternative Development Initiatives and Global Network for Social Threefolding.

Reich, Robert B. 1991. *The Work of Nations: Preparing Ourselves for 21st-Century Capitalism*. New York: Alfred A. Knopf.

Rohter, Larry. 2002. Brazilians Find Political Cost for Help from I.M.F. *New York Times*, August 11.

———. 2003. Brazil's Leader Steps Gingerly Onto World Stage. *New York Times*, May 31.

Sernau, Scott. 2000. *Bound: Living in the Globalized World*. Bloomfield, CT: Kumarian Press.

Simmons, P.J. 1998. Learning to Live with NGOs. *Foreign Policy* (Fall): 82–84.

Simpson, Glenn R. 2003. Multinational Firms Take Steps to Avert Boycotts Over War. *Wall Street Journal*, April 4.

Stevenson, Mark. 2003. Mexico Waging Trade War Against Chinese Imports: Resentment Grows Over Flood of Low-Cost Products. *Hackensack (NJ) Record*, November 24.

Stevenson, Richard W. 2002. Calculating Checks and Balances at the World Bank. *New York Times,* September 29.

Stiglitz, Joseph E. 2002. Think Global: Questions for Joseph E. Stiglitz. Interview with New York Times Magazine. *New York Times Magazine,* June 9.

Stromquist, Nelly P., and Karen Monkman, eds. 2000. *Globalization and Education: Integration and Contestation Across Cultures.* Lanham, MD: Rowman & Littlefield Publishers.

Tharoor, Shashi. 2003. Why America Still Needs the United Nations. *Foreign Affairs* 82 (September–October).

Thurow, Lester. 2003. *Fortune Favors the Bold: What We Must Do to Build a New and Lasting Global Prosperity.* New York: HarperCollins Publishers.

Turner, Bryan S. 2001. National Identities and Cosmopolitan Virtues: Citizenship in a Global Age. In *Beyond Nationalism? Sovereignty and Citizenship,* edited by F. Dallmayr and J.M. Rosales, 199–220. Lanham, MD: Lexington Books.

Vertovec, Steven, and Robin Cohen, eds. 2002. *Conceiving Cosmopolitanism: Theory, Context, and Practice.* New York: Oxford University Press.

Weiner, Tim. 2003. Wal-Mart Invades, and Mexico Gladly Surrenders. *New York Times,* December 6.

Woods, Ngaire. 2003. Holding Intergovernmental Institutions to Account. *Ethics & International Affairs* 17, no. 1: 69–80.

World Bank. 2005. http://www.worldbank.org (accessed June 6, 2005).

Yergin, Daniel, and Joseph Stanislaw. 2002. *The Commanding Heights: The Battle for the World Economy.* New York: Touchstone.

4

A Foundation for World Citizenship

We have inherited a large house, a great "world house" in which we have to live together—black and white, Easterner and Westerner, Gentile and Jew, Catholic and Protestant, Moslem and Hindu—a family unduly separated in ideas, culture and interest, who, because we can never again live apart, must learn somehow to live with each other in peace . . . we cannot ignore the larger world house in which we are also dwellers.

—Martin Luther King, Jr.
Where Do We Go from Here: Chaos or Community? 1967

If a gentleman always maintains reverence without ignorance, behaves with courtesy to others and observes the rules of ritual, then all within the Four Oceans are his brothers.

—Confucius
The Analects, Fifth Century B.C.

Where Do We Go From Here?

Globalization breaks down barriers, provides new links across borders, and, in the process, reduces the influence of the nation-state. Changes are racing at breakneck speed, producing tremendous opportunities and equally monumental challenges.

Globalization is a reality. We are operating in a new context; we see the world through new and different frames. What should we do with this new understanding? How do we as individuals react to both the challenges and the opportunities? How can we further connect the dots? What insights and skills do we need to succeed in this new environment?

The short answer is that a world without boundaries requires us to start thinking outside national perspectives. In other words, responding

91

to globalization means adopting a global view. Succeeding in a globalized world means becoming a global or world citizen.

But few things in life are that simple. What exactly does it mean to have a global view and be a world citizen? Is this a new concept? Is it really necessary, or even possible, to look beyond the limits of our local landscape to adopt a planetwide attitude and outlook? Does it mean we must abandon our national identities? Does everyone believe world citizenship is the answer?

Corporations have seized the opportunities provided by technology for years, and now they look more and more at possibilities outside their domestic borders. Their employees are increasingly called upon to operate in different cultures. Those who want to prosper in the global economy must learn how to be world citizens.

However, while there are examples of corporate global agility, there are numerous instances in which a local product or view failed when exported abroad, and perhaps an effort to understand, appreciate, and connect with the local culture would have been particularly beneficial.

The Parker Pen Company once advertised a new bottled ink product with copy that concluded, "to avoid embarrassment in your social correspondence, be sure to use Parker SuperQuink." The product was exported to Mexico and twenty thousand metal signs were imprinted in Spanish with that slogan. In Spanish, however, the words formed a special phrase that, when translated, read, "to avoid *pregnancy,* use Parker SuperQuink" (Axtell 1999, 119).

There is a widely cited legend that, some time ago, Chevrolet tried to export its successful Nova car model to Latin America. What was a recognizable name brand in the United States, however, did not translate quite so well in Spanish-speaking countries: In Spanish, *no va* means "it doesn't go" or "it doesn't work." Hardly the best name for an automobile.

Like the actual experience of the Parker Pen Company, the mythic Nova tale contains a fundamental truth. Not viewing the situation through the eyes of others is a formula for disaster. In business, the ramifications of thinking solely within a national context could be financial ruin.

Beyond the pragmatism of global commerce, people and nations cannot combat global crises by working in isolation. The problems of environmental degradation or international terrorism require global cooperation. With globalization should come a greater realization that our fates are now linked. We must connect the dots of this new world to understand today's interconnections and shared destiny.

Quite simply, becoming a citizen of the world is an economic, political, practical, and moral imperative. It is an issue of our very survival.

Seeking a Definition of World Citizenship

If world citizenship is so important, how do you get a passport? If you are born in the United States, you automatically become a US citizen. Since we were all born on the same planet, it would seem that world citizenship should be similarly automatic.

But it is not that easy. You have to apply to receive a passport from your country, and affirm agreement with certain principles and responsibilities. You must recognize and acknowledge your geographic citizenship. In declaring world citizenship, you must also acknowledge and accept a set of principles and responsibilities.

A Multinational Study

A few years ago, the influential *American Educational Research Journal* published a fascinating article entitled "Educating World Citizens: Toward Multinational Curriculum Development." The piece summarized the findings of a multinational research team that surveyed 182 scholars, practitioners, and policy leaders from many countries and across many fields. The purpose of the study was to determine the major global crises facing humanity in the next quarter-century. From that base, the authors asked what skills and characteristics would be needed to meet those challenges.

The dominant theme identified was "increasing inequality coupled with increasing resource scarcity" (Parker, Ninomiya, and Cogan 1999, 123). The seven top challenges cited were:

1. "The economic gap among countries and between people within countries will widen significantly"
2. "Information technologies will dramatically reduce the privacy of individuals"
3. "The inequalities between those who have access to information technologies and those who do not will increase dramatically"
4. "Conflict of interest between developing and developed nations will increase due to environmental deterioration"

5. "The cost of obtaining adequate water will rise dramatically due to population growth and environmental deterioration"
6. "Deforestation will dramatically affect diversity of life, air, soil, and water quality"
7. "In developing countries, population growth will result in a dramatic increase in the percentage of people, especially children, living in poverty" (Parker, Ninomiya, and Cogan 1999, 124)

Globalization has aggravated and accelerated, if not initiated, many of the pressing problems we must confront in the twenty-first century. Many of these problems are obviously global in scale. Other challenges could be added to the above list, particularly in the wake of the attacks of September 11, 2001, but those seven items are certainly not in dispute. And the common element for all seven—as with problems like conflict and terrorism, AIDS and other infectious diseases, global warming, and ozone depletion—is that their effects do not stop at national borders.

It should therefore be no surprise that the team found that the most important characteristic needed in today's global era is "the ability to deal with serious worldwide problems as a member of a worldwide society" (Parker, Ninomiya, and Cogan 1999, 125). In other words, the ability "to look at and approach problems as a member of a global society."

Just behind that necessary trait, the authors suggested, are the following:

- "Ability to work with others in a cooperative way and to take responsibility for one's roles/duties within society"
- "Ability to understand, accept, appreciate, and tolerate cultural differences"
- "Capacity to think in a critical and systematic way"
- "Willingness to resolve conflict in a nonviolent manner"
- "Willingness and ability to participate in politics at local, national, and international levels"
- "Willingness to change one's lifestyle and consumption habits to protect the environment"
- "Ability to be sensitive toward and to defend human rights" (Parker, Ninomiya, and Cogan 1999, 125)

The critical theme of world citizenship emerged as a necessity. The authors do not discount the importance of a national identity, but they rightly note that citizens must understand and embrace other identities as well. As they describe it,

> The challenges of the 21st century transcend national boundaries . . . Persons and groups who are going to face those challenges together . . . must be able to think and act flexibly within multiple community affiliations. (Parker, Ninomiya, and Cogan 1999, 127)

Embracing Multiple Identities

The *American Educational Research Journal* study used the example of a person of Canadian citizenship, Japanese-Canadian culture, Catholic faith, and Asian race, but who above all is a mother. We understand and are familiar with possessing strong identities as family members, friends, career professionals, and members of local communities and nations. We instinctively and readily switch among our roles as wife, husband, daughter, son, friend, worker, town resident, and national citizen without losing sanity. So how hard can it be to absorb the ultimate identity of world citizen?

We recently shared a conversation with a five-year-old in a group of adults. He was asked the typical question: "What do you want to be when you grow up?"

Michael immediately replied, "The ten things I want to be are:

- An astronaut
- A daddy
- A boat man
- A shop man
- A fireman
- A policeman
- A pilot
- A farmer/grower
- A teacher
- And an American idol."

Five-year-olds have little humility, but clearly understand that they can play many roles and hold many positions. We all can relate to some extent. Outline your own different or desired identities.

In today's environment, multiple identities are not a sign of mental illness; they mean you are normal. They are an inherent part of a complex world. The ability to recognize and acknowledge your multiple identities might be the first concrete step toward gaining world citizenship. Acknowledging simultaneous identities—ethnic, racial, sexual, occupational, and social—leads away from the traditional notion of a citizen as one who has membership in a political entity, and toward the concept of a world citizen.

Exploring Definitions
Citizenship is certainly a complex issue. How to define the term, and whether the emphasis is on one's duties or one's rights, has been the subject of much debate throughout the centuries. Before venturing into the unbounded territory of world citizenship, some discussion of basic citizenship is in order.

Citizenship can be described in many ways, but let's start with a simple linguistic definition. A citizen is most often defined as:

   a. An inhabitant of a city, town, or place
   b. A member of a state or nation
   c. A native or naturalized person who owes allegiance to a particular government and is entitled to protection from that government

It is common to trace citizenship to a particular geographic location or group association, and to link it with specific rights, privileges, and responsibilities. Many learn about that in elementary school. Often, though, what is imparted is a very limited and passive notion of citizenship. It is no surprise, then, "when upper division college students are asked to list the citizenship skills they have learned . . . they inevitably list the same five 'skills':

   1. Vote
   2. Obey the law
   3. Pay taxes
   4. Salute the flag, and
   5. Say the pledge of allegiance" (Andrzejewski and Alessio 1999)

But citizenship should include more active exercises, such as dialogue, deliberation, and community-building. As philosophy professor

Mark Kingwell contends, citizenship is a powerful emotional concept, "a way of meeting one of our deepest needs, the need to belong; it gives voice and structure to the yearning to be part of something larger than ourselves" (Kingwell 2000, 5).

That "something larger" is usually implied to be our political community, defined by a governing body and including everyone under it who is subject to national laws, tax requirements, and, when the nation calls, military service. Through citizenship, we gain rights and duties, but we also gain something much more important: identity and a sense of commitment and belonging to a particular community.

Today, traditional models of citizenship are outdated. The need to belong is as relevant as ever, but in an era of globalization, constraining our civic responsibilities and rights to political boundaries limits the richness of human opportunity and potential for our world. If it was ever valid to tie citizenship to the land—like gang members bonded to their "turf" or animals wedded to their territory—today's global age makes such an association impractical at best.

It is important to keep in mind that the history of citizenship has been one of exclusion and subordination, based primarily on race and national identity. At the height of the Roman Empire, there was a great divide between citizens and noncitizens. "Barbarians" had few rights and privileges. In the seventeenth and eighteenth centuries in India, the lowest British imperial army private had more civil rights and privileges than any rajah. Commonly seen as a gateway to a new life for millions, Ellis Island was actually an inspection station that screened applicants for potential citizenship, and many were sent back home because they did not qualify.

For women, minorities, and the impoverished, gaining rights or even just recognition as citizens has taken centuries of struggle. But despite— or perhaps because of—this long tradition of exclusion, we still tend to think of citizenship in terms of who is among us and who is not, who has certain rights and who does not. It is time for something better.

Cosmopolitanism

If globalization helps us overcome geographic barriers, why should citizenship remain exclusively tied to a particular territory? It is time to loosen the link bonding citizenship to the nation-state, and expand our sense of community and belonging to all of humanity.

The solution, says Bryan Turner, lies in cosmopolitanism, which "is the necessary cultural envelope for the cultivation of transnational obligations of care and respect" (Turner 2001, 217). By its definition, this sense of cosmopolitanism involves an outlook and concern that goes beyond any particular area or territory.

Cosmopolitanism literally means being a citizen of the world, and commonly includes or implies a global awareness and ethic. We use the term frequently in the following discussion as a synonym for world citizenship, although we understand that cosmopolitanism has often been used to describe elite circles of world travelers and consumers not exactly preoccupied with moral rights and responsibilities. For that reason, in other places, we prefer to use the term "world citizen" or "global citizen."

As we develop a sense of cosmopolitanism and expand our notion of citizenship to other places and peoples, we must also move beyond the symbolic exercises that too often pass for loyal citizenship, such as paying taxes or saluting the flag. What is needed today is a new model "based on *the act of participation itself,* not on some quality or thought or right enjoyed by its possessor. . . . Citizenship, if it means anything, means *making our desire for justice active*" (Kingwell 2000, 12, 19).

As a democratic society, we need to do a better job of encouraging active citizenship and democratic participation. In a world of increased connections, we cannot limit our sphere of responsibility to a local or even national ruling government. Globalization and the new technologies that bring us closer together blur geographic and political boundaries and definitions. These developments have created avenues for political and civic expression that go beyond the traditional connection between citizen and state.

Richard Falk notes that the growth of information technology has given rise to an interesting identity he calls a "netizen" (Falk 2002, 16). Netizens cross borders at will and link to fellow humans everywhere. Such an identity, he adds, is particularly important and "relevant to an assessment of new configurations of belief and allegiance." As our ability to act and communicate across long distances increases, we need to enlarge our framework of citizenship beyond the local landscape.

But technology is simply the vehicle. The key is to understand that the realities of globalization compel us to expand our association with fellow citizens beyond those traditionally defined by the state. There must be no more barbarians.

Defining World Citizenship

Falk, an international law scholar, introduces the notion of "citizen pilgrims" who move away from exclusive allegiance to states and toward an allegiance to values. These pioneers, he suggests, will form "a community of believers in the collective destiny of the human species" (Falk 2002, 28).

What characteristics define passport qualifications for world citizenship? Perhaps world citizens must focus upon positive change. What unites us as a species is more binding than geographic borders. All humans possess equal rights and equal worth without regard to nationality, ethnicity, or religion. World citizens can have multiple identities, simultaneously embracing national citizenship while recognizing and working to solve problems that transcend geographic borders.

The authors of "Educating World Citizens" define a world citizen as "one for whom the commonwealth is not only a local or national political community but, alongside these, a transnational civic culture concerned with global problems and global problem solving" (Parker, Ninomiya, and Cogan 1999, 130).

Oxfam, an organization working in more than one hundred countries to combat poverty and suffering, includes as part of its definition of global citizenship someone who:

- "is aware of the wider world and has a sense of their own role as a world citizen"
- "respects and values diversity"
- "is willing to act to make the world a more equitable and sustainable place"
- "takes responsibility for their actions" (Oxfam 1997)

These definitions are the foundation of world citizenship.

Measure Your Boundaries by the Sun

Martha Nussbaum, a professor of law and ethics at the University of Chicago, is one of the leading thinkers in the school of global citizenship. Using the foundation laid by the Greek Stoics, she has forcefully put forward the notions of cosmopolitanism and a global humanity whose interests are aligned across countries and continents.

She uses as a base Diogenes' reply to the question of where he came from: "I am a citizen of the world." (Socrates said virtually the same thing.)

The Stoics would not be confined to local and group identities. Instead, they viewed themselves "in terms of more universal aspirations and concerns" (Nussbaum 1996a, 6–7). They argued that

> each of us dwells, in effect, in two communities—the local community of our birth, and the community of human argument and aspiration that "is truly great and truly common, in which we look neither to this corner nor to that, but measure the boundaries of our nation by the sun" (Seneca, *De Otio*). (Nussbaum 1996a, 7)

Seneca, in *Letters From A Stoic* (62–65 A.D.), added that we should adhere to the creed, "I wasn't born for one particular corner: the whole world's my home country."

Stoic thought was predicated on the notion of a universal citizenry. Anything less is born of an irrational prejudice.

> The accident of where one is born is just that, an accident; any human being might have been born in any nation. Recognizing this, his [Diogenes'] Stoic successors held, we should not allow differences of nationality or class or ethnic membership or even gender to erect barriers between us and our fellow human beings. We should recognize humanity wherever it occurs, and give its fundamental ingredients, reason and moral capacity, our first allegiance and respect. (Nussbaum 1996a, 7)

We are indeed accidents of birth. Which one of us decided where we were born? Why such arrogance based upon the geography of our natal experience? (The word nation in fact derives from the Latin word meaning "to be born.") It is almost the same as if we were to give certain special rights to those with whom we share a first name, hair color, or height. Imagine the reaction if you claimed special privileges because your first name was John or Mary. Our national identities, like our names or most of our physical characteristics, are largely acts of fate (excepting those who emigrate). They should not bind our behavior or limit our world.

We must look beyond local governments and national identities toward the "moral community made up by the humanity of all human beings. . . . One should always behave so as to treat with equal respect the dignity of reason and moral choice in every human being" (Nussbaum 1996a, 7–8).

This does not imply that citizens of the world must abandon their local identities. Even if that were possible—which is highly doubtful—such local ties add immeasurable pleasure and satisfaction to life. "There's no place like home" is more than a sentimental closing line from a beloved tale. It expresses the profound sense of attachment and belonging to the familiar, to that which we know best. Even those comfortable with criticizing their family members or their nation will close ranks when a relative or their homeland is denounced by others and become fierce defenders of the familiar.

The sense of belonging and security found most often at home cannot and should not be diminished.

The Circle of Humanity
The Stoics suggested the use of concentric circles to describe our personal worlds. The first one encircles the self; the next takes in the immediate family; then the extended family; and then neighbors, town and country dwellers, and so on, until you get to the outermost and largest circle, that of humanity.

World citizens believe we should seek to bring all the circles closer to ourselves. But how do we move the outer circle of humanity closer to our inner circle of concern?

We must continue to respect and relish the particular relationships and identifications that make us unique. They are part of the multiple identities we all have as individuals. At the same time, however, we must recognize that all human beings are connected. That connection is an equally important part of our definition. All humanity deserves special attention and concern.

This is a challenging proposition. How does one go about developing this type of personal acknowledgment and global inclusion?

An Educational Imperative

The Stoics believed that the main task of education is the "vivid imagining of the different" (Nussbaum 1996a, 9–10). Consider the advice offered by Roman emperor Marcus Aurelius, which could be the basis for cosmopolitan education: "Accustom yourself not to be inattentive to what another person says, and as far as possible enter into that person's mind" (VI. 53) (Nussbaum 1996a, 10).

It is imperative that we learn to look at problems through the eyes of others. This is one of the core requirements of what political science professor David Held calls "cultural cosmopolitanism." He says a cosmopolitan citizen must:

1. Recognize "the increasing interconnectedness of political communities in diverse domains including the social, economic and environmental"
2. Develop the "understanding of overlapping 'collective fortunes' that require collective solutions" and
3. Celebrate "difference, diversity and hybridity while learning how to 'reason from the point of view of others' and mediate traditions" (Held 2002, 58).

Expanding on the Stoics' case for global citizenship, Nussbaum suggests four arguments for making cosmopolitanism or world citizenship the focus for civic education.

- *"Through cosmopolitan education, we learn more about ourselves."*
  Adopting different perspectives contributes to greater understanding and self-awareness. When we learn about others, it

helps us understand what we have in common and what makes us different. We cannot gain this awareness in isolation. If we are ignorant of the rest of the world, we are ignorant of ourselves.

- *"We make headway solving problems that require international cooperation."*

  As is so clearly illustrated by the war on terrorism, international problems that threaten us require international cooperation. Numerous other challenges call on us to join hands with others who are very different from us. These international coalitions can only be successful if we have some understanding of others' traditions and positions.

- *"We recognize moral obligations to the rest of the world that are real and that otherwise would go unrecognized."*

  Believing that all humans have equal worth and certain rights carries with it implicit ethical guidelines. Of course, one may continue to show special concern for that which is close geographically and emotionally, but if we believe others, too, have the right to life, liberty, and the pursuit of happiness, then we must learn about the concerns of others and consider how our social, political, and economic choices affect others.

- *"We make a consistent coherent argument based on distinctions we are prepared to defend."*

  There is nothing magical about a national border that gives people rights within it and indifference outside it. If people as different as those in New York City and Omaha, Nebraska, are entitled to equal consideration, then is not that same diversity worthy of respect across national boundaries? Humanity transcends such boundaries, yet unless we are given the tools to cross them in our minds, the impression can easily be gathered that special respect must be afforded Americans first. (Nussbaum 1996a, 11–15)

It is very natural to embrace the comfortable and stay confined within warm and emotionally secure boundaries. It is also natural to want to bask in the security of those nearest to us, and uncomfortable to venture from the security of close ties.

But then again, if we always followed the comfortable path, what kind of lives would we lead? Don't we need to challenge ourselves, to sometimes venture into the unknown and explore the unfamiliar if we are to improve as a society, as a species?

Building from the Stoics and writing more than two centuries ago, American revolutionary leader Thomas Paine enthusiastically endorsed the notion of world citizenship. He embraced multinational identities and allegiances. "My country is the world, and my religion is to do good," he wrote in his classic work *Rights of Man* (1791–1792).

Paine's famous efforts to help the United States gain its independence have effectively tied him, for history's sake, to one country's cause. Paine himself, however, wished to be remembered as a citizen of the world, and referred to himself as someone who "considers the world as his home." He declared throughout his life that his interests were "universal. My attachment is to all of the world, and not to any particular part" (Fruchtman 1994, 440, 108).

While Paine was writing on behalf of the American cause, he set forth what he believed were universal principles. The goal, as he saw it, was "a universal society, whose mind rises above the atmosphere of local thoughts" (Paine, Letter to the Abbé Raynal; in Fruchtman 1994, 145).

Universal Aspirations

In many ways, Paine's "universal society" was a grand vision ahead of its time. His work and ideas anticipated the views of other American internationalists such as Woodrow Wilson and Franklin D. Roosevelt, and the formation of collective organizations such as the United Nations. Paine's life offers a road map for world citizens, a way to merge the often contradictory impulses of nationalism and cosmopolitanism. Biographer Jack Fruchtman, Jr., wrote,

> Thomas Paine was at once conscious of the contradictions that might have existed inherently in his American nationality and his internationalism. Emotionally, as he himself testified more than once, he was an American; but intellectually he was an internationalist" (Fruchtman 1994, 440–441).

Paine was able to merge his universality and his nationalism. "He brought them together in a manner that allowed him at once to say that while his nationality was American, his mind was always on the whole world" (Fruchtman, 441).

Like the Stoics and Paine, other great thinkers have similarly identified with universal aspirations, ranging from Confucius and

Gandhi, to Emerson and Thoreau, to Martin Luther King, Jr. Another such thinker was Enlightenment philosopher Immanuel Kant.

Kant said actions should be judged in terms of their universal applicability, and not on the basis of any particular interest to individuals or nations. As described by Mark Kingwell, Kant believed that "a human being is worthy of respect simply by virtue of being alive. And that worthiness extends without borders to encompass every individual, ignoring all particularities" (Kingwell 2000, 52).

Kant saw the need for an international global ethic. "His was a cosmopolitanism of spirit and intellect—it had no relation to place" (Delanty 2000, 55). In *Perpetual Peace,* published in 1795, Kant wrote,

> Since the narrower or wider community of the peoples of the earth has developed so far that a violation of rights in one place is felt throughout the world, the idea of a cosmopolitan right is no fantastical, high-flown or exaggerated notion. It is a complement to the unwritten code of the civil and international law, necessary for the public rights of mankind in general and thus for the realization of perpetual peace. (Third Definitive Article for Perpetual Peace)

H.G. Wells called for adoption of a global mindset, a "mental cosmopolis," and thought of himself as a citizen of the world. Martin Luther King, Jr., also called himself a citizen of the world, declaring famously in his 1963 *Letter from Birmingham City Jail,* "We are caught in an inescapable network of mutuality; tied in a single garment of destiny."

There have been many other expressions of world citizenship. The Dutch humanist and theologian Erasmus, for example, attacked national identities as "very stupid labels" that only breed division. He wrote, "My own wish is to be a citizen of the world, to be a fellow-citizen to all men" (Carter 2001, 19–20).

Recall the stirring lines from John Donne's *Devotions Upon Emergent Occasions* (XVII), written in 1624:

> No man is an island intire of itselfe, every man is a piece of the Continent, a part of the maine . . . any man's death diminishes me, because I am involved in Mankinde; and therefore never send to know for whom the bell tolls; it tolls for thee.

Almost 250 years later, Dostoyevsky echoed those sentiments in *The Brothers Karamazov,* writing that "every one is really responsible to all men for all men and for everything." He also wrote, "Until you have become really, in actual fact, a brother to everyone, brotherhood will not come to pass."

Another Russian writer, Alexandr Solzhenitsyn, believed,

> . . . mankind's sole salvation lies in everyone making everything his business; in the people of the East being vitally concerned with what is thought in the West, the people of the West vitally concerned with what goes on in the East. (Solzhenitsyn 1970)

Philosopher Kwame Anthony Appiah expressed a similar world-view. In discussing African identity, he wrote, "We will only solve our problems if we see them as human problems arising out of a special situation, and we shall not solve them if we see them as African problems generated by our being somehow unlike others" (Appiah 1992, 136).

Even American leaders mired in Cold War politics were able to pronounce cosmopolitan sentiments. Former president Dwight D. Eisenhower, in his 1959 State of the Union Address, said, "We seek victory—not over any nation or people—but over the ancient enemies of us all; victory over ignorance, poverty, disease and human degradation wherever they may be found."

The Buddhist association Soka Gakkai International, which has more than twelve million members in 190 countries and territories, is firmly committed to global solidarity and world citizenship. Its president, Daisaku Ikeda, said, "The work of fostering global citizens . . . concerns us all. It is a vital project in which we all are participants and for which we all share responsibility" (Ikeda 1996).

The array of individuals who embraced the concept of a global community is wide and deep. The concept continues to emerge in radically different geographic locations, and across hundreds of years of time.

The Bengali poet, novelist, and philosopher Rabindranath Tagore, who lived through the Indian struggle for independence, is widely considered to be the greatest modern writer in India. The winner of the Nobel Prize for literature in 1913, he looked forward to international harmony.

Tagore saw artificial divisions plaguing humankind. That is why he spoke against individuals adopting a narrow group identification. "Whether that group was religious or racial, whether it was a caste or a nation. For Tagore, the function of such identification was invariably exclusion, hierarchy—and violence" (Hogan 2003, 16).

Tagore believed the key virtue of internationalism lay in breaking down those walls and fusing the ideals of East and West. He wrote that

> during the evolution of the Nation the moral culture of brotherhood was limited by geographical boundaries . . . the time has come . . . to make another great moral adjustment which will comprehend the whole world of men and not fractional groups of nationality. (Tagore 1917, 122–123)

As Tagore scholar Bandana Purkayastha relates,

> Tagore's model requires formally recognizing multiple allegiances, making it possible to respect one's own country without strident patriotism and cultural isolation. His model requires being deeply committed to one's own culture without creating walls of sectarianism or viewing culture as fixed. It calls for attention to tradition without becoming enslaved by outdated rules. It requires seeing the home in the world. (Purkayastha 2003, 61)

Tagore was careful to emphasize that cultures should retain their unique heritages and identities. He was not seeking a colorless cosmopolitanism, as he phrased it, but instead a vibrant exchange of people and ideas—a loose constellation of groups that remained diverse, but could reconcile their differences with their common interests, humanity, and destiny.

There is, he wrote, a "universal standard of justice to which all men irrespective of their caste and colour have their equal claim" (Tagore 1917, 30).

The call for world citizenship is strong. It comes from many voices across centuries. The message appeared even before there were effective communication systems that today encourage dialogue and discussion about new ideas.

The Critics Speak

Even though this thread of global thought spans time and cultures, proponents of world citizenship have always faced substantial numbers of detractors. Betty Jean Craige framed the issue in terms of

political holists and political dualists. She defines political holists
as having

> an appreciation of human society as a continuously evolving
> global system of ethnically and ideologically diverse, interde-
> pendent individuals and groups, whose interests are more likely
> to be advanced by cooperation than by hostile competition.
> (Craige 1996, 3)

On the other hand, tribalists, who believe in political dualism,
see the world divided between "us" and "them," and possess "un-
questioning allegiance to one's group, the belief in the inherent superiority of the group, and the tendency to view other groups as alien
competitors" (Craige 1996, 4).

Perhaps we all possess characteristics of both, or perhaps it is
true that, in the words of Danish poet Piet Hein, "We are global citizens with tribal souls" (Barnaby 1988, 192). In other words, we all
may have the responsibility, but neither the capacity nor the imagination, to fulfill the duties of world citizenship. In any case, the division between those who embrace their global side and those who prefer to think tribally is real.

Globalization, while bringing people together, mainly through
technology, has intensified the battle lines between globalists and
tribalists. Although globalization creates incentives for cooperation
and outlets for universal aspirations, it also is seen to threaten the
autonomy of individual cultures.

With new forums for cooperation and exchange also comes the
potential for exploitation and homogenization. And technology not
only affords the chance for greater interaction, but greater devastation. It should not be surprising that, like globalization itself, the
notion of world citizenship has spawned numerous critics and generated radical and emotional opposition.

A common position is that anyone who promotes this world
idea is incredibly naïve. What sort of utopian, idealistic vision is this
quest for world citizenship? It is more like a wild fantasy, a pipe
dream that has no chance of becoming a reality, critics charge. That
it still remains only a vision after people have been talking about it
for thousands of years proves that it is impossible to realize.

Four recurring themes form a foundation of objections and concerns about world citizenship. While some of the criticism is grounded

in fear and prejudice, a good deal of it is based on thoughtful observations of human nature and current political realities. It is valuable to review these positions.

Position One: Only Nation-States Can Protect Us

Critics of world citizenship first point to the continuing relevance of the nation-state. If the forces of globalization are sometimes destructive, then the only thing powerful enough to combat those forces are nation-states—particularly the most influential ones. The nation-state, they add, is the only force that could truly protect its citizens and thus bestow rights upon them.

They concede, of course, that the nation-state is not the all-powerful actor that it used to be. But they maintain that its power is still greater than the fledgling and often less-than-effective existing transnational bodies. That being the case, loyalties to nation-states must remain paramount. They are natural, understandable, and desirable in an uncertain and violent world. We need to think of our nation first.

Position Two: Absence of a Worldwide Institution

Some argue that citizens have an inherent need to relate to a specific political community and ruling body. If world citizenship is so important and compelling, they ask, where is the worldwide institution that provides the relevant framework? Where can I sign up?

There is no world government, they argue, and nothing even close on the horizon, so it is premature to discuss world citizenship. The concept is meaningless without a corresponding world organization, which simply does not exist.

The United Nations is a world assembly, but its power and authority are decidedly limited. It is true that the United Nations allows many opportunities for collective agreements and global participation. Still, its potential remains largely untapped. In any event, even a more powerful and effective United Nations would not be comparable to a global governing body.

Position Three: Family Always Comes First

Critics further insist that it is human nature for us to embrace what is closest to us. Therefore, the family will always have our ultimate loyalty, followed by our friends, the local community, the nation, and the world. The world is in last place in the hierarchy of our attachments.

Like the Stoics, Alexander Pope described this circle of attachments in his classic *An Essay on Man* (Epistle IV, 1733–1734).

> God loves from whole to parts: but human soul
> Must rise from individual to the whole.
> Self-love but serves the virtuous mind to wake,
> As the small pebble stirs the peaceful lake;
> The centre mov'd, a circle strait succeeds,
> Another still, and still another spreads,
> Friend, parent, neighbor, first it will embrace,
> His country next; and next all human race.

While Stoics would seek to draw the outer edge of the circle closer, critics answer that the outer edge will always remain the outer edge, and thus always be of lesser importance.

Position Four: Global Citizenship Is a Dull Exercise
Others say that, while desirable on several counts, the notion of world citizenship is a barely tangible ideal that offers nothing approaching the emotionally satisfying relationship a citizen has with a nation. Where is the flag? What anthem do we sing?

Because there is no particular worldwide governing entity, the notion of citizenship is stripped of its political and practical connotations. World citizenship is only a stand-in for a "moral agent," a vague and hollow construct much weaker than the traditional form of citizenship. The result is a citizenship without duties, rights, and, worst of all, feeling. Some have said that world citizens are without roots, and by claiming to be citizens of everywhere, they become citizens of nowhere. They lack a sense of engagement and attachment to their communities. Others contend that without a shared culture, there can be no true sense of community.

The scholar Richard Rorty accused proponents of multiculturalism of rejecting "the emotion of national pride" (Rorty 1994). He further argued that "humanity" and "planetwide justice" are empty abstractions, and that people's actions should be guided by local, concrete solidarities (Robbins 1999, 131).

For Gertrude Himmelfarb, cosmopolitanism above all "obscures, even denies . . . the givens of life: parents, ancestors, family, race, religion, heritage, history, culture, tradition, community—and nationality" (Himmelfarb 1996, 77).

The Globalist Response

In any debate, there are always at least two positions. It is valuable to review the cosmopolitan responses to these objections to world citizenship.

Position One: The Nation-State Is Important
Cosmopolitans acknowledge the importance of the nation-state. There is no question that it is still a vital power structure that can exert positive influence and affect many different situations. It has important legal and institutional advantages and, in many cases, is the most powerful vehicle for addressing problems. We will continue to rely heavily on its normal functioning for years to come.

But it also cannot be denied that the nation-state has seen its power decline, and in isolation, it cannot guarantee its citizens' well-being, economic prosperity, and cultural identity. It is plainly suffering from a case of what Richard Falk calls "diminished autonomy" (Falk 1996, 54). Nowhere has this been more evident than when states with a long history of humanitarian policies cave in to the imperatives of the global marketplace. For example,

> If Sweden can no longer be Sweden because of the pressures being exerted by global capital to reduce taxes, hold wages, downsize welfare, and avoid any kind of judgmental posture in foreign policy of the sort previously associated with Swedish neutrality, then to continue to rely on a nationalist orientation in the quest for political fulfillment seems increasingly to be a courtship with self-delusion. (Falk 1996, 55)

Most significantly, any nation-state acting in isolation is doomed to failure. In our interconnected world, it has become essential that nation-states work together, acting multilaterally as good international citizens. Doing so—working together across borders to forge global solutions—is exactly what a world citizen would want. Nation-states legitimize countless international efforts and guarantee the success of many transnational ones.

We agree that states are the only available entities that can make international laws, treaties, and other multinational agreements credible. World citizenship does not desire the elimination of the nation-state. In fact, it often seeks to work within the corridors of power aligned by nation-states. As Bruce Robbins has written, "Using the machinery of the nation-state to try to control the predatoriness of global capital is a clear example, and a crucial one, of a necessary tactic that may be simultaneously nationalist and internationalist" (Robbins 1999, 34).

We must continue to value our countries, but world citizens need to overcome narrow parochial prejudice. They also have to judge foreign policy a little differently. Actions that exclusively serve national interests at the expense of international goals should be increasingly less desirable. Because of globalization, though, most actions that ignore the international community may eventually result in unfavorable long-term consequences for the nation in question. In other words, nations acting solely out of self-interest and national advocates thinking myopically will not prosper in the long run. Besides endangering others, thinking and acting in isolation endangers the actors as well.

What is needed is not a form of citizenship that replaces the bond with the nation, but an added dimension of citizenship that reaches out to others beyond the nation.

The United Nations, while not a world governing body, is a forum that seeks to combine these two forms of allegiance. All UN efforts, whether to prevent diseases, maintain peace, or combat terrorism, contain both national and international emphases. The organization is rooted firmly in the continued effectiveness of individual states. At the same time, it increasingly provides venues for multilateral cooperation and opportunities for NGOs and citizens to act globally.

Position Two: Supranational Open Roads
It is true that governing institutions direct citizen activity and provide avenues for expression and representation. But other global gateways are open as well, despite the absence of a world governing body. With globalization and the advent of the information revolution, the possibilities for citizen action are abundant. As discussed in chapter 3, individuals or citizen groups can start powerful movements without relying on any particular state or governing body. The incredible growth of transnational NGOs, other supranational forces, and regional organizations, to say nothing of the technological advances that facilitate international collaboration, are more than adequate beginnings for the exercise of international citizen activities.

Through the opportunities created by globalization, citizens can navigate physically and virtually beyond borders and express themselves on behalf of ideas and issues they deem important. Within this growing global civil society, individuals can act as world citizens. We believe the widespread adoption of world citizenship would inspire the creation of many more international forums. As Nigel Dower summarizes, a world citizen is "someone who sees herself as ethically committed to global goals, to using existing institutions appropriate to this and/or to creating and strengthening institutions to the same end" (Dower 2000).

Global connections mandate that we work together across cultures and boundaries to forge global solutions. When avenues for global cooperation exist, we should take advantage of them. When they do not, we should build them.

The fact that a world state does not exist does nothing to diminish the possibility of citizens acting for the world. We must emphasize that we are not arguing for the development of a world government, and do not believe world citizenship requires such an entity. In fact, "considering oneself as a global citizen does not depend on anything other than identification of oneself as a member of the human race with an interest in its survival" (Hutchings 2002, 57).

Once again, it really boils down to your definition of what constitutes a citizen. As Fairleigh Dickinson University philosophy and political science professor Jason Scorza emphasizes, citizenship, at its root,

> means being a full and equal member of a community. In this sense, there is no reason to think one can be a citizen only of a state. From this perspective, we are able to imagine ourselves as a citizen of any number of different kinds of communities including a global community, with equal rights, responsibilities and hopefully, the capabilities, skills and virtues to fulfill our responsibilities and enjoy our rights. (Scorza 2003)

It is important to note that regional movements creating broader expressions of citizenship are already tremendously popular and successful. They are being spearheaded not just by world citizens or even global corporations, but also by states themselves. The European Union is the most obvious example.

The European Union is not only a supranational forum for political and civic expression; it has created opportunities for a European citizenship that effectively broadens national rights beyond national borders. The union includes nearly five hundred million people and twenty-five nations that have agreed to incorporate themselves into a single market with a common currency and certain common policies. There is a parliament, a court system, and a central bank. Every person belonging to a member nation has specific rights, including the right to work and travel freely among member states, vote in local and European Parliament elections, and bring cases before the European Court of Justice.

The union, while respectful of state sovereignty in some areas (such as foreign policy), ignores it in others. For example, the union's judiciary can override national law. The point is that citizens have formal rights beyond the boundaries of the nation-state.

There are, of course, limits to this example. First, the rights available are far from comprehensive. In the European Union, citizenship is dependent on being a citizen of a particular nation, and thus the nation-state remains in control. And so far, there is little expected in the form of duties or citizen obligations.

Finally, even within the European Union, people overwhelmingly continue to act within their national context and resist further integration. Most continue to identify primarily with their nations. Very few consider themselves first and foremost as Europeans. Still, we believe that the European Union and efforts like common markets take important steps toward aligning notions of citizenship beyond traditional political borders. They do not seek to obliterate local variations, but instead to forge a common commitment to the greater good. They have encouraged cooperation and compromise among both countries and individuals, and hold great potential to broaden identities and bridge the gap from national citizenship to world citizenship.

Position Three: Extending the Circle
Critics are absolutely correct to assert that we form loyalties to those we live and grow close to. World citizenship is not meant to replace those bonds. Instead, it complements them with an understanding of the attachments we have to all beings, regardless of the accident of birth. We are adding bonds, not replacing them.

Belief in the importance of universal reason, equal justice, and the inherent worth of all humans does not in any way deny us the capacity to feel strongly for those closest to us. It is impossible to diminish those precious ties. Parents have special attachments, duties, and responsibilities to their children above all others. But this does not mean that they should view other families and other children as having fewer rights or not being worthy of equal respect and understanding.

There is nothing wrong with pride and identification with familial heritages, local communities, and the nation-state. In fact, it can be argued that only through such pride in a particular identity can we grasp what is distinctive and universal about the human experience. The emotional connections to community and national identity are important. They inspire civic involvement.

But an emotional bond based on shared interests with a world community can easily coexist with the emotional ties to the nation-state. Think how closely many in the United States identify simultaneously with their state and their nation. We are also able to take great pride in our local town or city as well. And our ties to those entities do not replace familial bonds, or our special relationships with close friends. They represent additional levels of attachment and coexist quite naturally. Citizens in the United States have a long tradition of embracing hybrid identities, as African-Americans, Greek-Americans, or Asian-Americans, for example.

If world citizenship precluded special relations with certain people or even groups, then the price would be too high. But nothing in the case for global citizenship requires the dismantling of local bonds and relationships. Humans are capable of maintaining multiple allegiances and identities. If this were not the case, we would be in serious trouble as a species. As Hilary Putnam writes, "We do not have to choose between patriotism and universal reason; critical intelligence and loyalty to what is best in our traditions, including our national and ethnic traditions, are interdependent" (Putnam 1996, 97).

Isabelle de Courtivron, a professor of foreign languages and literatures, makes an interesting analogy between proficiency in multiple languages and identities.

> Linguists will tell you that, in bilingual speakers, one language may recede for a while if it is not being used, or needed, but that it will be revived in another context or at a later time; it can even become dominant again under the influence of any number of geographical, emotional, professional, or familial factors. So, too, with identities. We can switch from one to another without fear that we will lose any. (de Courtivron 2000)

We will always have special relationships. And we also must continue to preserve and encourage diversity, which is fundamental to the richness of the human experience. A world citizen does not desire the homogenization that globalization sometimes threatens us with. Being a world citizen means understanding and accepting culturally and ideologically diverse groups. We believe it is possible to do this while still relishing those unique ties that bind us to our inner circle of associations.

But if it is natural to seek comfort close to home, isn't it also natural to be curious about how others think and live? Isn't it also natural to want to embrace humanity wherever it is found?

As research across cultures has shown, all humans have specific predispositions for social bonding. Young children possess a powerful sense of empathy toward others, showing a high degree of concern and an incredible ability to cooperate with all types of people. It is as a child grows that he or she is taught nationalistic rituals and pride, and sometimes prejudice toward a certain culture, identity, and nation.

The last ring appearing on the Stoics' Circle of Humanity—concern for the human species—may well be the first to form in a young child.

> Long before children have any acquaintance with the idea of a nation, or even of one specific religion, they know hunger and loneliness. Long before they encounter patriotism, they have probably encountered death. Long before ideology interferes, they know something of humanity. (Nussbaum 1996b, 143)

Position Four: Emotional Solidarity
This leads us to address the critique that world citizenship is somehow devoid of deep feeling and too abstract a notion to embrace. There is no question that national identities inspire strong emotional attachments. Unfortunately, some nationalist attachments and passions have led to tremendous destruction and murder, while alienating and separating people who otherwise would have no reason for animosity. Other national visions, such as the "American Dream," prompt initiative, action, and achievement.

George Orwell made the valuable distinction that patriotism is "devotion to a particular place and a particular way of life" that one

does not wish to force upon others, while nationalism "is insepara-
ble from the desire for power." Orwell had little use for nationalism;
it "is power-hunger tempered by self-deception," he wrote. "Every
nationalist is capable of the most flagrant dishonesty, but he is also—
since he is conscious of serving something bigger than himself—
unshakably certain of being in the right" (Orwell 1945).

In his pivotal book on the subject, *Nationalism,* Tagore also did
not mince words. Nationalism, he wrote, is a "great menace" and "a
cruel epidemic of evil that is sweeping over the human world of the
present age, and eating into its moral vitality" (Tagore 1917, 133,
28). Nations too often put walls around themselves, he believed, and
deny the underlying reality of our world: that we are all interdependent. "But those who can see," he wrote, "know that men are so
closely knit, that when you strike others, the blow comes back to
yourself" (Tagore 1917, 97).

Nationalism and strong collective identities have many times
led to xenophobia and hostility toward others. And too often, nationalism is associated with uncritical acceptance of the nation's actions
and blind obedience to its government's policies.

But the same forces of patriotism and nationalism, based on a
shared heritage, language, or religion, have been a source of tremendous loyalty and commitment for citizens and have led to great
achievements. They can be grounded in noble human aspirations.
Poll after poll reveals that the vast majority of people in our country
are very proud to be Americans and have strong allegiances to their
national identities and communities. We feel the same emotions. We
do not have to relinquish that heartfelt attachment to the nation-state.
But patriotism does not mean slavish devotion to a government or
nation, no matter the consequences. We can love our country just as
we love a family member, without agreeing with every action taken.
We can especially love it for efforts that enhance the general welfare
of humanity. But we have to get beyond unquestioned loyalty to
the nation-state if world citizenship is to flourish. And blind allegiance is more than just an impediment to world citizenship; it is per-
ilous to an effective democracy. Critical thinking is the bedrock of
progress.

Also, the arrogance based on a selective and overly positive
interpretation of one nation's achievements must be reduced. This
type of linear thinking prevents an appreciation of the rich diversity

of human accomplishments and the sense of common identity and shared worldwide citizenship.

Benedict Anderson describes nationhood as "the most universally legitimate value in the political life of our time" because people will sacrifice their lives for it. "Who," he asks, "will willingly die for Comecon [the now dissolved Council for Mutual Economic Cooperation, which arranged trade among the former Communist countries] or the EEC [the European Economic Community]?" (Anderson 1991, 3, 53).

We agree that the nation is a great source of emotional attachment, and that emotional ties across borders can sometimes be difficult to build. But the above argument ignores the need for a broader international consciousness in today's age, as well as the many international causes that have inspired great passion—from efforts to abolish slavery, to movements that enhance women's and children's rights, to environmental campaigns.

Just like nationalists, world citizens can be emotionally tied to people and objectives. After all, as Robbins points out, nationalists somehow form passionate allegiances and bonds of fellowship with millions they never meet. "If there can be an 'emotion of national pride,' then why not emotions of international pride, based on a horizontal comradeship across the formal equality of nations?" (Robbins 1999, 70).

The notion of world citizenship does depend upon a corresponding sense of community, but we believe that there is a developing global community that can also be a source of passion, solidarity, and identity. Some will continue to question the strength of international commitments and the ties that bind the international community. Certainly, these ties need to be further developed. But critics underestimate the strength of the foundation in place, as well as the capacity of people to understand what is at stake and respond with unbelievable commitment and creativity.

Even without a shared culture, we have a shared commitment to addressing common concerns and problems. This commitment is the foundation for our international community and for world citizenship, and it has led to significant achievements, illustrated particularly in the work of the United Nations and the development of international law and treaties in the second half of the twentieth century. Yes, we remain in the beginning stages of global solidarity, but one cannot deny the growing consensus, or at least willingness to cooperate, on many issues among states and citizens throughout the world.

Global citizenship is something more than a vague notion of ethics. It provides a forum greater than the traditional nation-state, creating a larger umbrella of obligations and responsibilities. That is significant by itself. The strength of that association is entirely up to us, but one thing is clear: We are not working to advance the interest of an abstract notion of humanity. Instead, we are striving to improve the lives of real people. We should be able to identify with all of humanity, no matter where they were born or where they live now.

Common Human Rights: A Consistent Message

With world citizenship should come common fundamental rights. We know that certain basic values can be discussed without danger of cultural bias. Certainly, freedom from want, suffering and disease, oppression, degradation, and destruction would be valuable starting points. Everyone shares the need for nutrition, shelter, economic and physical security, a healthy environment, and a degree of autonomy. Our common needs and vulnerabilities should always take precedence over the differences that separate us.

To go a step further, it is probably fair to say that we all want responsive and stable political, civil, and legal institutions that provide meaningful opportunities for self- and collective expression. Each of us can identify appropriate common desires and hopes for all of humanity. Our list might differ—just a bit—and certainly cultural differences can be pronounced, but fundamental rights are without issue. They often, however, do not guide our individual behavior. How does one begin to translate common rights into action?

How does one take the first step toward world citizenship? Is there a primary ethical message about behavior for our species?

Actually, a consistent message appears throughout human history and in many different cultures. Inside and outside organized religious structures, a single powerful idea has been forwarded for thousands of years.

In Christianity, this basic concept is known as the Golden Rule, but interestingly, this same theme for human behavior appears at many points of time and different locations.

A Familiar Message
Across Cultures and Centuries

Buddhism
Do not offend others as you would not wish to be offended.

—*Undanavarga*

Christianity
Do unto others all that you would have them do unto you, because this is the sum of the law and of the prophets.

—*Jesus Christ, Gospel of Matthew*

Confucianism
Is there a maxim that one ought to follow all his life? Surely the maxim of peaceful goodness: What we don't want done to us we should not do to others.

—*The Analects*

Hindu Philosophy
All your duties are included in this: Do nothing to others that would pain you if it were done to you.

—*Mahabharata*

Islam
Not one of you will be a true believer who does not wish for his brother the same that he wishes for himself.

—*Sunnah*

Judaism
What you don't wish for yourself do not wish for your neighbor. This is all the law, the rest is only commentary.

—*Talmud Shabbat*

Taoism
Hold as your own the gains of your neighbor and as yours his losses.

—*T'ai-Shang Kan-Ying P'ien*

Assembled by the Golden Rule Insurance Company, Indianapolis, Indiana

The consistency of the message implies a universal ethic—a strong starting point for world citizens.

Building upon that principle, there is another, more detailed universal message to which we might all aspire. Adopted in 1948, the UN Universal Declaration of Human Rights establishes a strong foundation of common liberties and rights that should be bestowed across cultures and distinctive local traditions. Nearly everyone today agrees on those fundamental precepts, which include:

- The right to life, liberty, and security
- The right to equal recognition before the law and equal protection, including public hearings by independent tribunals
- The right to freedom of movement, freedom of thought, conscience, and of religion, opinion, expression, and assembly
- Economic, social, and cultural rights "indispensable for [one's] dignity and the free development of [one's] personality" and
- The right to property, and the right to an "adequate" standard of living and to education and equal pay for equal work (United Nations 1948).

The declaration also prohibits slavery, discrimination, torture, and degrading treatment and punishment, as well as arbitrary arrests. We understand that agreement on such rights in principle is not the same thing as enforcing them, ensuring their universal applicability, or even clearly defining them. But as a global dialogue expands, perhaps we can take these next steps.

Working toward these ends can be very meaningful, and we can think of few things more captivating and exciting. If we agree that basic universal rights exist, then our responsibilities as world citizens essentially involve acting to guarantee that people everywhere enjoy these rights.

What can be more inspiring than the notion of a common humanity striving together to preserve the rights of billions against forces of economic and political self-interest? An abstraction does not hold much emotional comfort, but when the links are made real, then the relationships and the sense of attachment can grow.

Wherever we are born, we are tied together through issues and events. We agree with scholars like Steven Vertovec and Robin Cohen, who believe that "only a cosmopolitan outlook can accommodate itself to the political challenges of a more global era." Through cosmopolitanism and global citizenship, they add, we have "the potential to abolish the razor-wired camps, national flags and walls of silence that separate us from our fellow human beings" (Vertovec and Cohen 2002, 21–22).

As we consciously cross borders and develop relationships; as we expand our capacity to imagine the different and identify what we have in common; as we foster international cooperation and collectively answer global challenges; as we make real the promise of global citizenship, then our passions for the cause will soar.

Traveling to New Horizons

Studs Terkel, the great oral historian, described the essence of world citizenship when discussing the famous picture of the Vietnamese girl screaming and running naked from an attack on her village. "That is OUR little girl," he declared. And when we all agree on that, the world will be united as a true global village. Considering that girl as one's own is the mark of a world citizen.

Today's level of interconnectedness and interdependence demands that we look beyond our near horizon and consider the impact of our actions on others throughout the world. We have rights and responsibilities that go beyond the nation-state. Although world citizenship is not a new concept, the need for it and the opportunity to express it have never been clearer than they are in our globalized era.

Even among advocates of global citizenship, there remains disagreement about the scope of our rights and obligations as world citizens. Are we all global citizens already, like it or not? Or do we have to choose to become world citizens? In some sense, both are true. We are bound together in a human community aboard a fragile planet with finite resources and mind-boggling destructive capacities, and thus we all have a responsibility to work toward global goals. On the other hand, there is no doubt that active world citizenship requires a concerted commitment to looking beyond the local and making international connections that contribute to a better world.

Some individuals do not have the capability or opportunity to do more than survive for themselves and their families. But many have such opportunities and are quite capable of accepting the responsibility to make the world a better place in which to live. It is this active form of world citizenship that we wish to encourage and expand.

The next generation may be in a better position than the current one to make global connections. They have been raised on the World Wide Web, satellite communications, international campaigns, and other instruments and manifestations of our global age. They may have less of a sense of rigid separation between national stakes and global interests, and may be closer to becoming globally aware and creating a global identity. It is hoped that they can connect the dots in new ways to find new solutions to the problems we face.

Becoming world citizens does not mean turning our backs on local identities and traditional communities—just as becoming a national citizen does not mean forsaking pride in our state. Our own United States provides the basis for optimism that a vast divergence of identities can come together for common interests. We do not have to relinquish local ties. But becoming a world citizen does mean expanding our circle of concern and attachment to those who are different and to those who are not our compatriots. It means being concerned about and acting on behalf of humanity everywhere.

References

Anderson, Benedict. 1991. *Imagined Communities: Reflections on the Origin and Spread of Nationalism.* Second edition. London: Verso.

Andrzejewski, Julie, and John Alessio. 1999. Education for Global Citizenship and Social Responsibility. *Progressive Perspectives* 1, no. 2 (Spring). Monograph Series. John Dewey Project on Progressive Education, University of Vermont.

Appiah, Kwame Anthony. 1992. *In My Father's House: Africa in the Philosophy of Culture.* New York: Oxford University Press.

Axtell, Roger E. 1999. *Do's and Taboos of Humor Around the World: Stories and Tips from Business and Life.* New York: John Wiley & Sons.

Barnaby, Frank, ed. 1988. *The Gaia Peace Atlas: Survival into the Third Millennium.* New York: Doubleday.

Boulding, Elise. 1988. *Building a Global Civic Culture: Education for an Interdependent World.* Syracuse, NY: Syracuse University Press.

Carter, April. 2001. *The Political Theory of Global Citizenship.* New York: Routledge.

Craige, Betty Jean. 1996. American Patriotism in a Global Society. Albany, NY: State University of New York Press.

Dallmayr, Fred, and Rosales, José M., eds. 2001. *Beyond Nationalism? Sovereignty and Citizenship.* Lanham, MD: Lexington Books.

de Courtivron, Isabelle. 2000. Educating the Global Student, Whose Identity Is Always a Matter of Choice. *The Chronicle of Higher Education,* July 7.

Delanty, Gerard. 2000. *Citizenship in a Global Age: Society, Culture, Politics.* Philadelphia: Open University Press.

Dower, Nigel. 2000. The Idea of Global Citizenship—A Sympathetic Assessment. *Global Society: Journal of Interdisciplinary International Relations* 14, no. 4 (October): 553–567.

Dower, Nigel. 2002. Global Citizenship: Yes or No? In *Global Citizenship: A Critical Introduction,* edited by N. Dower and J. Williams, 30–40. New York: Routledge.

Dower, Nigel, and Williams, John, eds. 2002. *Global Citizenship: A Critical Introduction.* New York: Routledge.

Eisenhower, Dwight D. 1959. Annual Message to the Congress on the State of the Union. January 9. Source: *Public Papers of the President: Dwight D. Eisenhower, 1959.* Published by the Office of the Federal Register, National Archives and Records Service, and the General Services Administration.

Falk, Richard. 1996. Revisioning Cosmopolitanism. In *For Love of Country: Debating the Limits of Patriotism,* edited by M.C. Nussbaum, 53–60. Boston: Beacon Press.

———. 2002. An Emergent Matrix of Citizenship: Complex, Uneven, and Fluid. In *Global Citizenship: A Critical Introduction,* edited by N. Dower and J. Williams, 15–29. New York: Routledge.

Fruchtman, Jr., Jack. 1994. *Thomas Paine: Apostle of Freedom.* New York: Four Walls Eight Windows.

Held, David. 2002. Culture and Political Community: National, Global, and Cosmopolitan. In *Conceiving Cosmopolitanism: Theory, Context, and Practice,* edited by S. Vertovec and R. Cohen, 48–58. New York: Oxford University Press.

Himmelfarb, Gertrude. 1996. The Illusions of Cosmopolitanism. In *For Love of Country: Debating the Limits of Patriotism,* edited by M.C. Nussbaum, 72–77. Boston: Beacon Press.

Hogan, Patrick Colm. 2003. Introduction: Tagore and the Ambivalence of Commitment. In *Rabindranath Tagore: Universality and Tradition,* edited by P.C. Hogan and L. Pandit, 9–23. Madison and Teaneck, NJ: Fairleigh Dickinson University Press.

Hogan, Patrick Colm, and Lalita Pandit, eds. 2003. *Rabindranath Tagore: Universality and Tradition.* Madison and Teaneck, NJ: Fairleigh Dickinson University Press.

Hutchings, Kimberly. 2002. Feminism and Global Citizenship. In *Global Citizenship: A Critical Introduction,* edited by N. Dower and J. Williams, 53–62. New York: Routledge.

Ikeda, Daisaku. 1996. Thoughts on Education for Global Citizenship. Address delivered at Teachers College, Columbia University, June 13. http://www.sgi.org/english/President/speeches/thoughts.htm (accessed September 14, 2005).

King, Jr., Martin Luther. 1967. *Where Do We Go From Here: Chaos or Community?* New York: Harper & Row.

Kingwell, Mark. 2000. *The World We Want: Restoring Citizenship in a Fractured Age.* Lanham, MD: Rowman & Littlefield Publishers.

Nussbaum, Martha C. 1996a. Patriotism and Cosmopolitanism. In *For Love of Country: Debating the Limits of Patriotism,* edited by M.C. Nussbaum, 3–17. Boston: Beacon Press.

———. 1996b. Reply. In *For Love of Country: Debating the Limits of Patriotism,* edited by M.C. Nussbaum, 131–144. Boston: Beacon Press.

Nussbaum, Martha C., with respondents. 1996. In *For Love of Country: Debating the Limits of Patriotism,* edited by M.C. Nussbaum. Boston: Beacon Press.

Nussbaum, Martha C. 1997. *Cultivating Humanity: A Classical Defense of Reform in Liberal Education.* Cambridge, MA: Harvard University Press.

Orwell, George. 1945. Notes on Nationalism. http://orwell.ru/library/essays/nationalism/english/e_nat (accessed September 14, 2005).

Oxfam. 1997. What is Global Citizenship? http://oxfam.org.uk/coolplanet/teachers/globciti/whatis.htm (accessed September 14, 2005).

Paine, Thomas. 1995. *Collected Writings.* Edited by Eric Foner. New York: The Library of America.

Parker, Walter C., Akira Ninomiya, and John Cogan. 1999. Educating World Citizens: Toward Multinational Curriculum Development. *American Educational Research Journal* 36, no. 2 (summer): 117–145.

Purkayastha, Bandana. 2003. Contesting the Boundaries Between Home and the World: Tagore and the Construction of Citizenship. In *Rabindranath Tagore: Universality and Tradition,* edited by P.C. Hogan and L. Pandit, 49–64. Madison and Teaneck, NJ: Fairleigh Dickinson University Press.

Putnam, Hilary. 1996. Must We Choose Between Patriotism and Universal Reason? In *For Love of Country: Debating the Limits of Patriotism,* edited by M.C. Nussbaum, 91–97. Boston: Beacon Press.

Robbins, Bruce. 1999. *Feeling Global: Internationalism in Distress.* New York: New York University Press.

Rorty, Richard. 1994. The Unpatriotic Academy. *New York Times,* February 13.

Rotblat, Joseph, ed. 1997. *World Citizenship: Allegiance to Humanity.* New York: St. Martin's Press.

Scorza, Jason. 2003. Address. Developing Global Competencies in Higher Education. A conference presented by Fairleigh Dickinson University and the Internationalization Collaborative of the American Council on Education, April 4–5.

Solzhenitsyn, Alexandr. 1970. Nobel Lecture address. http://nobelprize.org/literature/laureates/1970/solzhenitsyn-lecture.html (accessed September 14, 2005).

Tagore, Rabindranath. 1917. *Nationalism.* New York: The MacMillan Company.

Turner, Bryan S. 2001. National Identities and Cosmopolitan Virtues: Citizenship in a Global Age. In *Beyond Nationalism? Sovereignty and Citizenship,* edited by F. Dallmayr and J.M. Rosales, 199–220. Lanham, MD: Lexington Books.

United Nations. 1948. Universal Declaration of Human Rights. http://www.un.org/overview/rights.html (accesssed October 13, 2005).

Vertovec, Steven, and Robin Cohen. 2002. Introduction: Conceiving Cosmopolitanism. In *Conceiving Cosmopolitanism: Theory, Context, and Practice,* edited by S. Vertovec and R. Cohen, 1–22. New York: Oxford University Press.

Vertovec, Steven, and Robin Cohen, eds. 2002. *Conceiving Cosmopolitanism: Theory, Context, and Practice.* New York: Oxford University Press.

5

GLOBALIZATION AND WORLD CITIZENSHIP AFTER SEPTEMBER 11

You can not spill a drop of American blood without spilling the blood of the whole world . . . No: our blood is as the flood of the Amazon, made up of a thousand noble currents all pouring into one. We are not a nation, so much as a world; for unless we may claim all the world for our sire . . . we are without father or mother.

—Herman Melville
Redburn, 1849

In retrospect, the millennium marked only a moment in time. It was the events of September 11 that marked a turning point in history, where we confront the dangers of the future, and assess the choices facing humankind.

—Tony Blair, 2001

A Personal Experience

I had the opportunity to visit Ground Zero, the place where the buildings of the World Trade Center had stood, just ten days after the tragedy. Amid so many powerful, overwhelming images, one scene was particularly strong.

A long, polished, black marble wall stood on a street adjacent to the disaster's epicenter. The wall was covered in dust, dirt, and ashes hurled against the stone during the collapse of the towers. People had written messages in the dust:

"The Oakland Fire Department is here to help"

"Carlos, you are our hero, we love and miss you"

"Damn it, we must be brave"

"Pray for a better world"

The wall struck me as a metaphor for the tragedy—and perhaps for life. Through our actions and lives, we individually and collectively write messages for the world. We try to influence and make better what we can touch.

Our lives, however, and our messages for the world, are not permanent. They can be erased in an instant. Our messages can only endure through the connections we make with our fellow humans to improve the world.

A New View of Ourselves and Our World

"Our world changed on September 11." It's been said so many times by so many that it is an undisputed fact for most Americans. But what exactly changed, and what does it mean for the future of globalization? Does it strengthen or weaken the United States and other nation-states? And what of world citizenship after September 11? Is it still as desirable, or even possible?

September 11 was an Earth-shattering event, with tragic consequences that will be felt for years to come. For the victims and their families, the toll was devastating. Our first thoughts should always be of their loss and enduring pain. For justice on their behalf especially, the search to apprehend those responsible should continue. And for their sake and ours, all possible resources should be used to prevent any such tragedy from occurring again.

But the impact has been significant on an even broader scale. Some say our nation's innocence was lost that day, and to a large extent, it is true. For millions who either had not given it much thought or who were sedated by the illusion of invulnerability, the United States appeared to be an impregnable fortress, immune from such horror. Aside from the attack on Pearl Harbor, it had been nearly two hundred years since an enemy made a direct assault on our soil (in 1814, the British army burned public buildings in Washington, including the White House).

Further, the idea that the United States could represent an evil to be attacked with such ruthlessness was incomprehensible to many. We learned differently. We understand our vulnerability better now, and we also are more sensitive to the disdain and outright hatred that exists toward the United States.

Shashi Tharoor, the United Nations under-secretary-general for communications and public information, believes history will record September 11 as the true beginning of the twenty-first century. Its main importance, Tharoor says, lies in its effect on the relationship between America and the rest of the world: "If only by bringing home to Americans the end of their insulation from the history and geography that bedeviled the rest of the globe, September 11 changed the world forever" (Tharoor 2002).

In the immediate aftermath of the tragedy, there surfaced a great desire among many to become more engaged with the rest of the world, and to try to learn exactly why we are so hated.

Some of the reasons for the hatred are rooted in nothing more than intolerance and ignorance, but some are inspired by real and perceived grievances. In any event, nothing justifies such atrocities, but the search for explanations was under way. It seemed that the country was at least—and probably at long last—on the verge of a critical self-examination. Many abroad and some at home long decried the arrogance of the United States and its lack of involvement with the world community. Could such isolationist tendencies be thwarted by a growing recognition that, in many ways, we are just as vulnerable and fragile as the rest of the world?

Tharoor adds, "After September 11, there could be no easy retreat into isolationism, no comfort in the illusion that the problems of the rest of the world need not trouble the United States. Americans now understand viscerally the old cliché of the global village" (Tharoor 2002).

Rallying 'Round the Flag

That growing recognition appeared alongside a wave of patriotism and "America first" sentiments. Certainly, the conspicuous display of patriotism was understandable in the wake of such a horrifying attack. Americans rallied like a nation at war, which in many ways was appropriate considering the violent attack and warlike declarations from al-Qaeda. The media and government portrayed the attacks as a tragedy that happened to our nation, and the context of the battle was set in terms of "America's War on Terror."

The danger, though, was in framing a complex situation purely in nationalist terms, in painting a gray picture in terms of black and white, "us" against "them." Such concepts often lead to expressions of arrogance and supremacy. They imply a sense of otherness and alienation from others that contributes nothing to the solution. Such an attitude only aggravates the tension between America and other parts of the world.

This is wrong not only from an ethical standpoint, but also from a practical position. A purely nationalist view of the current conflict and pursuit of criminal organizations and individuals will not make the United States any safer. In our interconnected world, where a few individuals can have such an impact against governments and nation-states, the answer is not found in traditional battles between countries. You cannot invade an idea or emotion.

The answer, much like that for a coordinated criminal hunt, is more multinational cooperation, more tentacles stretching among countries and greater links between governmental and civic bodies. It is hard to imagine any lasting gains in the war on terrorism without extensive collaboration among police officials, bankers, and immigration and customs officers from multiple national governments. This is the only way to ferret out underground networks operating clandestinely among and across many countries.

The al-Qaeda network supposedly has operated in more than sixty countries (Sassen 2002; Haass 2001). It has neither a home country nor a central location, but instead is a decentralized network connected by communication technologies. Its members cross borders with ease. And its victims are not exclusively Americans. On September 11, more than seventy-five nations besides the United States suffered casualties (Haass 2001).

Subsequent attacks by al-Qaeda and its allies have targeted people across the globe, in places such as Egypt, Morocco, Saudi Arabia, Tunisia, and Turkey. On October 12, 2002, a car bomb exploded outside a nightclub in Bali, Indonesia, killing 202 people, including many foreign tourists. On March 11, 2004, three days before Spain's general elections, multiple bombings on trains and train stations in Madrid killed 191 people and wounded approximately 1,500. On July 7, 2005, a series of bombings struck the London public transport system, killing more than 50 people and injuring about 700. Winning the war on terrorism will require a global effort.

Re-examining Globalization

But for our discussion, the question remains: What will become of globalization after September 11? The assassination of Archduke

Franz Ferdinand in 1914 not only started World War I, but heralded the end of the earlier era of globalization. War, violence, and nationalism, accompanied by trade protectionism and immigration restrictions, all ensued, and it took decades for globalization to pick up steam again. Will history repeat itself? In attacking the World Trade Center's Twin Towers, perhaps the global economy's most symbolic structure, did the terrorists derail globalization itself?

Sociology professor Saskia Sassen suggests that there have been some countervailing trends to globalization since September 11. "We are seeing a renationalizing of governments' efforts to control their territory after a decade of 'denationalizing' national economies. But we are also seeing new types of cross-border government coalitions in legal, policing, and military arenas" (Sassen 2002).

Some aspects of globalization led to our increased vulnerability in the first place. But this is not new. Increased trade and migration have always brought exposure to diseases, instability, and, perhaps most dangerous of all, new ideas. The scale of the potential influence and destruction, however, is much greater today.

The affluence created by global economic forces has aroused the envy and wrath of those who do not need much justification to unleash their frustrations. Even more alarming is how easily the global network can be damaged. It is clear, as Sassen notes, that great wealth and complex, interlinked infrastructures "offer insufficient protection against bombs loaded with carpenter nails, elementary nuclear devices and 'homemade' biological weapons, not to mention computer hackers and hijackers." Today, small groups and individuals have destructive power previously available only to nations and governments.

> Much, though by no means all, global business has come to thrive increasingly on deregulation and privatization. But the terrorists' use of the financial system, along with money laundering and tax evasion by drug barons and other criminal groups, all suggest the limits of liberalization and privatization, and the need to re-insert governments in the global financial system. (Sassen 2002)

Sassen, though, does not advocate that states should act in isolation, but rather with each other, as was done in the antiterrorist financial clampdown carried out by the United States and the European Union after September 11.

Security remains the main concern following September 11, and the only way to achieve that is through multinational efforts. For security reasons, trade and financial transactions must be closely monitored. This may raise the cost of business and therefore influence where that business takes place. But few believe that the major trading nations and corporations will or can pull back because of the obvious potential for wealth still existing in the system.

It is true that economic growth slowed, particularly after September 11, and that trade clashes were not hard to find. After a decade of rapid gains, exports and foreign direct investment (FDI) declined. But globalization was not expected to end the inevitable swings of the business cycle and most experts did not see the declines as permanent. Even with a significant drop in FDI (from $1.49 trillion to $735 billion), the flow of money in 2001 was the highest of any year before 1999 and nearly double its 1995 level (*Foreign Policy* 2003). In 2002, FDI was "down" to $651 billion (*Foreign Policy* 2004). The same pattern applies to trade: The small drops followed dramatic rises. And trade levels, like economic growth, soon picked up. World trade grew by only 3.5 percent in 2002, but rose by 5.5 percent in 2003 and 9.9 percent in 2004 (*Economist* 2005).

For the first time since World War II, travel and tourism declined globally in 2001. But travel levels rebounded the next year. In addition, international telephone traffic continued to reach record levels, and the number of Internet users grew at dynamic rates (*Foreign Policy* 2004).

After September 11, political integration became more common, most notably as countries formed coalitions to fight a number of battles, particularly the war on terrorism. And, membership in international organizations continued to expand.

Thomas Friedman said that the attack on September 11 "slowed down the system a little bit." He phrased it well when he added, "It's put sand in the gears of the system" (Friedman 2003). But Friedman and others are quick to accurately add that the fundamental processes of globalization are not going away. Capital movements will continue to ebb and flow. Global trade will find ways to adapt. People will continue to journey and interact with other cultures, and governments and nations will continue to need to work with other nations. As *Foreign Policy* concluded, "Despite all its travails, the world was more—not less—integrated at the end of 2002 than it had ever been before" (*Foreign Policy* 2004).

Many other ancillary connections, brought about through communications and technological advancements in particular, are bringing peoples together. How would one turn back the clock on the globalization of technology? Worldwide integration, fueled by technology, continues with irreversible force.

Rebound of the Nation-State?

Some view September 11 as reason to return to the primacy of the nation-state over multinational coalitions. Christopher Hill, a lecturer in international affairs, says, "Pick any problem out there—AIDS, the environment or terrorism. If the state isn't effective in its jurisdiction, then the problem isn't going to get solved" (Stille 2002). John Gaddis, a history professor, says the response to the attacks reaffirms the importance of states. "It suggests that reports of the death of states have been exaggerated. The whole reason we have states is protection against anarchy—9-11 shows that states are rather good things to have around" (Stille 2002).

States are most definitely still good to have around, and it remains obvious that global problems must be effectively combated at the state level, as Hill suggests. It is critical to keep in mind that the successful coalitions formed to combat the scourge of terrorism are made up of states. But despite September 11, nothing has changed the realities that chapters 2 and 3 describe. The power of the nation-state in relation to international forces, particularly regarding economic issues, has declined. To succeed, people must think globally and deal with institutions and individuals throughout the world.

In a complex, borderless world, where finances and information flow effortlessly and complex issues overlap with borders, states working in isolation, no matter how powerful, cannot hope to overcome major problems. That belief is echoed by scholars such as Joseph Nye, who said, "The fact that information technology decentralizes power and puts it in the hands of individuals scattered around the world means you are going to need a lot of people who will cooperate with you" (Stille 2002).

And, as Benjamin Barber notes, the dialogue has noticeably shifted in this direction after September 11 as "'idealistic' internationalism has become the new realism." After September 11,

> What alone has become clear is that we can no longer assign culpability in the neat nineteenth-century terms of domestic and foreign. And while we may still seek sovereign sponsors for acts of terror that have none, the myth of our independence can no

longer be sustained. Nonstate actors, whether they are multi-national corporations or loosely knit terrorist cells, are neither domestic nor foreign, neither national nor international, neither sovereign entities nor international organizations. (Barber 2002)

As Barber also observed, the United States is vulnerable, like many other nations, because of its extensive interconnectedness with the rest of the world. Our technological advances and economic systems can be used against us by terrorists, just as they can be used to spread injustice and inequality. The circle is becoming smaller, and few actions, malicious or otherwise, can take place in a vacuum. That is ultimately a good thing, because both those engaging in acts of murder and those engaging in oppressive and exploitative practices need to be held accountable.

Many have noted that, as globalization continues, people in wealthy nations must help create opportunities for growth and expression for others. The risk of leaving them behind is too great. This is part of the lesson of September 11, even if the denial of opportunity was not the driving force behind the maniacal hijackers that cruel morning. Those crazed forces of destruction can ultimately only find support and assistance for their heinous acts among those who are desperate. And oppression breeds desperation.

A Tradition of Going It Alone

While police and military antiterrorism work continues, we can and should be doing more. That at least includes improving our country's standing as a responsible and compassionate neighbor, acting as global citizens in a diverse world, proud of our identity as Americans but aware of our responsibility to all. In this vein, it is important to return to that process of self-examination that simultaneously looks inward and outward. We must better understand other cultures: In the process, we gain an appreciation for what makes our culture different from others, and most vitally, what we have in common with all who share this planet. And we must recognize our own limitations and acknowledge our mistakes.

This may not come easy for many Americans. We have long been known for a fierce willingness to march to our own beat, as Barber notes.

From the Monroe Doctrine to our refusal to join the League of Nations, from the isolationism that preceded World War II, and from which we were jarred only by Pearl Harbor, to the isolationism that followed the war and that yielded only partially to the cold war and the arms race, and from our reluctance to pay our UN dues or sign on to international treaties to our refusal to place American troops under the command of friendly NATO foreigners, the United States has persisted in reducing foreign policy to a singular formula that preaches going it alone. (Barber 2002)

That assessment might be a little harsh. After all, the United States has been influential in forming many multinational efforts that today are held up as the standards for international cooperation, ranging from the United Nations to the WTO. Still, there is no denying a distinctly independent streak that has a strong historical tradition (both George Washington and Thomas Jefferson, among others, viewed alliances with suspicion) and has often proven successful. It might be unrealistic to expect the world's dominant power to avoid acting selfishly apart at times and with hard-edged realism, aligned perfectly with national goals. Previous world powers were no different.

Many observers hoped September 11 might steer the American government away from its historic inclination to go it alone and toward the rest of the world. And there were positive signs. At least in formal declarations and pronouncements, many US leaders recognized the global scope of the threat and the need to join forces with allies throughout the world.

Richard Haass, writing in 2001 when he was the US State Department's director of policy planning, made a similar point when, following the attacks, he said that the United States needed to work closely with others to triumph over terrorism.

Like a virus, international terrorism respects no boundaries— moving from country to country, exploiting globalized commerce and communication to spread. We therefore need to take appropriate prophylactic measures at home and abroad . . . no matter how much we may want to solve the problems that face us entirely by ourselves, we cannot single handedly wage a successful campaign against international terrorism. In that respect, terrorism is like many other challenges of this globalized era, like combating HIV/AIDS, stymieing the proliferation of weapons of mass destruction, or halting the trafficking in humans and illicit drugs. Global problems require global solutions. (Haass 2001)

In 2002, the United States unveiled its updated National Security Strategy to account for the emerging new threats in the world. While widely discussed and criticized as an affirmation of the US right to act preemptively and unilaterally to defeat its enemies, the document repeatedly stressed the need for multilateral cooperation. The document affirms the United States' commitment to international institutions such as the United Nations, noting that "no nation can build a safer, better world alone." Later, it adds, "There is little of lasting consequence that the United States can accomplish in the world without the sustained cooperation of its allies and friends" (National Security Council 2002).

After being elected for a second term, US President George W. Bush forcefully articulated his commitment to global cooperation, saying, "The first great commitment is to defend our security and spread freedom by building effective multinational and multilateral institutions and supporting multilateral action" (Douglas 2004). In his second inaugural address, he stressed the obvious interconnected nature of our world when he said, "The survival of liberty in our land increasingly depends on the success of liberty in other lands. The best hope for peace in our world is the expansion of freedom in all the world."

While such sentiments might be dismissed as mere rhetoric, they are significant because they were issued by a president and an administration often criticized for their willingness to go it alone. That the Bush Administration can officially articulate such positions and readily agree on the reality of our interconnected world emphasizes the pressing importance of forging alliances and international friendships.

Still, actions speak louder than words, and following September 11, it was clear that many governmental leaders disregarded or at least downplayed the importance of multilateralism. Some have made a forceful case that the United States after September 11 should act unilaterally to protect its interests and preserve its security. They argue that building its power, acting outside alliances, and applying military force preemptively are necessary in a more volatile world.

The United States' real power, though, derives not just from economic and military might, but from ideals of equality, freedom, and liberty, which speak to not just individual or national opportunities, but collective security and prosperity. As US President Franklin D. Roosevelt said, the four essential freedoms—of speech and expression, of worship, and from material want and fear—are freedoms to which all people can aspire. Advancing those ideals abroad and preserving them at home requires extensive cooperation, strong bonds of friendship, and close alliances throughout the world. There is no other way to advance American ideals.

In writing about the burdens of empire and the increased emphasis on American military might after September 11, Michael Ignatieff suggested,

> This sort of projection of power, hunkered down against attack, can earn the United States fear and respect, but not admiration and affection. America's very strength—in military power—cannot conceal its weakness in the areas that really matter: the elements of power that do not subdue by force of arms but inspire by force of example. (Ignatieff 2003)

The guiding principle that relies on cooperation only when convenient is exactly the wrong one needed for the twenty-first century, and the wrong lesson learned from September 11.

The Relevance of the United Nations

The terrorist attacks and subsequent crises, particularly the US invasion of Iraq, have changed the way many in the United States view their country's relationship with the United Nations. Some have questioned the relevance of the United Nations in the new world.

The United Nations was created in large part by the efforts and leadership of the United States. President Franklin D. Roosevelt's vision and dedication was decisive in forming the world body. He even coined its name. Former US Secretary of State Cordell Hull won the Nobel Peace Prize mainly for his role in creating the institution. President Harry S. Truman supported Roosevelt's vision with equal devotion to the cause. The American delegation at the founding conference in San Francisco, led by then-Secretary of State Edward Stettinius, worked feverishly to resolve complex disagreements among the nations represented. Their efforts succeeded.

On the stage of the San Francisco Opera House, on June 26, 1945, representatives from fifty countries signed the charter (Poland added its signature later, bringing the original membership to fifty-one nations). In Washington, where the Senate had earlier rejected membership in Woodrow Wilson's League of Nations, there were no reservations. The charter was quickly ratified on Capitol Hill, with the Senate voting 89 to 2 in favor.

The vision of the United Nations, articulated in the preamble to the charter, was "to save succeeding generations from the scourge of war," "to reaffirm faith in fundamental human rights," "to establish conditions under which justice . . . can be maintained," and "to promote social progress and better standards of life . . ." (United Nations 1945). The charter adds that the United Nations has four purposes:

1. "to maintain international peace and security"
2. "to develop friendly relations among nations"
3. "to achieve international cooperation in solving international problems" and "in promoting and encouraging respect for human rights and for fundamental freedoms" and
4. "to be a center for harmonizing the actions of nations in the attainment of these common ends" (United Nations 1945).

The United Nations is the most ambitious step to forge a world community in humankind's existence. It has succeeded most in preventing the horror of a third world war, encouraging multinational dialogues and the development of international law, and giving a voice to numerous governmental and nongovernmental entities. Among many other efforts, it is active in peacekeeping, disarmament, economic development, environmental preservation, education, and disease prevention.

Its quest for peace has not been without setbacks, but its vision of a world free from conflict remains. That vision had special meaning for Truman, who carried with him several stanzas of his favorite poem, Alfred Lord Tennyson's *Locksley Hall* (1842) (Schlesinger 2003, 5–6). The poem includes these powerful lines:

> For I dipt into the future, far as human eye could see,
>   Saw the Vision of the world, and all the wonder that would be; . . .
>   Till the war-drum throbb'd no longer, and the battle-flags were furl'd
>   In the Parliament of man, the Federation of the World.

All acknowledge that the institution is far from perfect. It has aggravated tensions just as often as it has brought nations together. At its essence, though, the United Nations is not really a singular entity; it is merely a forum for groups and countries to engage each other. It has six main parts:

1. The Security Council
2. The General Assembly
3. The Economic and Social Council, which coordinates the economic and social work of the many UN-related organizations
4. The Trusteeship Council, which no longer meets because the territories under its supervision have all achieved self-government or independence
5. The Secretariat, which under the Secretary-General handles the administrative work, and
6. The International Court of Justice, also known as the World Court, which decides disputes between countries.

In addition to these main bodies, the United Nations system includes:

- Specialized agencies, such as the United Nations Educational, Scientific, and Cultural Organization (UNESCO), WHO, the IMF, and the World Bank
- Various programs and funds, such as the United Nations Children's Fund (UNICEF), UNDP, and the Office of the United Nations High Commissioner for Refugees (UNHCR)
- Related organizations, such as the WTO and the International Atomic Energy Agency (IAEA)

These agencies, offices, and organizations have their own governing bodies and budgets, and they operate autonomously.

When discussing the United Nations, most attention focuses on either the Security Council or the General Assembly. The Security Council is primarily responsible for maintaining peace and security. It is the only UN body that can pass binding resolutions. The structure and policies of the Security Council, however, often render it ineffective and leave much open to criticism. The Council has fifteen members, five permanent and ten elected by the General Assembly for a two-year term. The five permanent members are China, France,

Russia, the United Kingdom, and the United States. This configuration is often considered an anachronistic legacy of World War II. Of special concern for many countries is the veto provision: Any one of the five permanent members, with its veto, can derail the will of the entire world community. Since the United States has veto power, worries about threats to American sovereignty are overblown, while international resentment of certain powers is easily understood.

The General Assembly, which includes delegates from all member nations, is sometimes referred to as a parliament of nations. It has the authority to review and approve the budget, and it elects the members of other UN bodies. Its resolutions can express the voice of the world community. They are, however, not legally binding. Assembly members often become mired in tedious debates. Committee chairs and memberships are regularly made on a rotating basis, with equal weight given to sometimes very unequal participants. And because of the one state, one vote rule, majorities can represent very little of the world's population and hardly reflect the realities of international opinion or the distribution of power in the world. For example, the 127 least-populated nations in the world body, representing just 8 percent of the world's total population, can deliver the two-thirds majority needed to pass a major resolution (Schwartzberg 2004, 9).

Madeleine Albright, former US ambassador to the United Nations and former secretary of state, says she used to joke "that managing the global institution was like trying to run a business with 184 chief executive officers—each with a different language, a distinct set of priorities, and an unemployed brother-in-law seeking a paycheck" (Albright 2003).

So the United Nations often struggles to remain on track, torn by its many divisions and structural deficiencies and reflecting the weaknesses of its many members. But in the words of its second secretary-general, Dag Hammarskjöld, the United Nations was not established "to take humanity to heaven but to save it from hell" (Tharoor 2003). So far, it has done that.

While the United Nations certainly deserves criticism, the alternative, a world where nations fight to preserve their own self-interest, is not only undesirable, but has been rejected by the vast majority of world opinion. As another former U.S. ambassador to the United Nations, Richard Holbrooke, says,

> Can any serious policy maker actually think that the world—and especially the United States—would be better off without this

organization? Its record of achievement—from specialized agencies like UNICEF and WHO to successful peacekeeping operations in such places as Namibia and East Timor—is substantial; without the United Nations the world would be in far worse shape. (Holbrooke 2003)

Albright agrees, noting that the global body "is still the best investment that the world can make in stopping AIDS and SARS, feeding the poor, helping refugees, and fighting global crime and the spread of nuclear weapons" (Albright 2003). She points out that in 2003, the IAEA reported that Iran had violated the Nuclear Nonproliferation Treaty, and WHO successfully responded to the global threat of SARS.

Meanwhile, the World Food Programme has fed more than 70 million people annually for the last five years; the U.N. High Commissioner for Refugees maintains a lifeline to the international homeless; the U.N. Children's Fund has launched a campaign to end forced childhood marriage; the Joint U.N. Programme on HIV/AIDS remains a focal point for global efforts to defeat HIV/AIDS; and the U.N. Population Fund helps families plan, mothers survive, and children grow up healthy in the most impoverished places on Earth. (Albright 2003)

The United Nations is a forum for both nation-states and NGOs to air grievances and address global injustices, from environmental degradations to apartheid to the exploitation of women and children. All of these can be taken to the world community, exposed to the light of day, and remedied or alleviated through international alliances. International conventions have forged multilateral agreements to progress in areas such as disarmament, human rights, and environmental preservation.

It is less commonly known that the United Nations also handles international labor standards, international aviation safety provisions, international mail flow issues, and international copyright laws—all of which significantly aid Americans. The United Nations also facilitates educational exchanges and international research projects.

The United Nations represents the best hope for our developing world community. By enshrining the principle of self-determination alongside guidelines and provisions to secure and preserve common interests, it has dramatically advanced many causes. And it is the best source of international legitimacy. When the United Nations acts, particularly when the Security Council passes a resolution, it is not only legally binding, but widely respected.

Even when the American government might prefer to avoid dealing with the multinational community, it invariably finds itself appealing to it. The situation in Iraq was just one example. The United States ultimately dismissed pursuing the approval of the United Nations to attack Iraq, but after the attack, it quickly sought to involve the United Nations in nation-building efforts.

As journalist James Traub wrote, it may be true that the United States does not need the United Nations. But, he adds, "The U.S. does, however, need other countries; and the other countries we need believe in the U.N. whether we do or not" (Traub 2003).

We are convinced, though, that the United States does need the United Nations. As the most powerful country on Earth, the United States would benefit greatly from tackling global problems like international terrorism, environmental threats, and disease. These problems threaten everyone, and working with other countries and the United Nations to solve them is not only desired by world citizens who view global problems as shared responsibilities, but is perfectly consistent with US national self-interests. Holbrooke notes that despite the flaws of the United Nations, it "still serves American foreign policy interests far more than it hurts them" (Holbrooke 2003).

Although the United States has been at odds with the United Nations, it has great influence there. The United Nations has served US interests in many cases, supporting the dispatch of forces to Korea, the 1991 incursion into Kuwait to expel Iraqi forces, and the attack on Afghanistan in 2001.

Nowhere is the UN alliance with US interests more evident than in the war on terrorism. After September 11, UN resolutions "provided an international framework for the global battle against terrorism," wrote Tharoor. Resolution 1373 in particular "required nations to interdict arms flows and financial transfers to suspected terrorist groups, report on terrorists' movements, and update national legislation to fight them." Tharoor adds,

> Without the legal authority of a binding Security Council resolution, Washington would have been hard-pressed to obtain such cooperation "retail" from 191 individual states, and it would have taken decades to negotiate and ratify separate treaties and conventions imposing the same standards on all countries. (Tharoor 2003)

John Negroponte became the US ambassador to the United Nations one week after the terrorist attacks. Three years later, he was quoted as saying,

> I'm struck by the relevance of the UN to United States foreign policy and national security interests. . . . To those who would question the relevance of the UN, my answer would be: absolutely the UN is relevant, no question about it, all you have to do is look at our agenda. The degree of UN involvement in any specific issue will vary from case to case, but there will always be a UN role. (Fasulo 2004, 204)

Cosmopolitans and world citizens desire a US foreign policy that strongly considers national security and national goals, but also includes concerted action with other countries to further global aims. World citizens also desire US leadership to improve and enhance international agreements and organizations, beginning with the United Nations. Perhaps alone among powerful countries, the United States has the necessary clout and capability to power the reform and continued vitality of the United Nations.

But on an even more basic level, paying dues on time and contributing more financial support would certainly be a start. Among nation-states, the United States is the largest financial contributor to the United Nations. Still, its overall contribution to the world body "is just one-third of the level provided by the EU, which has an economy of comparable size" (Patrick 2003, 50–51). While the United States accounts for approximately 30 percent of the world's total GNP, it is responsible for 22 percent of the UN budget (Schwartzberg 2004, 13).

Ultimately, by working multinationally through the United Nations, the United States can enhance its standing and further its interests. As Stewart Patrick noted, "By providing weaker countries with a voice and reassuring them against exploitation or abandonment, Washington can increase the legitimacy of its global leadership" (Patrick 2003, 53).

The World and US

With great American power and influence come American responsibilities to address global concerns. In certain areas, too, such as producing greenhouse gases or nuclear waste, the United States bears its share of the responsibility and must lead in finding remedies and forging coalitions.

True or not, many around the world have the impression that the US government, particularly after September 11, views collective action, alliances, and treaties with distrust, and works with others only when its direct interests are at stake and it can dictate the terms. That does not bode well for future global harmony or the prosperity and security of our country. Nor does the increasing anti-American sentiment around the world, whether in the form of suicidal terrorists or global protests against the United States.

After September 11, there was a tremendous outpouring of support throughout the world. Since then, though, things have changed. Several surveys show the United States' popularity declining. The Pew Global Attitudes Project has repeatedly reported that anger toward the United States is pervasive in Muslim countries, but also that the United States' favorability ratings dropped markedly since 2002 in the United Kingdom, Canada, France, and Germany. The organization noted that

> anti-Americanism is deeper and broader than at any time in modern history. . . . the rest of the world both fears and resents the unrivaled power that the United States has amassed since the Cold War ended. In the eyes of others, the U.S. is a worrisome colossus: It is too quick to act unilaterally, it doesn't do a good job of addressing the world's problems, and it widens the global gulf between rich and poor. (Pew Research Center 2005, 106)

A 2004 GMI survey of eight thousand people from the world's major industrial nations revealed that more than half of respondents have an increasingly negative perception of the United States, and 67 percent believe that US policies are driven by self-interest and empire building. This antipathy has consequences beyond the political realm. Disturbingly, the GMI survey found, nearly 20 percent of foreign consumers say they will avoid purchasing US goods because of US foreign policy. This coincides with other research confirming a declining preference for American brands, and growing negative attitudes toward American firms.

Government policies are not the entire cause of anti-American sentiments, however. Our cultural exports are not beloved by all, and the behavior and attitudes of American businesses and travelers overseas are not always exemplary. A group called Business for Diplomatic Action has formed to combat the problem, enlisting help from the business community to spread goodwill and developing educational guides for American travelers. Among its core messages is that Americans should not try to dictate or even teach others, but instead, learn to listen.

We must stop the tide of hostility that seems to be growing against us. This should be viewed as a national pursuit with global implications. We all have a role to play. Abroad, we should view ourselves as goodwill ambassadors. At home, we should view ourselves as both Americans and world citizens, with the right and privilege to act as participants and partners on the world stage.

The world continues to heavily support the United Nations. In a 2005 BBC World Service poll that questioned more than twenty-three thousand people from twenty-three countries, an overwhelming majority was in favor of the United Nations becoming "significantly more powerful in world affairs." It is heartening that a majority of Americans, 59 percent, viewed this positively; however, the bad news is that 37 percent of Americans—the second-highest percentage in any nation polled—thought this development would be mainly negative.

Despite these numbers about the United Nations specifically, it does appear that a large proportion of the American public values multilateral efforts. According to a 2004 survey, 77 percent of the nation believes that the most important lesson of September 11 is that the United States needs to work more closely with other countries to fight terrorism, rather than act alone (Todorov and Mandisodza 2004).

The main avenue for multilateral efforts remains the United Nations. For all its weaknesses, it is an indispensable body, through which our hopes for international peace and prosperity can be fulfilled. Truman knew that the United Nations was not perfect upon its creation; the challenge, as he saw it, was for the next generation to improve what was born that day in June 1945 (Holbrooke 2003). That challenge remains for the next generation.

"Humanity is Indivisible"

September 11 sadly revealed the worst face of humanity. It showed the anger and destruction that can be unleashed when intolerance and ignorance come together. Intolerance and ignorance remain our real enemies. They breed hatred and fanaticism. They are not confined to any geographic or political region, but spread like wildfire across frontiers when stoked by righteousness.

Yet anyone looking for signs of hope could find them from the very onset of the attacks. From those selflessly running into burning buildings to aid others, to those sorting through debris, and still more rushing to give blood or money, the efforts of good people were extraordinary. These heroes brought light to darkness and left us with indelible images of the power of the human spirit to prevail.

The key notion here is *human* spirit. Many came forward because of the attack on the United States. On a local level, New Yorkers joined hands in compassion and resolve. But above all, we witnessed humans caring for humans, without checking their passports first. The impulse to help one another, no matter the origin or beliefs of that person, stems from the first human emotions of kindness and concern shown by infants. Unless it is warped and distilled by artificial notions of separateness, that impulse stays with us throughout life.

Upon accepting the Nobel Peace Prize in 2001, U.N. Secretary-General Kofi Annan said,

> We have entered the third millennium through a gate of fire. If today, after the horror of 11 September, we see better, and we see further—we will realize that humanity is indivisible. New threats make no distinction between races, nations or regions. A new insecurity has entered every mind, regardless of wealth or status. A deeper awareness of the bonds that bind us all—in pain as in prosperity—has gripped young and old. (Annan 2001)

He added, "Today, no walls can separate humanitarian or human rights crises in one part of the world from national security crises in another."

The hope for the triumph of peace ultimately rests with this "deeper awareness" of our interconnections. It relies on the natural impulses we so vividly witnessed on September 11 to come to each other's aid and comfort, regardless of background or origin. This is part of the essence of a world citizen, and, we would argue, part of the essence of a human being who is concerned with the future of the entire planet.

To combat ignorance and intolerance requires more than a return to some basic instincts of compassion. It requires an education, one that is inclusive, open, and responsive, that nurtures our awareness of global society, our global problems, and our global kinship. In other words, we need a global education.

It is a sad commentary that after September 11, there were desperate calls for Arabic scholars to help make sense of what had happened, and for Arabic speakers to help translate the voices of a world so little understood. Not only did we not understand their view of the world; we did not even have a sufficient corps who spoke their language. We were both mute and blind.

But from disaster, opportunity often emerges, and we have one before us now. If seized, it can make the United States and its citizens more conscious of their membership in a global community. Some signs suggest that our government understands this, but other troubling signals indicate that we have a long way to go.

The danger remains that some Americans will only extend their compassion as far as the national border because of fears stemming from the September 11 tragedy. But we must extend our circle of compassion beyond the immediate and include the world.

Multinational efforts, the United Nations, international legitimacy; in the wake of September 11, these things remain more than relevant. Ignoring the need for multilateralism and acting apart from the United Nations will not make the United States safer. On the contrary, it will cause more people to distrust and even dislike our nation, while weakening our international influence. The United States cannot afford or accept that environment.

The case for world citizenship did not suffer a blow on September 11. Instead, it was shown to be the only way to answer those who try to divide and destroy us. Working together across cultures and countries, we can accomplish anything and overcome all challenges.

With Great Resolve

September 11 was a pivotal event whose importance cannot be overstated. The tragedy gives us pause when considering our optimistic notions about the future of a peaceful planet. Still, the nightmare must not stop us from uniting in common pursuits, seizing the benefits of globalization while working together to mitigate its costs. The magnitude of the horror may increase awareness of our interconnected world. Certainly, it illustrates the necessity of world citizenship and global education.

In the words of Shashi Tharoor,

> . . . the twenty-first century will be the century of "one world" as never before, with a consciousness that the tragedies of our time are all global in origin and reach, and that tackling them is also a global responsibility that must be assumed by us all. Interdependence is now the watchword. The terrorist attack was an assault not just on one city but, in its callous indifference to the lives of innocents . . . around the world, an assault on the very bonds of humanity that tie us all together. To respond to it effectively we must be united, and out of the solidarity that the world has demonstrated with the victims of this horror, a unity may emerge across borders that will also mark the new century as different from the ones that preceded it. (Tharoor 2002)

Eva Campbell gave birth to Mitchell Graff Campbell on September 11, 2001. His father, Mark, held his new son in his arms and watched the first tower at the World Trade Center come down on television. It was a wrenching, emotional experience, with the conflicting emotions of the joy of a healthy birth and fear for the future of young Mitchell.

Both parents solemnly wondered what kind of world Mitchell would face. What would his future hold?

Sometime later, I was visiting Thanu Kulachol, the president of Bangkok University in Thailand. As frequently happened in that first year after the tragedy, we asked each other where the other was on September 11. Thanu told me that September 11, 2001, was his sixtieth birthday, and his friends had gathered for a celebration.

I told Thanu about Mitchell Campbell's birth and the experience of his parents. Thanu smiled and said, "Isn't that wonderful?" I confess to being a bit surprised, since that was not the typical reaction. In fact, most Americans thought the story sad, and shared the Campbells' fear for Mitchell's future.

I asked Thanu to explain his reaction. He replied,

> Mitchell's birth is demonstration of the resiliency of human life. Our species will achieve, succeed and survive, no matter the ills of our world. Each year his birthday, like mine, should be a celebration of the strength of human confidence, resolve and continuation.

We deeply mourn the events of September 11, but as Thanu advises, we celebrate those who are resolved to make tomorrow better and forge lasting memorials of humanity, liberty, and justice for all. From the toughest of life's trials, together we can emerge stronger and renewed in our commitment to world citizenship and education as the path to peace.

References

Albright, Madeleine K. 2003. Think Again: The United Nations. *Foreign Policy,* no. 138 (September–October): 16–24.

Annan, Kofi A. 2001. Nobel lecture. December 10. http://nobelprize.org/ peace/laureates/2001/annan-lecture.html (accessed September 14, 2005).

Barber, Benjamin R. 2002. Beyond Jihad vs. McWorld: On Terrorism and the New Democratic Realism. *Nation,* January 21.

BBC World Service Poll. 2005. 23-Country Poll Finds Support for Dramatic Changes at UN and for Increased UN Power. http://www.pipa.org/ OnlineReports/BBCworldpoll/032005/html/bbcpoll4.html (accessed September 14, 2005).

Blair, Tony. 2001. Address at the Labour Party conference. October 2. http:// www.politics.guardian.co.uk/labour2001/story/0,1414,562006,00.html (accessed May 3, 2003).

Bush, George. 2005. Inaugural Address. January 20. http://www.cnn.com/2005/ ALLPOLITICS/01/20/bush.transcript (accessed September 14, 2005).

Douglas, William. 2004. Bush Thanks Canada, Presses for More Support in War on Terror. Knight Ridder Newspapers, December 1. http://www. realcities.com/mld/krwashington/news/columnists/william_douglas/ 10315121.htm (accessed March 10, 2005).

Economist. 2005. *The World in Figures.* London: *Economist.*

Fasulo, Linda. 2004. *An Insider's Guide to the UN.* New Haven, CT: Yale University Press.

Foreign Policy/A.T. Kearney. 2003. *2003 Globalization Index.* Washington, D.C.: *Foreign Policy.*

———. 2004. *2004 Globalization Index.* Washington, D.C.: Foreign Policy.

Friedman, Thomas L. 2003. Terrorism May Have Put Sand in Its Gears But Globalization Won't Stop. Interview with Nayan Chanda. *YaleGlobal Online,* January 30. http://yaleglobal.yale.edu/display.article?id=870 (accessed September 14, 2005).

Global Market Insite (GMI). 2004. Unpopular U.S. Foreign Policies Threaten Revenue, Diminish Global Market Share for Many American-Based Companies. News release, October 21.

Haass, Richard N. 2001. The Bush Administration's Response to Globalization. Remarks to the National Defense University, Washington, D.C., September 21.

Holbrooke, Richard. 2003. Last Best Hope: Stephen C. Schlesinger Tells the Story of the Meeting Out of Which the United Nations Emerged.

Review of *Act of Creation: The Founding of the United Nations. New York Times Book Review,* September 28.

Ignatieff, Michael. 2003. The Burden. *New York Times Magazine,* January 5.

Leonhardt, David. 2003. Globalization Hits a Political Speed Bump. *New York Times,* June 1.

National Security Council. 2002. National Security Strategy of the United States of America. http://www.whitehouse.gov/nsc/nssall.html (accessed September 14, 2005).

Patrick, Stewart. 2003. Beyond Coalitions of the Willing: Assessing U.S. Multilateralism. *Ethics & International Affairs* 17, no. 1: 37–54.

Pew Global Attitudes Project. 2004. *A Year After Iraq War: Mistrust of America in Europe Ever Higher, Muslim Anger Persists.* Washington, D.C.: The Pew Research Center for People and the Press.

Pew Global Attitudes Project. 2005. *U.S. Image Up Slightly, But Still Negative.* Washington, D.C.: The Pew Research Center for People and the Press.

Pew Research Center. 2005. *Trends 2005.* Washington, D.C.: The Pew Research Center for People and the Press.

Sassen, Saskia. 2002. Globalization After September 11. *Chronicle of Higher Education,* January 18.

Schlesinger, Stephen C. 2003. *Act of Creation: The Founding of the United Nations.* Boulder, CO: Westview Press.

Schwartzberg, Joseph E. 2004. *Revitalizing the United Nations: Reform Through Weighted Voting.* New York: Institute for Global Policy, World Federalist Movement.

Stille, Alexander. 2002. What Is America's Place in the World Now? *New York Times,* January 12.

Tharoor, Shashi. 2002. The Global Century. *American Scholar* 71, no. 1 (Winter): 66–68.

———. 2003. Why America Still Needs the United Nations. *Foreign Affairs* 82, no. 5 (September–October).

Tickner, Neil. 2002. Globalization From Both Sides of the Barricades After 9-11. *College Park, The University of Maryland Magazine* 13, no. 2 (Spring): 20–25.

Todorov, Alexander, and Anesu N. Mandisodza. 2004. Public Opinion on Foreign Policy: The Multilateral Public that Perceives Itself as Unilateral. *Public Opinion Quarterly* 68, no. 3 (Fall): 323–348.

Traub, James. 2003. The Next Resolution: If You Think the United Nations Is Irrelevant Now in Iraq, Wait and See What Hawkish Policy Makers Are Planning for Any Sequel. *New York Times Magazine,* April 13.

United Nations. 1945. Charter. http://www.un.org/aboutun/charter/ (accessed October 13, 2005).

6

A GLOBAL EDUCATION: SCHOOLING WORLD CITIZENS

> The universities go out to meet the tremendous challenges of our social and political life, like men who go out in armour with bows and arrows to meet a bombing aeroplane.
>
> —H. G. Wells
> *World Brain*, 1938

> Education should not make us specialists for some particular future professional job, but should make us citizens, social citizens, citizens today of the whole world. As citizens of the whole world we have to have some understanding of the world as a whole and especially of those parts whose tradition is very different from ours and again, especially of those parts, which, owing to present short-lived but very acute international tensions, we regard as our opponents or even as our outright enemies.
>
> —Arnold J. Toynbee, 1965

Bucky's Worldview

Buckminster Fuller was considered by many to be a twentieth-century Renaissance man. He was one of the first and most important futurists, a philosopher, poet, architect, and inventor. Expelled from Harvard twice as an undergraduate, Fuller would go on to design the geodesic dome, the Dymaxion car, and a new world map. He was the prolific author of more than twenty books and hundreds of essays and articles.

One of his most popular books was *Operating Manual for Spaceship Earth,* written in 1963. With only a bit of satirical humor, he suggested that our planet was actually a spaceship, but that we had

151

lost the instruction manual. Bucky, as he was known to his friends, had a unique worldview.

In 1975, at a dinner in my home, Bucky held my two-year-old son, Benjamin, on his lap. He enjoyed it, saying, "I like contact with young life. It gives confidence in the future of the species." .

I asked him if he had any recommendations for how to educate Benjamin to prepare him for the millennium, which was twenty-five years away. He replied,

> It is critically important that Ben understand we live on a sphere. Everything is intimately related. Events at one point of the globe affect people and events everywhere else.
>
> How we view our world is how we describe it. The corollary is that how we describe the world can change how we view it. Language is simultaneously limiting and powerful.
>
> For example, if you live on the surface of a ball, the concepts of "up" and "down" have no meaning. "Up" and "down" apply only on a flat surface—a plane. On a sphere, the appropriate language is "in" and "out." You either go in toward the center or you go out away from the center.
>
> In my home, we don't go "upstairs" or "downstairs." We go "instairs" and "outstairs."
>
> My recommendation is that you shape your language so Ben grows up describing his world as global, complex and inter-related.

Ben, now in his thirties, is always aware that he is living on a planet as a citizen of the world.

Fuller also objected vehemently when people talked about the Sun setting. "The Sun never sets or goes down," he would exclaim, "the sun eclipses, and the correct term would be that we sunsight in the morning and sunclipse in the evening" (Zung 2001, xiii).

Bucky Fuller's worldview and recommendations for language and education are as relevant today as they ever were. Well before globalization entered our vocabulary, Fuller described how revolutionary technological changes could bring people together and help unite the global village. As he said, 99.9 percent of humanity used to think only in terms of their local region, but new technologies have altered the landscape and created a greater awareness of each other. He believed that the grip of nationalism and the state is strong on individuals and creates barriers to global understanding. He said that this "'national' claim upon humans born in various lands leads to ever more severely specialized servitude and highly personalized identity classification" (Fuller 1963, 19).

All humans share residence on a planet traveling sixty thousand miles an hour, wrote Fuller. More than the concept of national identities, what distinguishes us is the fact that "we are all astronauts" (Fuller 1963, 46).

Fuller was concerned that as the pursuit of specialization increased, individuals would lose sight of the big picture and become alienated and dysfunctional. Over-specialization, he observed, leads to extinction. The trick, he said, was to start thinking in terms of "wholes."

How do we think in terms of "wholes?" Bucky said that our nature already programs us to examine the whole. Children are interested in the universe and ask universal questions. They are "natural comprehensivists," he wrote, with the desire to understand the principles governing interrelationships. Anyone who has spoken with a small child knows of the stream of global questions:

"Where does the moon go during the day?"
"Why is the sky blue? Why is the grass green?"
"If the world is round and spinning, how come we don't
    fall off?"
"Why are these countries divided this way on the map?"
"How can we tell who belongs to our country?"
"What country does the sun belong to?"

But something happens during our schooling years. We seem to unlearn spontaneity and the ability to comprehend and question the whole. Our early classroom experiences center, as we recall, on conformity, group harmony, socialization, and the sequential development of a common skill set—"readin', writin', and 'rithmetic." Those are necessary skills, but the schooling somehow changes the way we see our world and the questions we ask.

When Fuller talks of specialization, he is speaking of an educational system that defines narrow paths of study to the exclusion of broad and deep understandings. While our educational system must deliver a common base of knowledge and offer great depth within fields, it should not destroy our natural yearnings to understand and question the whole. It must provide what Fuller termed a "comprehensivity curriculum" to integrate the various disciplines.

One way to comprehend the whole is through simple devices like Fuller's Dymaxion world map. This unique map, which has no right way up, shows the continents as nearly contiguous land masses with the least amount of visual distortion, thereby helping people to see the world as an interdependent network of relationships.

Fuller urged young people to not just worry about earning a living, but instead focus on what needs to be done. For Fuller, our future ultimately will be decided by whether humans fulfill their responsibilities to each other. The "evil" systems people like to blame for their troubles are ultimately not the problem, he said. "Whether humanity is to continue and comprehensively prosper on Spaceship Earth depends entirely on the integrity of the human individuals and not on the political and economic systems" (Zung 2001, 380).

He believed, "We are not going to be able to operate our Spaceship Earth successfully nor for much longer unless we see it as a whole spaceship and our fate as common. It has to be everybody or nobody." Bucky Fuller was the epitome of a world citizen.

What is the Purpose of Education?

Bucky Fuller believed that education must cultivate a global mentality. With the full-speed onslaught of globalization, it is vital that we adopt global views and become world citizens. But how does someone learn to be a global citizen? What do educational systems need to do? The question is one often posed by educators and thinkers concerned with the future: What is the purpose of education? Should it serve the individual? Should it serve the state or society in general? Invariably, the answer leads down one of two paths: toward the development of personal skills that have practical value, or toward the cultivation of a sense of wisdom or humanity. It is the professionals versus the humanists.

The debate is not a novel one. The ancient Greeks themselves grappled with the purpose of schools. Plato's Academy was devoted to seeking truth and universal knowledge, while the Sophists focused on useful, practical skills, individual improvement, and success in life.

Increasingly in our society, social prestige is associated with employment. When we meet someone, a common question posed to us is, "What do you do?" We are not asked whether we play bridge, watch films, or eat at McDonald's. The question is about our profession or job, and the point is to determine our position in the social

FULLER PROJECTION

Dymaxion™ Air-Ocean World

REVERSING THE TRANSFORMATION: from Two to Three Dimensions

hierarchy. Many believe that your job, your professional status, and your income level represent the primary source of your identity. Occupation and identity are tied together early on. Who cannot remember being asked at entirely too young an age, "What do you want to be when you grow up?" The questioner is trying to learn which occupation will define you. The question is then repeated countless times to students as they progress through the educational system. The lesson is unmistakable: Choose a career and define your identity.

One outcome of this attitude in our society is a growing interest in education as the foundation for future employment. The primary purpose of a college, in the view of the vast majority of Americans, is to develop the skills necessary to get a good job. The strength of those who advocate skills training has grown in our more specialized world.

By the latter stages of the twentieth century, as renowned university president Clark Kerr pointed out,

> Many students came to college looking for job training, not a philosophy of life . . . Enrollments in engineering, business administration, and computer science went up drastically, and the departments involved became among the most dominant on campus. (Kerr 2001, 203)

And education has become very good at propelling people to prestigious positions and lucrative salaries. Studies linking higher education to advanced wealth and prestige validate education's success as an instrument for advancement.

But there remain others who believe the purity of education is sullied by crass objectives like making money. The cry for a return to a liberal education as the true measure of worth is loud and strong. The problem here, though, is that no one agrees exactly what constitutes a liberal education. The term usually leads to confusion, and is often used interchangeably with the liberal arts.

Scholars, however, can point to the distinction between the two: namely, that "the liberal arts" refers to specific disciplines, while a "liberal education" is categorized by a philosophy of learning that encourages a broad range of knowledge, critical thinking, self-examination, and social responsibility.

The values of a liberal education and professional training are undeniable. There is nothing wrong with aiming for professional success and desiring greater wealth and income through education. On the other hand, a good liberal education that imparts a broad understanding of the human experience is fundamental to all human pursuits. And when information changes so fast, and people change careers so readily, it is apparent that such an understanding and an appreciation for inquiry and lifelong learning are indeed vital.

Almost two thousand years ago, the Roman philosopher Seneca wrote,

> Why "liberal studies" are so called is obvious: it is because they are the ones considered worthy of a free man. But there is really only one liberal study that deserves the name—because it makes a person free—and that is the pursuit of wisdom. (Seneca, *Letters From A Stoic*, 62–65 A.D.)

We agree with the merits of a liberal education. But when liberal education is defined as the pursuit of wisdom, that basically covers everything, which leaves one with nothing.

So if liberal education is fraught with such ambiguity, and if we cannot get our two sides together on what the goal of education is, perhaps we should change course and leave the debate for a moment. We suggest a truce in the battle between liberal education and professional studies. Despite seeming like polar opposites, there is great value in linking the two. Linking them, in fact, will enhance the power of each.

Perhaps it is not an either-or question. There might be value in an education that embraces both positions.

Rethinking What It Means to Be Educated

Perhaps we can try to find some common ground in exploring the equally important question of what defines an educated person. What should the skill set of an educated person in a global society be? If we can identify the outcomes, then we might be able to define mutually agreeable paths or routes to those ends.

For hundreds of years, educators and scholars have presumed that education is based on owning information. We sat in classrooms and listened to and learned from a teacher who gave us information. We digested data, dates, and definitions. And we were judged by our ability to give back that information. The measure of ownership is assessed by the ever-present "test." As we memorized more facts, and passed more tests, we advanced through a system that repeated the process, but with increasingly complex information. Pass enough tests and you graduate. You might even receive a diploma certifying ownership of sufficient knowledge to be labeled "educated."

But how meaningful is a diploma, and how important are memorized facts in a world characterized by change, continual advances, and complex interrelationships? What level of knowledge, insights, or skills does a college diploma certify today? And what must education do to respond to globalization? Historian and writer Henry Adams, in *The Education of Henry Adams* (1907), wrote, "Nothing in education is so astonishing as the amount of ignorance it accumulates in the form of inert facts." It is not all about the facts.

In our society, information is changing and advancing so fast that no one can possibly absorb even a small percentage of it. Derek de Solla Price, in his book *Science Since Babylon,* noted the massive amount of information published in scientific journals. He wrote that as early as 1830, there was so much new scientific information being published each year that a person could not keep pace and stay conversant with it all (Price 1961, 96–98). And that was more than 175 years ago. Can you imagine how much more difficult it is today to learn all the information in a given field?

With the dazzling rate in the expansion of information, specialized knowledge has a half-life—the time a piece of information stays current—as short as five years. And then we need to consider that the average American will change jobs and careers as many as six times (Rhodes 2001, 86). The number of those committed to one field over a lifetime is rapidly shrinking. Thus, education needs to be based on more than just owning information.

We agree that there should be skills that all schools emphasize. Communication and language concepts, basic math and science principles, and facility with technology and computer literacy are all essential. We do not discount the importance of learning a core body of information, but in today's digitized world, in which information overflows in every field, memorizing and owning facts is not nearly as important as it used to be.

It is more important to be able to find, analyze, and synthesize information to advance knowledge and solve problems. The workers and citizens of the twenty-first century will be successful not because they own more information, but because they locate and use information to find solutions.

Even more critically, educated people in the twenty-first century must understand the individual's role in our global society. An educated person is someone who can look beyond the local and identify the global parameters of each and every question; someone who can embrace other identities and comprehend other viewpoints; someone who understands complex interrelationships and is comfortable in diverse environments. Being educated means being able to connect the dots and gain a sense of the big picture.

To keep pace with the forces of globalization requires a global education.

What is a Global Education?

A global education is much more than studying abroad or learning about another country. It is an education that ensures that individuals will be able to succeed in a world marked by interdependence, diversity, and rapid change. A global education provides knowledge and understanding of cultures, languages, geography, and global perspectives. A global education enables us to understand our roles in a global community and teaches us how our actions affect people across the world. It also demonstrates how events around the world affect us as individuals, and therefore cannot be ignored.

Put simply, a global education clearly reveals the connections that characterize our world. From the local to the national to the global, from the cultural to the political to the financial, world citizens can connect the dots that draw our world together and form new patterns of understanding.

A global education considers the world as a whole, with a rich (and sometimes unpleasant) interplay of nations, cultures, and societies. The concept is gaining ground as more educators espouse an education "that brings the world into the classroom, where teachers teach from a world-centric rather than an ethno-specific or nation-state perspective" (Kirkwood 2001).

Graham Pike and David Selby note that a crucial part of global education is what has been called "worldmindedness," which, they explain, is "a commitment to the principle of 'one world,' in which the interests of individual nations must be viewed in light of the overall needs of the planet" (Pike and Selby 2000, 11).

As education has long been tied to citizenship, a global education provides the basis for world citizenship. To become such citizens, students must learn to make global connections. Audrey Osler and Kerry

Vincent write, "Learners will require skills and attitudes which allow them to make connections between different contexts and situations, and to respond to constant change" (Osler and Vincent 2002, 124).

The American Forum for Global Education agrees with the importance of making connections. Along with learning about global challenges and studying diverse cultures, the group lists global connections as one of the main approaches to global education.

> For better or worse, this web of interconnections suffuses economic activities, religious groups, and social and community organizations. Students should develop such skills as recognizing, analyzing, and evaluating the interconnections among local, regional, and global issues and between their personal lives and global events. (Smith 2002, 41)

Perspective is everything, and such knowledge and skills will not only prepare individuals to live and work globally, but will contribute to a sense of responsible world citizenship.

The Elements of Global Education

How can a global education best cultivate world citizens? Or a little more specifically: What are the components or elements of a global education?

Robert Hanvey lays out the five major components of a global education as follows:

1. Perspective consciousness: Students need to understand that their view is not shared universally. They must develop the ability to see the world through the perspective of others.
2. "State of the planet" awareness: Students have to learn basic information about the world and the issues facing human beings today, including an understanding of the causes of events and their effects on different nations and peoples.
3. Cross-cultural awareness: Students should become familiar with other cultures and must be able to relate to those from other backgrounds, while appreciating the many varieties of cultures.
4. Knowledge of global dynamics: Students need to understand the world as a system and comprehend how societies are linked together.

5. Awareness of human choices: Students need to understand the responsibilities, realize the choices facing individuals and nations, and learn how to act as world citizens. (Hanvey 1976)

In some sense, a global education should do what great teachers have long been doing. It should break down boundaries, expand horizons, and introduce learners to the breadth of human achievement and diversity.

Merry Merryfield, a professor of social studies and global education, believes global educators share a number of certain traits and strategies:

> . . . they confront stereotypes and exotica and resist simplification of other cultures and global issues; foster the habit of examining multiple perspectives; teach about power, discrimination, and injustice; and provide cross-cultural experiential learning. (Merryfield 2002, 18)

Building from Hanvey and others, Merryfield included eight elements in her description of global education, namely,

- Human beliefs and values
- Global systems
- Global issues and problems
- Cross-cultural understanding
- Awareness of human choices
- Global history
- Acquisition of indigenous knowledge
- Development of analytical, evaluative, and participatory skills. (Kirkwood 2001)

Many proponents of global education believe that the most important strategy is to focus on understanding multiple perspectives, even when they conflict (basically, Hanvey's first point), enabling students to imagine what it is like to be in another person's shoes, in another place, or even in another time.

> Even when students all agree with one side of an issue, they come to appreciate points of view that they disagree with in order to fully understand the event or issue from a global perspective.

This habit of seeking out diverse perspectives and primary sources from the culture under study is central to global education. (Merryfield 2002, 19)

For global educators Nancy Bacon and Gerrit Kischner, understanding multiple perspectives is the foundation of a global curriculum for the twenty-first century. "Students begin to view themselves as global citizens in a rapidly changing world when they encounter, compare, experience, and adopt multiple international perspectives" (Bacon and Kischner 2002, 48). Bacon's Global Classroom program features a network of nearly one thousand teachers in the Seattle, Washington area, devoted to integrating such elements into the curriculum as the study of and exposure to diverse cultures and experiences, and the opportunity to apply that learning.

There is a good deal of agreement about the common elements to include in a global education. And it is easy to lengthen the list. But the key is to help students develop a global viewpoint and the ability to understand and work alongside others throughout the world.

The Answers Lie in the Questions

Chapter 4 reported the findings of a multinational research team focused on defining the educational outcomes needed in our globalized world. The authors concluded, you might recall, that the most important characteristic needed for the challenges of the twenty-first century "is the ability to deal with serious worldwide problems as a member of a worldwide society" (Parker, Ninomiya, and Cogan 1999, 125). How do they propose that we develop that sense of global responsibility? Our first illustration of what a global education might include is based on their conclusions.

The study recommended support for the teaching of subjects in a manner that encourages critical thinking and fosters discussion and deliberation with others to reach consensus. This requires a teaching population with international experience and cross-cultural sensitivity. International programs are needed that foment dialogue among students of all backgrounds and nationalities. Students need to learn to use information technologies effectively. And schools need to focus on global issues and international studies.

The authors call for a multinational curriculum that focuses on complex worldwide problems and uses cross-cultural deliberation to address them. Their specific curriculum is multinational in two respects. Subject matter revolves around issues "that affect persons across national boundaries"; likewise, the projects are designed to be implemented "across national boundaries."

The primary subject matter takes the form of six ethical questions that the research team derived from its study of recurring trends in the world. The questions are:

1. "What should be done in order to promote equity and fairness within and among societies?"
2. "What should be the balance between the right to privacy and free and open access to information in information-based societies?"
3. "What should be the balance between protecting the environment and meeting human needs?"
4. "What should be done to cope with population growth, genetic engineering, and children in poverty?"
5. "What should be done to develop shared (universal, global) values while respecting local values?"
6. "What should be done to secure an ethically based distribution of power for deciding policy and action on the above issues?" (Parker, Ninomiya, and Cogan 1999, 129)

The research team recommends that courses in different nations feature these questions and have students from different cultures deliberate and engage in "cooperative discussion with an eye toward decision" (Parker, Ninomiya, and Cogan 1999, 135). Such an exercise has great potential to foster a variety of skills and attitudes, not the least important of which is the willingness to listen to opposing points of view.

The authors add, "When students within classrooms in several nations are deliberating roughly the same set of cross-culturally felt problems, then a larger multinational relation—a global civil society—emerges" (Parker, Ninomiya, and Cogan 1999, 134).

This cross-cultural dialogue is pivotal. Students then become learners and teachers, understanding their common traits and breaking down stereotypical notions of the other. This gets at the heart of what it means to be educated. The use of ethical questions across cultures is an intriguing way to create global understanding. Deliberation is the key.

One of the study's authors, education professor Walter Parker, says deliberation is coming together to make collective decisions about our future. He adds that

> In school settings, deliberation is not only an instructional means but a curriculum outcome itself, for it spawns a particular kind of democratic community—a public culture among the deliberators wherein the norms include listening as well as talking, trying to understand where someone else is coming from, sharing resources, forging decisions together rather than only advocating positions taken earlier, coming to agreement and disagreement . . . (Parker 2002, 27)

Through these exchanges, participants must learn about each other and understand the basis for different viewpoints. This deliberation, where diversity and differences are valued as advantages to finding solutions, not only enlightens, Parker says, but engages, and therefore enables people to become more active citizens. Elementary and middle school students "should be deliberating classroom and school policies together" (Parker 2004, 454). Students should be deliberating both global and local issues.

In any dialogue, it is fundamentally important not to impose our own view of the world on others. We can easily assume that our upbringing was the "right" way or "best" environment. If someone has a different background, then it might be viewed as "wrong."

Differences should not be the basis for value judgments. We should not assume our experiences deliver the correct answer to others' questions. Our ownership of "truth" or the only "right" answer is arrogant, offensive, and often wrong.

Cornell University President Emeritus Frank Rhodes cites a classic example of such arrogance in the Virginia colony that, in the 1770s, invited a local Native American community to send six of their members to Williamsburg College. Here is the reply from the Native Americans:

> We thank you heartily. But you, who are wise, must know that different nations have different conceptions of things, and you will therefore not take it amiss, if our ideas of education happen not to be the same as yours. We have had some experience with it. Several of our young people were formerly brought up at

your colleges; they were instructed in all your sciences; but, when they came back to us, they were bad runners, ignorant of every means of living in the woods, unable to bear either cold or hunger, knew neither how to build a cabin, take a deer, or kill an enemy, spoke our language imperfectly, were therefore neither fit for hunters, warriors, nor counsellors, they were totally good for nothing.

We are, however, not the less obliged by your kind offer, tho' we decline accepting it; and to show our grateful sense of it, if the gentleman of Virginia will send us a dozen of their sons, we will take care of their education; instruct them in all we know and make men of them. (Rhodes 2001, 205–206)

Despite cultural barriers, multinational deliberation and discussion can offer exciting lessons in world citizenship. But there are many ways to learn about each other. Rhodes and others have stressed the "need for comparative understanding of other times and cultures. *How* such understanding is achieved will be a local decision . . . *That* such understanding should be achieved seems to me a desirable expectation for all institutions" (Rhodes 2001, 106).

Rhodes' vision for the future of the American university might be applied to all educational organizations.

The successful university will be . . . international in its orientation and cosmopolitan in its character; its graduates will pursue their careers within an increasingly global economy and an increasingly diverse workforce. Both its curriculum and its membership will reflect this diversity; . . . both the student and faculty bodies will become conspicuously international in their membership; and living productively in a diverse community will increasingly come to be regarded as a "job skill." (Rhodes 2001, 236)

Yale President Richard Levin agrees when he writes,

. . . we must recognize that the leaders of the twenty-first century, in virtually every calling and profession, will operate in a global environment. To prepare our students for leadership, our curriculum needs to focus increasingly on international concerns; our student populations must have strong international representation, and our students should have ample opportunities for study abroad. (Levin 2003, 165)

A Rising Demand

The public appreciates the need for global learning. So do students. In 2001, the American Council on Education (ACE) found that 93 percent of the public believes that knowledge of international issues will be important for the careers of their children and other young people. That same percentage said it would be important to understand other cultures and customs to compete successfully in a global economy. Approximately 90 percent of high school seniors think that international skills and competencies will help them work with people from different cultures and provide a competitive edge in their careers (Hayward and Siaya 2001).

The study also found strong interest in and tremendous support for learning foreign languages and studying abroad, while international students were viewed as enhancing the learning environment of US students.

The report concludes that the public and the current generation of students

> understand that success as citizens and in their professions depends on how well they understand other people, nations, cultures, economies, and languages. The graduates of our colleges and universities must have the ability to move seamlessly through other cultures, economies, and systems. To do that, our graduates need much more international knowledge, strong training in languages, and deeper cultural understanding than most of them are getting at the present time. (Hayward and Siaya 2001)

Another ACE report, written one year after September 11, found that support for academic programs focusing on international issues remained very strong. Contrary to those who thought the tragedy would cause Americans to turn inward, support for international education remained high, and in fact, increased in some areas. The survey revealed that almost 75 percent of respondents thought higher education should teach students about international issues and other cultures. In addition, 77 percent supported international course requirements in college (the same percentage as in 2000), 74 percent agreed that there should be a foreign language requirement (up slightly from 2000), and 79 percent thought that college students should be immersed in a study abroad program (up slightly from 2000) (Siaya, Porcelli, and Green 2002). So Americans understand the benefits.

That understanding has been illustrated time and time again. In 2000, the Olathe, Kansas public school district went to parents, students, and representatives of business groups and higher education to ask what type of academic programs would be most important in the new high school being built. According to Craig Colgan's account in *Education Digest,* "there was one content area that ended up being requested over and over: international studies." He added, "The dialogue that resulted was so positive that the district decided that each of its four high schools would offer new international studies and beefed up language programs" (Colgan 2003).

Olathe is the best of Middle America. The community each year celebrates the Johnson County Fair; holds the Old Settlers Festival, with musical entertainment, carnival rides, and a parade; hosts Mahaffie's Wild West Show, with historical reenactments and stagecoach rides; and looks forward to the KC Pumpkin Patch event, which includes pumpkin picking, a petting zoo, a John Deere tricycle track, a haunted barn, a hay loft and barn swings, a mine shaft hill slide, and punkin' chunkin'.

More than a thousand miles from the nearest international border, the citizens of Olathe recognize that there is a world beyond themselves. Jan Heinen, the district's director of middle-level education, was quoted as saying, "Our community understands that many problems we will face in the twenty-first century will have only international solutions" (Colgan 2003).

The bad news, however, is that many colleges and schools have not aggressively offered international lessons. A 2003 ACE report revealed that only 28 percent of the 752 institutions surveyed identified internationalization as a top strategic priority. Also, just two out of five institutions required undergraduates to take an international course (Siaya and Hayward 2003).

A panel convened by the Academic Council on the United Nations System at Yale University concluded, "Colleges and universities across the United States are not offering adequate courses in international relations which reflect current global affairs nor are they meeting student demands for a curriculum that is relevant to today's questions" (ACUNS 2002).

As described by University of Michigan President Emeritus James Duderstadt,

> Despite the intellectual richness of our campuses, we still suffer from the inherited insularity and ethnocentrism of a country

that for much of its history has been protected from the rest of the world and self-sufficient in its economy—perhaps even self-absorbed. We must enable our students to appreciate the unique contributions to human culture that come to us from other traditions—to communicate, to work, to live, and to thrive in multicultural settings whether in this country or anywhere on the face of the globe. (Duderstadt 2000)

On the bright side, more colleges are beginning to take seriously the need to offer a global education. In 2004, a Harvard faculty and student panel completed the first thorough evaluation of Harvard's undergraduate curriculum in nearly three decades, and urged that greater opportunities be offered in international studies.

William Kirby, dean of the faculty of arts and sciences and co-chair of the Steering Committee leading the review process, wrote that Harvard must prepare students to be "citizens not only of their home country, but also of the world, with the capacity not only to understand others but also to see themselves, and this country, as others see them" (Kirby 2004).

Still, international studies are far from flourishing at the collegiate level. Enrollment in foreign languages is low and largely limited to Spanish. International courses are only a small part of the curriculum, and study-abroad opportunities are not sufficiently emphasized. The primary and secondary education levels are not any better.

It thus should be no surprise when reports reveal that American students are less than knowledgeable about the world around them. Even basic facts are elusive. Someone once remarked that war is God's way of teaching Americans geography. But even war and looming global threats do not appear to be helping Americans learn simple facts, such as where other countries are located.

According to the National Geographic-Roper 2002 Global Geographic Literacy Survey, only 17 percent of young adults (18- to 24-year-olds) in the United States could find Afghanistan on a map. Only 13 percent could find Iraq. On a world map, Americans could find on average only seven of sixteen countries. Even more appalling, about 11 percent of young citizens could not find the United States on a map, and 29 percent could not locate the Pacific Ocean. More than half could not find Japan, France, or the United Kingdom. Of the nine nations surveyed, the United States finished next to last (Trivedi 2002).

These results—and other studies similarly depicting our deficiencies—speak less to the intellectual capabilities of our students than to the alarming lack of emphasis on global learning in our educational system. Perhaps most disturbing from our standpoint, in a 2003 survey of college freshmen, only 24 percent described themselves as "appreciating the interconnectedness of everything" (Young 2004).

With such little emphasis, can we really say that we are giving students the skills to understand the world? Instead, we make it too easy to develop narrow views of people from other cultures. We will not develop any form of global solidarity or world citizenship without a global education.

Chapter 3 discussed the declining influence of the nation-state, which challenges the comfort of nationalism. However, schooling world citizens may be the most patriotic act of all. Our nation's future will be tied to the global awareness and skills possessed by the next generation.

Particularly after September 11, 2001, many lamented the lack of US experts and government personnel who were knowledgeable about non-European cultures and languages. A 2003 report by NAFSA: Association of International Educators emphasized that Americans' lack of knowledge about the world has become a "national liability." It stressed,

> We are unnecessarily putting ourselves at risk because of our stubborn monolingualism and ignorance of the world. As strong as our country and our economy are, we cannot remain prosperous and secure if we do not understand the words and actions of our international neighbors. . . . Americans need enhanced international skills and knowledge to guarantee our national security and competitiveness. (NAFSA 2003)

That premise was articulated long before September 11, though. As early as 1982, the National Council for the Social Studies (NCSS) made a compelling case for global education. The group stated, "The growing interrelatedness of life on our planet has increased the need for citizens to possess the knowledge and sensitivity required to comprehend the global dimensions of political, economic, and cultural phenomena." But the group also directly appealed to our patriotic self-interest. "Our nation's security, prosperity, and way of life are dependent in large part on citizens developing the capacity to comprehend transnational, cross-cultural interactions and to participate constructively in decisions influencing foreign policy" (NCSS 1982).

Particularly in the United States, which has an influence that permeates the globe, our citizens need to understand other peoples, other nations, and the economic, political, and social events that connect our fates. Understanding issues and events in a broader context not only makes a person a global citizen, but a better national citizen.

Despite the need and the demand, American schools lag in embracing internationalization as a process and world citizenship as a goal. The business community regularly looks beyond national interests and encourages its leaders to think in terms of the whole world. Unfortunately, so do terrorists. They move across borders, learn the workings of other cultures, and forge international alliances to advance their nefarious goals. It is time for teachers and students to think beyond borders as well.

Scaring Saber-Toothed Tigers

Unfortunately, institutions designed to educate the leaders of tomorrow often cannot escape from the past. Many educators have a rigid set of assumptions that they will not reconsider. They are often guilty of using yesterday's answers for today's questions. This trend has been both lamented and lampooned.

The Saber-Tooth Curriculum, by J. Abner Peddiwell (a.k.a. Harold Benjamin), should be required reading for anyone interested in educational reform. Published in 1939 and even more relevant today, the book offers a tongue-in-cheek description of a supposedly groundbreaking discovery of a Paleolithic school system. According to Peddiwell's "research," the original purpose of schooling was to provide basic life skills to young people:

- Saber-toothed tiger scaring
- Fish-grabbing
- Clubbing woolly-horses

The entire education system was built around developing these core skills.

As the ice age passed, the saber-toothed tigers succumbed to pneumonia, silt from receding glaciers made streams too murky to see fish, and the small horses went east to the dry plains. Yet, Peddi-well described, schools continued to teach the same basic life skills, maintaining that they defined an educated person. Educators who suggested that there was no relationship between real life and fish-grabbing were branded as heretics.

The lesson of Benjamin's satire is unmistakable and almost universally applicable. Education must become more flexible and adapt to the world of today and tomorrow. That means having the courage to rephrase the routine questions and alter the usual vocabulary. It means changing the assumptions of the formula, building more bridges among peoples and cultures, and ensuring that we produce citizens of the world. Yet schools and colleges have been slow to respond to globalization and many continue to teach a saber-toothed curriculum.

This is not exactly surprising. While many view schools in general and universities in particular as hotbeds of radicalism and springboards for change, the reality is that educational institutions are often rooted firmly in the past. In his 1962 study of American colleges, Frederick Rudolph commented that "resistance to fundamental reform was ingrained in the American collegiate and university tradition" (Kerr 2001, 72).

Universities in fact may be the institutions most likely to resist change. Clark Kerr wrote, "Universities are among the most conservative of all institutions in their methods of governance and conduct and are likely to remain so" (Kerr 2001, 220). He added that about eighty-five institutions in the Western world established by 1520 exist today in some recognizable form with similar roles. Among them are the Catholic Church, the Parliaments of the Isle of Man, Iceland, and Great Britain, several Swiss cantons, and a whopping seventy universities (Kerr 2001, 115). Universities are not bastions of change.

We like the fact that universities and educational institutions endure. We just need to make sure they adapt to the world around them and prepare students to help the human race endure. Despite the immense developments resulting from globalization, the way we teach and what we teach have barely changed. In the words of history professor Ross Dunn,

> We need a curriculum for our border-crossing, migration-prone, multiple-identity-taking planet, not one that relies on old-fashioned, essentialist, historically lifeless categories that only deter students

from tackling the marvelous complexities of current affairs and the
human past. (Dunn 2002, 13)

The challenge is great, but there is no other option. We must be
global or risk being irrelevant. We must update the saber-toothed curriculum, or suffer the fate of the saber-toothed tiger.

Examples of Global Education

There is no single path, sequence of experiences, or curriculum that
defines a global education. An ancient Hindu saying wisely notes that
all rivers flow to the ocean.

How you view what you are doing is most critical. Ideas and
activities grow from your aims, intent, and goals. Elements of global
education should be tailored to a particular institution's geographic
location, institutional mission, and regional resources and strengths.

Introducing a global education cannot be an event. It must be a
continual process that touches every part of the learning environment. For both faculty and students, the adventure of global education holds the promise of not just understanding our connected world,
but bringing it closer together. The challenge, though, is to provide
an expanded view of the world.

What is the difference between a process and an event? Some
recommend doing away with "diversity day." We all know this event,
commonly held on many college campuses. It is the day that we wear
ethnic clothing, eat ethnic food, and dance ethnic dances. At the end
of the day, most say, "Whew, I'm glad that's over and we don't have
to do it for another year." The celebration of diversity should take
place every day. But we do not need ethnic clothing, food, or dances
to learn about the wonderful differences within our species.

No two individuals learn in the same way, and schools can take
many roads to offer a global education. We already highlighted one
possibility: namely, the use of ethical questions and deliberation
among students from different countries. Of course, knowledge of
the history, traditions, and values of other cultures is imperative. And
the rich differences, while being celebrated, should not exclude the
important elements we share. Otherwise, we look at others as exotic
creatures very much separate from us.

Global views and global issues must be incorporated throughout the educational community and the curriculum. They should not

be ancillary courses or separate parts of courses or textbooks. Scott Sernau called this the "blue box syndrome," in which global issues are placed in those blue separate sections of textbooks while the main story remains what happens in the United States. "Global education will really have arrived," he says, "when it's not just a specialty course tacked onto the curriculum but when every course has global elements to it. It needs to permeate the courses" (Sernau 2003).

This cannot be a piecemeal approach. There must be institutional commitment, resources, and opportunities. There must be shared convictions and shared responsibilities.

Worthy Subjects

It is commonly said that history is written by the victors. And it was George Orwell who wrote that those who control the present control the past, and those who control the past control the future. So history is usually a good place to start if you want to work on providing alternative viewpoints. This is certainly not news.

With the five hundredth anniversary of Columbus' arrival in the new world, much debate focused on the need to balance the heroic presentations of the "discovery" with the other side of the tale. This is being done now to a greater extent, but the impact on indigenous peoples and their view of the story remains underemphasized. That period of history also needs to be linked to a present in which colonial effects still linger in many parts of the world. Similarly, in social studies and foreign affairs, international perspectives need to be introduced. How else can you comprehend international issues? It is important to understand the rich legacies of other nations. But how many great leaders from other nations can the average student name?

We noted how dismal our students' knowledge of geography is. All too often, we let people such as Osama bin Laden or Saddam Hussein teach us geography, and even that sometimes is not enough. Until a crisis develops, we fail to learn not just where other people are found, but any sense of their history and culture. We even fail to learn about those distant people and places that have played such a vital role in forming our country and culture. That has to change.

Global education, though, needs to go beyond history, social studies, and geography. Even in mathematics and the sciences, connections need to be made across cultures, and global viewpoints need to be understood. Both mathematics and the sciences feature a rich variety of contributions from individuals and cultures across the globe. These disciplines actually have long been considered as multinational activities. Many scientists already view each other as members of a global community dedicated to a common purpose. It is time for others to adopt that same mentality.

World Languages
Language is a critical instrument that shapes one's view of the world. Understanding the meaning of the words other people use yields perhaps the most insight into cultural differences. As the famous film director Federico Fellini observed, "A different language is a different vision of life."

Language both describes and limits what we see. The Alaskan Yupik Eskimos have fifteen different words for snow (Woodbury 1991). Because of their environment, they see differences and distinctions that might escape us. Learning another language offers another view of the world.

Looking statistically at this subject for a moment, there are both positive and negative signs. According to the *Digest of Education Statistics* (2002), the percentage of US students in grades nine through twelve who enrolled in foreign language courses increased from 29.4 percent in 1960 to 43.6 percent in 2000. Also, the number of foreign language programs in elementary schools has dramatically increased, from almost none in 1979 to thousands today (Smith 2002, 39). However, a major part of these increases are in offerings in just one language, Spanish, and foreign language programs still do not compare to offerings in other countries.

At the college level, the numbers also are rising. A Modern Language Association (MLA) study showed that almost 1.4 million students were studying at least one foreign language in 2002, a 17 percent increase over 1998. That also represents the highest proportion of students studying a foreign language since 1972. Yet that proportion (8.6 percent of all students) is still only about half of what it was in the 1960s (Welles 2004). Also, more than half of college students studying a language are enrolled in Spanish classes.

What does it say about our willingness to become engaged in the world if we underemphasize the importance of learning other languages? Are we saying that in this age of increasing international links, it makes no difference that we cannot communicate in other languages? Are we saying that our culture matters most?

Mari Wesche, a professor in second language education, believes that the study of languages, perhaps more than any other method, is a gateway to global understanding. She writes,

> Languages are the most comprehensive reflections of the complex cultures of the societies with which we share the planet. They offer us generous access to the experience of others . . . It appears that experiencing human relationships and daily life in a culture other than one's own, through a language whose words, structures, and discourse patterns reflect the shared experience and values of that group, may lead one to understand and accept other world views better. (Wesche 2004)

With the dominance of English in many parts of the world, many Americans can live and even travel to major cities without speaking a single non-English word. But while English is widely used, it is not spoken everywhere. The British Council promotes the fact that one in four people around the world speak English to some level, which sounds good; however, it also means that most of the world does not speak English at all (Chaker 2003).

As noted, the United States faces a shortage of multilingual experts, which can be a threat to national security. This was alarmingly evident after September 11, 2001, when the Federal Bureau of Investigation (FBI) urgently sought volunteers who could speak Arabic. To operate on the world stage, we need to speak other languages.

But language skills should not be considered solely to preserve national security. Mary Louise Pratt, a former president of the MLA, says that national security interests are driving renewed commitments to studying foreign languages. "But it would be tragic if national security became the center of gravity of our national investment in language." The reasons she cites include the fact that

> there are domestic needs for professionals and service people of all kinds who can operate in locally spoken languages within the United States. . . . In its external relations, North America needs area experts, diplomats, scholars, negotiators, aid workers, businesspeople and public servants with the ability to create and maintain relations of all kinds with the peoples of the world, whether or not they are considered strategic or critical at the moment. (Pratt 2004)

She adds convincingly that, in addition,

By the time a language has become a national security imperative, in a way it is already too late: The other has already been
defined as an enemy; the failures of communication and understanding have already done their damage. And if, at that point,
there are no experts who know the language and culture, it is too
late to create them. (Pratt 2004)

Wired into the World

As technology integrates economies and communities, it can connect
students to new worlds. Look at a satellite view of our continents at
night and determine what the concentrations of light tell us about the
distribution of populations and resources. Take a virtual tour of St.
Petersburg and "walk" the halls of the Hermitage. Use the World
Wide Web to monitor weekly UN updates on world issues, check out
a webcast of live and archived UN meetings and events, or download
data from WHO on the spread of infectious diseases such as AIDS or
SARS. Log on to the online editions of international newspapers and
learn how important events are covered differently around the globe.

The Internet has widely democratized knowledge with a world
of information about different peoples and cultures. It also can facilitate collaborations. Scholars and practitioners from afar can offer
viewpoints on the same issue via e-mail. Students in one country can
link up with students in other countries, becoming electronic pen
pals. Perhaps the greatest benefit of such technology is that it can
introduce individuals to ideas and people they would never have
otherwise met in Olathe, Kansas.

Look at the work of the International Education and Resource
Network (iEARN), a non-profit organization including more than
twenty thousand schools from over one hundred countries. iEARN's
goal is to help teachers and students "use the Internet and other new
technologies to collaborate on projects that both enhance learning and
make a difference in the world." The group currently offers more than
150 teacher-created projects that are rooted in real world problems,
international in scope, and targeted to students aged five though nineteen. Once a project is selected, teachers enter online forums to meet
one another and get involved with classrooms around the world working on the same project. Projects delve into many areas, from the
environment to social and cultural issues (iEARN 2005).

Each project features some concrete task, ranging from a letter-
writing campaign, a play, a publication, or producing a Web site. Edwin

Gragert, the executive director of iEARN-USA, says that the organization's emphasis on real experience "shows online education works—students can change how they view the world and make a difference" (Branzburg 2002).

The International Communication and Negotiation Simulations (ICONS) Project at the University of Maryland allows US students to interact with students in other countries using Web-based software. Students explore a range of global issues, assume the roles of decision makers from other countries, and enter into online negotiations with groups of students representing other countries. These interactions help students appreciate problems through the perspectives of others. And many universities are using technology to facilitate dialogues between students and teachers from different countries.

At Fairleigh Dickinson University, where global education is the cornerstone of our formal mission, the Internet and distance learning are viewed as integral parts of the learning process. In a groundbreaking distance-learning program, Fairleigh Dickinson University became the first traditional university to require all students to take one online course per year (one for every thirty-two credits).

While most universities view online learning as a vehicle to bring their programs to students throughout the world, Fairleigh Dickinson's main motivation, as part of its mission to prepare world citizens, is to use distance learning to bring the world to its students.

The first course in our core curriculum is The Global Challenge, which uses online learning to introduce our students to global issues and perspectives. This interdisciplinary course examines topics critical to our interdependent and interconnected world, such as global conflicts, AIDS, environmental challenges, and population issues. It also delves into the scientific method and moral reasoning.

As students explore these issues, they interact through the Internet with a network of international faculty members. Known as Global Virtual Faculty™, these scholars and practitioners hail from around the world and bring valuable insights to The Global Challenge and other courses.

Imagine a philosophy student examining how basic philosophical concepts such as rationalism and empiricism are applied to forensic investigations with a former head homicide investigator from Scotland Yard. Or a freshman in an e-mail exchange discussing the impact of globalization on Southeast Asia with an economics professor from Malaysia. Or a Nobel Prize-winning literature course taught by an American instructor with online contributions by an Arabic language and literature instructor from Egypt. Such interactions happen daily at Fairleigh Dickinson University.

While debates rage about the merits of online versus traditional learning, they are really just two different ways of learning. We are often asked if Fairleigh Dickinson is saying that online learning is better than the traditional classroom. We believe that is the wrong question. A great teacher in a classroom is magical. A bad teacher in a classroom is a tragedy. You can be taught well in the classroom and you can be taught poorly in the classroom. Physical walls and desks do not create great learning opportunities. Great teachers, no matter the environment, are the key ingredient.

Meanwhile, the Internet is here to stay and people must be prepared to use it well. They must learn how to gather and decipher information as well as collaborate online. The Internet can stimulate the most striking innovations in teaching and learning in recent history. Not only can it provide tremendous benefits for a lifetime of learning, but it also can bring people and cultures closer together.

A caveat regarding the Internet: it is not a panacea for the ills of insular outlooks. It can expand horizons, but it should supplement, not replace, the real person-to-person communications and connections that make life so rich.

Intellectual Odysseys

In *The Innocents Abroad* (1869), Mark Twain wrote that travel is "fatal to prejudice, bigotry, and narrow-mindedness." While technology can connect the classroom to the world in unique and meaningful ways, there is no substitute for living and learning within another culture. This encourages cross-cultural understandings by working at the core level of personal relationships.

If people know and understand each other, it is a lot harder for them to fight one another. One of the oldest study-abroad organizations in the world is AFS Intercultural Programs, which was founded as the American Field Service in 1914. AFS volunteer ambulance drivers risked their lives to rescue wounded soldiers during World War I and World War II. They saw the inhumanity of conflict and death, and sought to prevent the devastation of war from happening again.

To promote peace and understanding, the group's efforts expanded to international scholarships and cross-cultural exchanges. In 1947, AFS sent fifty-two students to study and learn in eleven different countries.

Nearly sixty years later, AFS offers 128 programs in over fifty countries, and typically places more than ten thousand high school students world-wide each year. The organization has found that AFS students significantly improve their intercultural and foreign language skills, while expanding their cross-cultural networks and friendships. Furthermore, as a result of their experiences, they have greater passion to understand different cultures and less anxiety about interacting with them (AFS 2003).

The impact on college students of studying abroad is equally powerful. Hubert Van Hoof and Marja Verbeeten, in a recent study that confirmed what many believe are the critical benefits from study-abroad programs, found that college students overwhelmingly valued their international experiences and believed it taught them how to live and work in different environments. Students felt that studying abroad

> brought them a greater understanding of other cultures, that it had helped them appreciate their own culture more, that it enabled them to learn more about themselves, and that it had enriched them personally. (Van Hoof and Verbeeten 2005, 56)

After September 11, 2001, there was a fear that antiterrorism efforts would slow the flow of students traveling abroad. But interest in studying abroad remains strong, and college students are studying overseas in growing numbers. Yet the overall percentage of college students studying abroad remains miniscule. Students must take advantage of these opportunities, and more opportunities must be made available.

Not all students can spend a full semester abroad. But there are alternatives. Many colleges and universities now offer short-term travel options, typically during winter break or summer session. If the group is small and students live in the local community, the learning and insights can approach the outcomes of a full semester's experience.

The point is to become immersed in a culture different from home—not as a tourist but as a community resident. The United States itself has many cultural pockets that offer opportunities to learn and appreciate differences among people and experiences. A month living and working in the Appalachian Mountains, on a Hopi reservation, or in Chicago's Chinatown will also bring important insights and experiences not found in the classroom.

The counterpart to studying abroad is to have international students in American classrooms. Sadly, the trend in this realm is not positive. In 2004, the Institute of International Education reported that for the first time in more than three decades, the number of foreign students studying in the country had declined (in this case by 2.4 percent from the academic year 2002–2003 to the year 2003–2004) (Institute of International Education 2004).

Because few Americans study abroad, having international students enrich our local environment is vitally important. We need to learn from them. We need to hear their voices and understand their perspectives.

Foreign students studying here not only learn about the United States, which can dispel myths when they return to their own nations; they also teach American students about their cultures. They are pioneers in embracing multiple identities and affiliations. They also often occupy significant positions of influence upon their return home, so consider what effect they could have if they enjoy a positive experience in the United States.

In a recent conversation with Mohamed Adbellah, president of the University of Alexandria in Egypt, he made a stunning remark: "I sent my son to Boston for four years for his undergraduate degree and he came home without one American friend. Shame on America." The condemnation applies to all of higher education. Coming to the United States is a study abroad experience for international students. As Americans, we cannot be insular. We must reach out to form personal relationships with foreign students. Universities should establish channels that encourage and support cross-cultural friendships.

The Humble Classroom

Classrooms come in all shapes, sizes, and configurations. Architecture, contemporary furniture, and creative interior design can make for an inviting, comfortable environment. New technological gadgets can be intriguing and fun. But whatever the specific features, the classroom remains the primary learning location for the majority of students at all levels.

Independent of the environment or tools, however, the most important force for learning and development is the teacher. The teacher orchestrates the experiences and guides the process. More than anything else, delivering a global education boils down to how the teacher views the world and wishes students to view it. Emphasizing an earlier statement, the critical issue is how teachers view what they are doing.

Learning is ultimately defined by the landscape of experiences and opportunities. However delivered, lessons must help students see the world through the eyes of others, understand multi-faceted viewpoints, and embrace multiple levels of identity.

Changes in the environment to introduce elements of global education need not be radical or complex. John Becker, professor emeritus of English at Fairleigh Dickinson University, recently spoke on how an American literature course might be adapted to better convey a global view. It could feature the works of global citizens, such as Henry David Thoreau. Thoreau, Becker noted, "traveled the globe in imagination" and "engaged in that dialogue of cultures which goes on . . . perhaps at the heart of all literatures."

> . . . my aim in teaching it [the course] would be to teach it as a literature engaged in dialogue with the literature of the rest of the world. I would try to arouse my students' curiosity about the oriental cultures that fascinated Emerson and Thoreau, about the rich and ancient Hispanic culture of the southwest, about the many cultures of the native Americans at the expense of whose lives we possess this land, about the Nordic epics that inspired Longfellow, about the culture of the Chinese who built our railroads. (Becker 2002)

American literature faculty have a wealth of work from which to choose. How they view what they are doing influences the final selection. If their view is that they are educating world citizens, they might select different books for study.

We know a business professor who requires reading the *Financial Times* for a market trends class. Another routinely uses the *Economist* as a basic classroom resource. Both follow the established course curriculum, but select resources that introduce an international view for each topic. Using periodicals that cover world issues and events can be a simple inclusion in nearly any course.

America is a country of immigrants. One faculty member, who teaches American history, asks students to write a paper on their family's countries of origin. If possible, she asks them to research and include the era of their ancestor's arrival and the reason they left. Her Native American students are an interesting challenge to that assignment. The subsequent classroom discussion is a fascinating exercise about different views of the same history.

Role-playing can encourage understandings of different perspectives. One prime example is the Model United Nations program, in which students assume the roles of leaders from different countries. In the humble classroom, some teachers ask students to write essays from the viewpoint of those they might never meet, such as a child laborer in Asia or a guerrilla leader in South America. When the Seattle protests occurred during the WTO meetings in 1999, educators in area schools "developed role-plays that put students in the shoes of Japanese apple growers, U.S. beef producers, Mexican tuna fisherman, and World Trade Organization judges" (Bacon and Kischner 2002, 50).

There is a calculus instructor we know who consistently includes cultural and historical material in his class. He loves to lead a discussion on the invention of the placeholder—we call it a zero—which might be the most significant invention in the history of our species. Certainly people have always understood the reality of having nothing, but in mathematics there was a time when zero had no corresponding notation. The first recorded use of the zero is by the Babylonians in the third century BC. Halfway around the world, in Central America, the Mayans later independently invented the zero. Then in the fifth century, it was again invented in India. This teacher traces the spread of the zero to Cambodia, into China, and then to the Middle East. Interestingly, the zero did not reach Western Europe until the twelfth century. This mathematics professor faithfully fulfills core math learning expectations, but introduces a multicultural element into the class. Students are entertained, informed, and intrigued by this new dimension. It is also humbling to learn that contemporary math is far from the exclusive domain of the Western world.

We opened this chapter by talking about children's natural ability to think in terms of whole systems. Bucky Fuller said that the key was to make global connections clear and cultivate appreciation of the "whole," including the extensive historical and cultural interrelationships that make up our world. Encouraging this view in the classroom need not be complex, disruptive, or painful. It is all about the vision and view of the individual teacher. The trick is to encourage a worldview within the context of normal classes and content. Only faculty can create this magic.

As pointed out by educator Linda Booth Sweeney, the idea of looking at the world as a whole has a rich history. "More than 2,000 years ago, the Greeks were describing reality in terms of wholes composed of related parts. Indeed, many cultures, including Native American traditions tend to see reality in terms of indivisible wholes, emphasizing inter-relationships and circular loops of causality" (Sweeney 2001, 15).

Sweeney adds that "wisdom is not about bits and pieces, but about relationships, and about the compassion that comes when we realize our deep relatedness" (Sweeney 2001, 7).

Today, our many creative and talented faculty and teachers have access to tremendous resources. Those in Olathe, Kansas can deliver the same global lessons as those in New York City, Paris, or Bangkok. It all relies upon the ability of individual faculty to conceive, create, and deliver exciting new ideas and applications within the context of their institution and geography. All we have to do is start the dialogue. Once we agree that the goal is to incorporate the global, we can let the adventure run its course.

Global Responsibilities and Common Bonds

In espousing a global education, we make no secret of our ultimate desire to foster greater connections among peoples, increase understanding of others, and ultimately, create a more peaceful world. We believe strongly that our lives are connected and that education can overcome the prejudices that lead to conflict.

But this is not a purely moral or philosophical vision, and it is hardly designed exclusively for those promoting a liberal education. In the classic sense, global education can be seen as an extension, a twenty-first century version, of a liberal education. But global education also can be approached from a different rationale, namely, that there are pressing career development issues at stake. As noted, both the general public and today's students overwhelmingly believe that the study of different cultures and international issues is needed for economic success. They are not mistaken. Corporate leaders tell us that the next working generation will need to be able to function as easily abroad and across different cultures as they can in this country. They commonly add that it is vital that their workers be comfortable with diversity and working with those from different backgrounds, while being able to understand issues from different points of view.

Fred Hassan, the chairman and CEO of Schering-Plough, said, "In the research-based pharmaceuticals industry, employees must have global attitudes if their companies are to survive." The same is true in nearly every field. Hassan points out that even having foreign language skills does not guarantee that someone has a global attitude. According to him, "Being yourself while also showing interest and openness is at the heart of a global attitude" (*Harvard Business Review* 2003, 41).

Jeffrey Immelt, the chairman and CEO of General Electric, says, "The business community has gone global, and it can't go back. Career decisions are no longer based on nationalism." He adds that the key is to find the best people, no matter where they hail from. "It's truly about people, not about where the buildings are" (*Harvard Business Review* 2003, 43).

Daniel Meiland, the executive chairman of Egon Zehnder International, predicts, "If you look ahead five to 10 years, the people with the top jobs in large corporations, even in the United States, will be those who have lived in several cultures and who can converse in at least two languages" (*Harvard Business Review* 2003, 45).

Students must be ready to flourish in this world. They must be able to appreciate diverse cultures and to succeed in the global marketplace. To do so, schools and universities must make understanding global issues an integral part of the learning experience. This will ultimately boost students' prospects for professional success. While the moral imperative is indeed strong, we should not overlook these practical considerations and career motivations, for they likewise necessitate a global education. *In fact, a global education is the common ground that reconciles the differences between advocates of professional degree programs and those of liberal education.*

While global education benefits students in many ways, it also should unite educators from all disciplines. Whether you believe schools and colleges should stress liberal education or professional studies, there is common need to more heavily incorporate global views, perspectives, and lessons. The ability to make global connections is fundamental for personal enlightenment, professional success, and ultimately, for the health and welfare of our planet. Whether or not society is up to the task of combating global challenges will depend upon the caliber of world citizens and global leaders our colleges and schools produce.

Careers and professional success will always matter. They should. But at the same time, as students prepare for professional success, they should be instilled with a sense of adventure and responsibility to make the world a better place in which to live and work, for people of all cultures. They should be able to take advantage of economic opportunities, but they should also be willing to help overcome economic inequalities and proceed with a responsible global ethic.

It is time to end the liberal education versus vocational debate. It has lasted long enough, without resolution or agreement. The dialogue itself dilutes the potential for true change and improvement. The common denominator is the need to make global connections.

Educating the Next Generation

Ahmad Kamal is an extraordinary man. He served as a professional diplomat in the Ministry of Foreign Affairs of Pakistan for close to forty years until his retirement in 1999. Among other offices, he held diplomatic posts in India, Belgium, France, the Soviet Union, and the United Nations. At the United Nations, he held many of the highest elected posts, including vice president of the General Assembly and president of ECOSOC. Today, he is president of The Ambassador's Club at the United Nations. Kamal has had a front-row seat for many of the world's most serious crises in the last fifty years. He knows what trends to brush aside and what challenges demand our earnest attention. He says that although it is an old process, globalization is now rapidly shrinking the world, and we must learn more about what is happening elsewhere "because the events that are taking place are crossing borders without passports and visas." Because of globalization, we need to think "about acting on a stage of a world that is a single home rather than one divided into pockets of nationalities and regions."

Kamal observes that most countries have come to terms with this reality, and "in fact have learned how to study the history of other countries, how to study other civilizations, how to study other languages. But for some reason, the United States has been relatively isolated in this work, and has a lesser tendency to interest itself in other ideas and other events and other languages."

Pointing to the emergence of the United States as the sole superpower, Kamal suggests that as the power of the United States grows, so too does its responsibility to use its power wisely. Unfortunately, he says, the United States has not been very successful in learning about the world. Thus, he adds, it becomes "absolutely vital to build up the knowledge inside the United States about the rest of the world. That is the *raison d'etre* of global education."

Because of globalization and the trends identified in earlier chapters, we believe that humanity is increasingly linked and that global education should be a priority everywhere. But perhaps the concept is even more critical in the United States. We agree with Kamal that global education is especially needed in the United States, precisely because of this country's current dominance on the world stage, its numerous international relationships, and its historical tendency to focus inward more than outward. Schooling world citizens cannot wait any longer.

Ambassador Kamal also maintains that a global education requires learning to think outside ourselves and overcoming the belief that we are the center of the world. "There is so much more of the world outside of you, that it is your duty to search for what the rest of the world has to offer. Global education is an exciting invitation to a rich world."

Bucky Fuller would echo that invitation. He would say that educated individuals understand the different dimensions of the world, and that language and other forces we take for granted routinely limit our perspectives. The metaphor of "instairs" and "outstairs" is, of course, intended to make that point. The job of expanding our perspectives and breaking down the barriers that separate people often falls to our schools. But make no mistake: This is a society-wide endeavor, and all aboard Spaceship Earth are responsible for cultivating the next generation of world citizens. Bucky Fuller understood well just how much was riding on developing a global view and educating world citizens.

It is pivotal for us in this country to begin asking global questions and making global links. It all comes back to that childhood skill of seeing the big picture, and not getting lost in isolation or specialization.

We have tried to suggest some guidelines and examples to spark those questions, but there is no shortage of methods to help students connect the dots about the world in which we live. There are numerous ways to develop active world citizens of all ages. Students can be transformed like Craig Kielburger from Canada. At age twelve, he read a news article about a Pakistani youngster's death. The boy, Iqbal Masih, was a former child laborer who had escaped and become a celebrated activist. Masih was shot and killed while working to improve conditions in the factories and set other child workers free.

Inspired by the boy's courage, Kielburger journeyed to South Asia to investigate child labor there, and helped launch an organization called Free the Children. Since 1995, this organization has spread to more than thirty-five countries, and more than one million people have taken part in its programs. These have included building schools, distributing health kits and medical supplies, campaigning against child abuses, and raising funds for education centers (Free the Children 2005).

Craig Kielburger recognizes the need for global education, and he says that one of the greatest challenges educators and teachers face "is to prepare your students to live in the new global village and to become active citizens of this world." He urges those responsible for helping to inspire and develop the next generation to "believe in us, the young people of today. Don't be afraid to challenge us to play a greater role in society, and please, don't underestimate who we are or what we can do. Our generation may just surprise you" (Kielburger 1996, 325–326).

We would not be surprised. In fact, we are counting on them. But first, we have to provide—and they have to seize the benefits of—a global education.

References

Academic Council on the United Nations System (ACUNS). 2002. US Colleges and Universities Are Not Meeting Student Demands. Summary of findings of a seminar held at the Yale Center for the Study of Globalization, New Haven, CT, November 22–23.

AFS Intercultural Programs (AFS). 2003. Assessment of the Impact of the AFS Study Abroad Experience. Designed and conducted by Mitchell R. Hammer. http://www.afs.org (accessed June 29, 2005).

Andrzejewski, Julie, and John Alessio. 1999. Education for Global Citizenship and Social Responsibility. *Progressive Perspectives* 1, no. 2 (Spring). Monograph Series. John Dewey Project on Progressive Education, University of Vermont.

Bacon, Nancy A., and Gerrit A. Kischner. 2002. Shaping Global Classrooms. *Educational Leadership* 60, no. 2 (October): 48–51.

Banks, James A., ed. 2004. *Diversity and Citizenship Education: Global Perspectives*. San Francisco: Jossey-Bass.

Barker, Carol M. 2000. Education for International Understanding and Global Competence. Report of a meeting convened by Carnegie Corporation of New York, January 21.

Becker, John E. 2002. I Have Traveled Much in Concord. Academic Con-
vocation Address, Fairleigh Dickinson University, September 25.

Benjamin, Harold. 1939. *The Saber-Tooth Curriculum.* New York: McGraw-
Hill Book Company.

Bigelow, Bill, and Bob Peterson, eds. 2002. *Rethinking Globalization: Teaching for Justice in an Unjust World.* Milwaukee: Rethinking Schools
Press.

Branzburg, Jeffrey. 2002. Reaching Around the Globe. *Technology and
Learning* (November): 41.

Burbules, Nicholas C., and Carlos Alberto Torres, eds. 2000. *Globalization
and Education: Critical Perspectives.* New York: Routledge.

Cassell, Brent. 2002. Prepping Global Citizens. *The Globalist,* November
28. http://www.theglobalist.com (accessed September 14, 2005).

Chaker, Anne Marie. 2003. Schools Say 'Adieu' to Foreign Languages. *Wall
Street Journal,* October 30.

Colgan, Craig. 2003. Interest in International Studies Is Back! *Education
Digest* 68, no. 8 (April): 61–64.

Collins, H. Thomas, Frederick R. Czarra, and Andrew F. Smith. 1995. Guidelines for Global and International Studies Education: Challenges, Culture, Connections. American Forum for Global Education. http://www.
globaled.org/guidelines/ (accessed September 14, 2005).

Duderstadt, James J. 2000. A Society of Learning: A Vision for the Future of
the Public University in the New Millennium. Address at the University of Wisconsin, Madison, WI, November 30.

Dunn, Ross E. 2002. Growing Good Citizens with a World-Centered Curriculum. *Educational Leadership* 60, no. 2 (October): 10–13.

Free the Children. 2005. http://www.freethechildren.com (accessed June 17,
2005).

Fuller, R. Buckminster. 1963. *Operating Manual for Spaceship Earth.* New
York: E.P. Dutton.

Gacel-Ávila, Jocelyne. 2005. The Internationalisation of Higher Education:
A Paradigm for Global Citizenry. *Journal of Studies in International
Education* 9, no. 2 (Summer): 121–136.

Green. Madeleine F. 2002. Going Global: Internationalizing U.S. Higher
Education. *Current* (July–August): 8–15.

Hanvey, Robert G. 1976. *An Attainable Global Perspective.* New York:
American Forum for Global Education.

Harvard Business Review. 2003. In Search of Global Leaders. *Harvard Business Review* 81 (August): 38–45.

Harvard University. 2004. *A Report on the Harvard College Curricular Review.* Boston: Harvard University.

Hayward, Fred M., and Laura M. Siaya. 2001. *Public Experience, Attitudes,
and Knowledge: A Report on Two National Surveys about International
Education.* Washington, D.C.: American Council on Education.

Holloway, John H. 2002. What Do Students Know? *Educational Leadership* 60, no. 2 (October): 85–86.

Institute of International Education. 2004. *Open Doors: Report on International Educational Exchange.* New York.

International Communication and Negotiation Simulations (ICONS) Project, University of Maryland. http://www.icons.umd.edu (accessed June 16, 2005).

International Education and Resource Network (iEARN). 2005. http://www.iearn.org (accessed June 16, 2005).

Kerr, Clark. 2001. *The Uses of the University.* Fifth edition. Cambridge, MA: Harvard University Press.

Kielburger, Craig. 1996. Kids Can Be Activists or Bystanders. In *Rethinking Globalization: Teaching for Justice in an Unjust World,* edited by B. Bigelow and B. Peterson, 325–326. Milwaukee: Rethinking Schools Press.

Kirby, William C. 2004. Letter introducing the Report on the Harvard College Curricular Review. In *A Report on the Harvard College Curricular Review.* Boston: Harvard University.

Kirkwood, Toni Fuss. 2001. Our Global Age Requires Global Education: Clarifying Definitional Ambiguities. *Social Studies* 92, no. 1 (January–February): 10–15.

Levin, Richard C. 2003. *The Work of the University.* New Haven, CT: Yale University Press.

Merryfield, Merry M. 2002. The Difference a Global Educator Can Make. *Educational Leadership* 60, no. 2 (October): 18–21.

NAFSA: Association of International Educators. 2003. *Securing America's Future: Global Education for a Global Age.* Washington, D.C.: NAFSA.

National Council for the Social Studies (NCSS). 1982. *Position Statement on Global Education.* Washington, D.C.: National Council for the Social Studies.

Osler, Audrey, and Kerry Vincent. 2002. *Citizenship and the Challenge of Global Education.* Sterling, VA: Trentham Books.

Parker, Walter C. 2002. The Deliberative Approach to Education for Democracy: Problems and Possibilities. *The School Field* XIII, no. 3/4: 25–42.

Parker, Walter C. 2004. Diversity, Globalization, and Democratic Education: Curriculum Possibilities. In *Diversity and Citizenship Education: Global Perspectives,* edited by J.A. Banks, 433–458. San Francisco: Jossey-Bass.

Parker, Walter C., Akira Ninomiya, and John Cogan. 1999. Educating World Citizens: Towards Multinational Curriculum Development. *American Educational Research Journal* 36, no. 2 (Summer): 117–145.

Pike, Graham, and David Selby. 2000. *In the Global Classroom: 2.* Toronto, Ontario: Pippin Publishing Corporation.

Pratt, Mary Louise. 2004. Language and National Security: Making a New Public Commitment. *Modern Language Journal* 88, no. 2 (Summer). Special Issue, *Teaching Languages and Cultures in a Post–9/11 World: North Amercan Perspectives* (268–291).

Price, Derek J. de Solla. 1961. *Science Since Babylon.* New Haven, CT: Yale University Press.

Ravitch, Diane, and Joseph P. Viteritti, eds. 2001. *Making Good Citizens: Education and Civil Society.* New Haven, CT: Yale University Press.

Ravitch, Diane. 2002. September 11: Seven Lessons for the Schools. *Educational Leadership* 60, no. 2 (October): 6–9.

Rhodes, Frank H.T. 2001. *The Creation of the Future: The Role of the American University.* Ithaca, NY: Cornell University Press.

Sammartino, Peter, ed. 1965. *An International Conference on Higher Education.* On the occasion of the dedication of Fairleigh Dickinson University's Wroxton College in Wroxton, England.

Sernau, Scott. 2003. Developing Global Competencies in Higher Education. Address at a conference presented by Fairleigh Dickinson University and the Internationalization Collaborative of the American Council on Education, April 4 and 5.

Siaya, Laura, and Fred M. Hayward. 2003. *Mapping Internationalization on U.S. Campuses.* Washington, D.C.: American Council on Education

Siaya, Laura, Maura Porcelli, and Madeleine F. Green. 2002. *One Year Later: Attitudes about International Education since September 11.* Washington, D.C.: American Council on Education.

Simmons, Jeff. 2001. Internationalization of U.S. Higher Education: Do We Prepare Graduates To Be Effective Global Citizens? *Hispanic Outlook in Higher Education,* September 10.

Smith, Andrew F. 2002. How Global Is the Curriculum? *Educational Leadership* 60, no. 2 (October): 38–41.

Stromquist, Nelly P., and Karen Monkman, eds. 2000. *Globalization and Education: Integration and Contestation Across Cultures.* Lanham, MD: Rowman & Littlefield Publishers.

Suárez-Orozco, Marcelo M., and Desirée Baolian Qin-Hilliard, eds. 2004. *Globalization: Culture and Education in the New Millennium.* Berkeley: University of California Press.

Sweeney, Linda Booth. 2001. *When a Butterfly Sneezes: A Guide for Helping Kids Explore Interconnections in Our World Through Favorite Stories.* Waltham, MA: Pegasus Communications.

Toynbee, Arnold J. 1965. The Importance of History. In *An International Conference on Higher Education,* edited by Peter Sammartino, 3–14. On the occasion of the dedication of Fairleigh Dickinson University's Wroxton College in Wroxton, England.

Trivedi, Bijal P. 2002. Survey Reveals Geographic Literacy. *National Geographic Today,* November 20. http://news.nationalgeographic.com/news/

2002/11/1120_021120_GeoRoperSurvey.html (accessed September 14, 2005).

Van Hoof, Hubert B., and Marja J.Verbeeten. 2005. Wine Is For Drinking, Water Is For Washing: Student Opinions about International Exchange Programs. *Journal of Studies in International Education* 9, no. 1 (Spring): 42–61.

Welles, Elizabeth B. 2004. Foreign Language Enrollments in United States Institutions of Higher Education, Fall 2002. *ADFL Bulletin* 35, no. 2 (Winter): 1–20.

Wesche, Mari. 2004. Teaching Languages and Cultures in a Post-9/11 World. *Modern Language Journal* 88, no. 2 (Summer). Special Issue, *Teaching Languages and Cultures in a Post–9/11 World: North American Perspectives* (268–291).

Woodbury, Anthony C. 1991. Counting Eskimo Words for Snow: A Citizen's Guide. http://www.princeton.edu/~browning/snow.html (accessed September 14, 2005).

Young, Jeffrey R. 2004. Students' Political Awareness Hits Highest Level in a Decade: Survey of Freshmen Shows a Continuing Shift to the Right and Middle. *Chronicle of Higher Education,* January 30.

Zung, Thomas T.K., ed. 2001. *Buckminster Fuller: Anthology for the New Millennium.* New York: St. Martin's Press.

7

GENETIC ROAD MAPS AND SPEED BUMPS ON THE ROUTE TO WORLD CITIZENSHIP

Oh, East is East, and West is West, and never the twain shall meet.

—Rudyard Kipling
The Ballad of East and West, 1889

I read somewhere that everybody on this planet is separated by only six other people. Six degrees of separation. Between us and everybody else on this planet. The president of the United States. A gondolier in Venice . . . A native in a rain forest. A Tierra del Fuegan. An Eskimo. I am bound to everyone on this planet by a trail of six people. It's a profound thought. . . . How every person is a new door, opening up into other worlds.

—John Guare
Six Degrees of Separation, 1990

A Matter of Degrees

The "small-world" principle says that we are all connected to each other by a short string of friends and acquaintances. Everyone has stories of meeting a stranger and learning that they know someone in common. In 1967, Stanley Milgram, a social psychologist, decided to test the theory.

The goal of his experiment was to measure the number of acquaintances linking two Americans who did not know each other. In a typical trial, an individual in the Midwest, called the source person, was given a letter to be delivered to someone in Massachusetts, called the target person. The source was told the target's name, address, and occupation, and asked to send the envelope to a personal

193

acquaintance who would be more likely to know the target person. Everyone receiving the letter was given the same instructions, and the process continued until the target received the message.

Milgram found the average number of steps from source to target was 5.5. He rounded the mean to six, and unintentionally created the "six degrees of separation" principle.

Though not scientifically conclusive, and limited to only one country, Milgram's findings have captured our collective imagination. John Guare popularized the idea with his 1990 hit play, *Six Degrees of Separation,* which was later made into a movie. The concept was further fueled by the Six Degrees of Kevin Bacon game, which asks players to link the actor to other movie stars. Are there really only six individuals between you and anyone else in the world?

In 2003, building on Milgram's work, Columbia University researchers conducted a similar worldwide experiment using e-mail. They found that the number of chains linking random people across the globe averaged five to seven steps—right in line with the six degrees principle. Only five to seven clicks on the "send" button separated most strangers around the globe. As geographic distances are reduced by technology, and as we expand our network of relationships through contemporary communication tools, humanity grows closer, and the degrees of separation decrease.

But if we are so connected, why are the opening lines of Rudyard Kipling's *The Ballad of East and West* so often expressed to describe our inability to understand each other and get along? Understanding and getting along is necessary for the very survival of our species. So what stops us? Why don't we understand that differences in background are not the basis for determining a person's worth? What stops us from learning to look at problems through the eyes of others? What stops us from connecting the dots?

One of the most common concerns is that we are incapable of extending emotional bonds beyond the nation. This points to the issue of human nature and whether our genetic blueprint precludes significant attachment to those who are distant. Does the fault lie in our genes, or are there other dimensions and institutions that influence our worldview?

The Tendency to Divide

Perhaps it is not so reassuring to be closely connected to everyone else in the world. Do I really have anything in common with an Aborigine in the Australian outback? To a Tutsi in Rwanda, a Sunni in Iraq, or a member of British royalty?

"West is West" can be a comforting notion. It gives us space to breathe, plants us on firm ground, and nicely organizes our world. We have a tendency to divide the world into two groups: "them" and "us." And if the "us" looks like us, it is even more reassuring.

It starts with the emotional security of our national identity. By itself, there is nothing wrong with celebrating the special identity that national citizenship provides. The problem occurs when such emotions translate into prejudices and narrow-minded acts of selfishness.

"My country, right or wrong!" must be replaced with the view that each country is part of a greater whole, a universal community that shares a common heritage and a common fate. The exaltation of national superiority simply justifies too much at the expense of the world community. It reinforces the artificial barrier between "us" and "them."

It is no secret that our species has been long dominated by tribal mentalities. Americans in particular have celebrated the notion that we have a special role and destiny. In 1630, Reverend John Winthrop delivered a sermon to settlers of the Massachusetts Bay Colony. He quoted from the Sermon on the Mount, saying, "We shall be as a city on a hill." His message was that the eyes and envy of the world would be upon this land.

Winthrop's message of the "city on a hill" has been part of our ethic and political posturing ever since. John Adams, Abraham Lincoln, John F. Kennedy, and Ronald Reagan have all delivered a "city on the hill" speech. We like believing that we are special.

Alexis de Tocqueville also pointed out how many Americans were convinced that they were exceptional and special compared to the rest of humanity. About such feelings, he complained, "It is impossible to conceive a more troublesome or more garrulous patriotism; it wearies even those who are disposed to respect it" (*Democracy in America* 1835/1840). This habit of celebrating our nation, our group, our tribe, is not an exclusively American tendency. It has flourished throughout human history. And it has almost always led to righteousness, followed unfortunately by conflict and violence. Will it continue to be that way? Or can we somehow overcome such narrow-minded thinking?

Pessimists will say we have always been at each other's throats, in Darwinian struggles that are embedded in our genetic makeup. It is human nature to resort to violence and seek protection from the family, the tribe, and today, the nation. Are we genetically capable of solidarity, cooperation, and world citizenship?

Nature versus Nurture: Round 7,899,999

How we view human nature is fundamental to how we respond to our world. Our assumptions about how humans develop and act guide our decisions in personal relationships and influence our interactions with others.

In the seventeenth century, British philosopher John Locke formed the idea of the *tabula rasa,* Latin for "blank slate." Locke contended that we are each born without predispositions, and that experience determines the essence of the individual. If you change the experiences, you can change the person. Locke believed we are essentially creatures of goodwill, and that our original state is perfectly compatible with freedom and equality.

Another British philosopher, Thomas Hobbes, strongly disagreed. He believed that the natural state of humans is marked by selfishness and violence. We are fundamentally vicious animals, Hobbes maintained. Only through the surrender of autonomy to a ruler or larger government can humans escape the violence that lies in their genes. Hobbes thought an authoritarian nation-state was necessary to overcome the vileness in humanity.

Joining the debate almost a century later, Jean-Jacques Rousseau forwarded the theme of "the noble savage." The concept was one of the most powerful ideas of the Enlightenment. Rousseau believed in the inherent goodness of natural man, arguing that it is only through the corrupting influence of society and civilization that cruelty emerges.

Many others have leapt into the human nature debate. Some cynics:

> One can make this generalization about men: they are ungrateful, fickle, liars, and deceivers, they shun danger and are greedy for profit . . . The bond of love is one which men, wretched creatures that they are, break when it is to their advantage to do so . . . (Machiavelli, *The Prince* 1513)

> It is just because human bloodthirstiness is such a primitive part of us that it is so hard to eradicate . . . (William James, American psychologist, *The Principles of Psychology* 1890)

It's silly to go on pretending that under the skin we are all brothers. The truth is more likely that under the skin we are all cannibals, assassins, traitors, liars, hypocrites, poltroons. (Henry Miller, American writer, *New York Times* op-ed, September 7, 1974)

Some idealists:

Man is not born wicked; he becomes so, as he becomes sick. (Voltaire, *Philosophical Dictionary* 1764)

All men are similar in body and soul . . . moral ailments are induced by the wrong sort of education, by all sorts of rubbish with which it has been the custom to stuff people's heads, by the monstrous state of society—in short, if society is put right, then the ailments will vanish. (Ivan Turgenev, *Fathers and Sons* 1862)

No one is born hating another person because of the color of his skin, or his background, or his religion. People must learn to hate, and if they can learn to hate, they can be taught to love, for love comes more naturally to the human heart than its opposite. (Nelson Mandela, *Long Walk to Freedom* 1994)

So which is it? Does human nature prescribe a future of continued selfishness, rabid nationalism, and destructive violence? Or do we possess more positive elements that can be nurtured?

Do we side with Confucius and Mencius, who taught that humans possessed inner goodness, or with another great Confucian, Hsun Tzu, who believed that our innate desires are selfish and that our natures are evil?

The camps aligned with and against the blank slate have debated each other viciously through the centuries. Supporters argue that humans are mostly malleable. Detractors claim that our essences are largely predetermined.

Hard-Wired Circuitry

As we learn more about humanity's genetic makeup, it does appear that we are born with certain tendencies. How else to explain the similarity of traits that appear everywhere?

Scientist and author Matt Ridley reports that the "same themes crop up in all cultures—themes such as family, ritual, bargain, love, hierarchy, friendship, jealousy, group loyalty and superstition" (Ridley 1996, 6). These cannot have developed solely from experiences. They must be part of who we are.

These inborn traits, unfortunately, include conflict and violence. In his seminal work *The Blank Slate: The Modern Denial of Human Nature,* Steven Pinker counters Rousseau's notion of a noble savage by writing, "A thoroughly noble *anything* is an unlikely product of natural selection, because in the competition among genes for representation in the next generation, noble guys tend to finish last" (Pinker 2002, 55).

Anthropologist Donald Brown identified a long list of human universals that include conflict, revenge, and dominance. But as Pinker notes, that sad reality "does not mean that our species has a death wish, an innate thirst for blood, or a territorial imperative. There are good evolutionary reasons for the members of an intelligent species to try to live in peace" (Pinker 2002, 58).

And certainly, there are other hard-wired skills we can rely on. In Pinker's words,

> . . . while conflict is a human universal, so is conflict resolution. Together, with all their nasty and brutish motives, all peoples display a host of kinder, gentler ones: a sense of morality, justice, and community, an ability to anticipate consequences when choosing how to act, and a love of children, spouses, and friends. Whether a group of people will engage in violence or work for peace depends on which set of motives is engaged . . . (Pinker 2002, 58)

While it appears that we are not exactly blank slates or noble savages, we are also not quite monsters at heart, nor are we slaves to our genes. We do have choices. Our destiny is not predetermined. We have innate features (instincts, if you will) that can lead to death and destruction, and we have other innate features that produce greater cooperation.

As historian Howard Zinn has noted,

> . . . human beings certainly have, from the start (genetically) a *potential* for violence, but also a potential for peacefulness. That leaves us open to all sorts of possibilities, depending on the circumstances we find ourselves in and the circumstances we create for ourselves. (Zinn 1990, 36)

Zinn has spent his career documenting the lives of people such as civil rights workers who peacefully changed the course of history. To those who repeatedly cite our history of violence, he replies,

> There is another history, of the rejection of violence, the refusal
> to kill, and the yearning for community. It has shown itself
> throughout the past in acts of courage and sacrifice that defied
> all the immediate pressures of the environment. (Zinn 1990, 46)

Author Robert Louis Stevenson captured the inherently conflicting natures within us in his classic story of Dr. Jekyll and Mr.
Hyde. The brilliant scientist Dr. Henry Jekyll sees life as a continu-
ous struggle between the two sides of our being, one representing all
that is pure and noble, the other empowered to act cruelly. Trying to
separate the two combative forces, Jekyll inadvertently unleashes the
monster within in the form of Mr. Edward Hyde.

We are made up of far more than just two forces, but Stevenson's story is nevertheless valuable. We are capable of both incredibly humanitarian deeds and desperately depraved acts. We have
choices.

Overcoming Tribal Desires

From the dawn of recorded history, humans have bonded in close-
knit groups. Family units and small bands initially formed for defense and protection. The tribal mentality is a powerful emotion,
strengthened by the presence of an enemy.

> Like chimps, we are xenophobic. All human preliterate soci-
> eties, and all modern ones as well, tend to have an 'enemy,' a
> concept of them and us. . . . Montagues and Capulets, French
> and English, Whig and Tory, Airbus and Boeing, Pepsi and
> Coke, Serb and Muslim, Christian and Saracen—we are irre-
> deemably tribal creatures. (Ridley 1996, 165–66)

Charles Darwin, in *The Descent of Man* (1871), made clear the
evolutionary advantage of this sort of thinking.

> A tribe including many members who, from possessing in a high
> degree the spirit of patriotism, fidelity, obedience, courage, and
> sympathy, were always ready to aid one another, and to sacrifice
> themselves for the common good, would be victorious over
> most other tribes; and this would be natural selection.

This tribal mentality has encouraged not only competitive
instincts, but also cooperative impulses. We have learned to work

alongside others. It could not be otherwise. Groups made up of purely selfish individuals would not be able to prosper. Because our genes have selfish motives—namely, to survive—we have learned the value of mutually beneficial partnership, or reciprocal altruism. We do things for others so that we may ultimately benefit.

As Ridley observes, "Cooperation was first used, not for virtuous reasons, but as a tool to achieve selfish results" (Ridley 1996, 152). Nevertheless, the result is the same. Our evolutionary design produced strong cooperative impulses. Ridley adds,

> Our minds have been built by selfish genes, but they have been built to be social, trustworthy and cooperative. . . . Human beings have social instincts. They come into the world equipped with predispositions to learn how to cooperate . . . this instinctive cooperativeness is the very hallmark of humanity and what sets us apart from other animals. (Ridley 1996, 249)

Our species is geared first and foremost toward preservation, and so self-interest dictates cooperation. In Adam Smith's famous phrase,

> It is not from the benevolence of the butcher, the brewer, or the baker that we expect our dinner, but from their regard to their own self-interest. We address ourselves not to their humanity but to their self-love. (*An Inquiry into the Nature and Causes of the Wealth of Nations* 1776)

When preservation necessitated cooperation within the tribe, we learned how to think in terms of us against them. In an interconnected world where planetary survival depends on it, global cooperation must trigger global mindsets. We must view ourselves as members of a global tribe.

It really is not that much of a leap from the tribe to humanity. While there are rich differences among cultures and groups, we have a set of shared values and a shared way of thinking and feeling that makes the entire world analogous to a single tribe. Just as the Golden Rule has emerged across cultures and nations, so too have other universal qualities and traits. Confucius was not off the mark when he wrote, "Men are close to one another by nature. They diverge as a result of repeated practice" (*The Analects* 5th century B.C.). Similarly, Voltaire observed, "Nature establishes unity, and everywhere settles a few invariable principles; the soil is still the same, but culture produces various fruits" (*Essay on the Manners and Spirit of Nations* 1756).

Rushworth Kidder, the president of the Institute for Global Ethics, interviewed influential leaders from nations and cultures around the world to identify a global code of ethics. He identified eight common values across cultures:

Love	Unity
Truthfulness	Tolerance
Fairness	Responsibility
Freedom	Respect for life

It should be noted that the value of unity included solidarity, cooperation, and group allegiance (Kidder 1994, 18–19).

While Donald Brown's list of universals included conflict, revenge, and dominance—among the nearly four hundred characteristics he found throughout human societies—he also cited empathy, admiration for generosity, gift giving, hospitality, fairness, and hope.

From an early age, striking similarities among people from vastly different cultures are obvious.

> Children as young as a year and a half spontaneously give toys, proffer help, and try to comfort adults or other children who are visibly distressed. People in all cultures distinguish right from wrong, have a sense of fairness, help one another, impose rights and obligations, believe that wrongs should be redressed, and proscribe rape, murder, and some kinds of violence. (Pinker 2002, 188)

Morality and virtue are as tightly tied to our natures as the worst features that the cynics cite. Pinker concludes, "For all its selfishness, the human mind is equipped with a moral sense, whose circle of application has expanded steadily and might continue to expand as the world becomes interdependent" (Pinker 2002, 299).

It is important to recognize that, while selfishness seems embedded in our nature, the values of altruism and unselfishness inspire praise throughout the world. All cultures frown upon selfishness and view nepotism with disdain. While many still believe it is acceptable to exalt one's nation above others, to celebrate group selfishness, perhaps we are closer to world citizenship than we think.

The question of nature versus nurture is the wrong one. We are obviously products of both. Instincts, of which we have many, interact with our experiences and produce the type of person we become. Human nature is far from being an obstacle to world citizenship; the roots of planetary cooperation and world citizenship already exist in it. The increasing acceptance of world citizenship would further strengthen those elements of cooperation and diminish tendencies toward selfishness.

We do not have to change human nature to achieve world citizenship, but we do have to cultivate those positive elements of human nature that already exist. How do we do that?

A Family Affair

Richard Rodgers and Oscar Hammerstein's *South Pacific* (1949) is among the most memorable musicals ever produced. It is also one of the first musicals to address racial prejudice, cultural conflict, and how humans are guided by their early training.

Set during World War II, the story centers around the relationship between Nellie Forbush, a Navy nurse from Arkansas, and Emile de Becque, a middle-aged French plantation owner. Nellie falls in love with Emile, but is shocked to learn that he is a widower with two mixed-race children.

Among the subplots is a forbidden romance between Lieutenant Joe Cable and a young Tonkinese woman. Cable emotionally summarizes the basis of the dilemma he and Nellie experience in the song "You Have to Be Carefully Taught."

> You've got to be taught
> To hate and fear . . .
> It's got to be drummed
> In your dear little ear
> You've got to be carefully taught.
> You've got to be taught to be afraid
> Of people whose eyes are oddly made,
> And people whose skin is a diff'rent shade . . .

If we are fortunate, we grow up in a secure and loving environment. Not all children are so fortunate. But for better or worse, we learn fundamental, long-lasting lessons from our family in our early years.

Ignatius of Loyola founded the Jesuits in the sixteenth century. He famously declared: "Give us a child until he is seven and he is ours for life." Ignatius and his brethren understood that the most formative and permanent ideas and attitudes are implanted while we are small children. Our view of ourselves and of our world begins taking shape even before we learn to speak. As Ana Maria Cetto writes, lessons on world citizenship

> . . . start when the child begins to learn that they are not alone in this world, and they gradually become aware of belonging to a family, a neighborhood, a group of children, a gender, an ethnic group, a cultural group, a socio-economic group, a community, a religion, a city, a country . . . a civilization, and to humankind. (Cetto 1997, 145)

What we teach our children in the home—the values we instill, the examples we set—may ultimately determine the future of world citizenship. If a child has been taught intolerance and self-centeredness at home, there may be no hope, no matter how hard educators work. Through normal, everyday events, children see how their parents and families view their world. And they are profoundly influenced.

Parents of young children are often startled by how much their children mimic their words and actions. Perhaps they are surprised because many do not see themselves as teachers and do not view their pre-toddlers and toddlers as students. But the teacher-student analogy must be acknowledged, not just by parents, but by older siblings, other relatives, and friends. The lessons that family members convey may be the most crucial in a children's life.

Child development expert Judith Myers-Walls suggests that both simple, routine actions and major lifestyle decisions influence a worldview.

> . . . parents have the ability to impact their children in many ways . . . They may choose where they will live, how they will earn a living, and where or if the child will attend school. They also choose how they will explain the world to their children

and how they will react to their questions. Families are providing education regarding global citizenship every day. (Myers-
Walls 2001, 12)

Myers-Walls illustrates this point with several commonplace
examples:

> A mother tells her son that he may not play with the children in
> the neighborhood who have dark skin. . . . A father complains to
> his family that the reason he lost his job is because immigrants
> are taking so many jobs that there aren't any left for the native
> citizens. . . . A grandfather tells his grandchildren how the cur-
> rent war started. . . . They are simple events, but each one plays
> a small part in the formation of the world . . . (Myers-Walls
> 2001, 3)

Parents take the lead in a child's development. And family members and friends play critical supporting roles. Everyone who enters
the child's environment has the opportunity to change the future.

Perhaps the greatest impact we have is through the force of
example. Take a strong interest in different cultures and world issues,
and continually show children how to translate values into action.
Always search for multiple perspectives and alternative viewpoints.
You will be surprised how rapidly children follow the lead.

By the end of *South Pacific,* Nellie accepts both Emile and his
children. Prejudice can be overcome. It would be easier, however, if
we learned the lesson from birth that we are world citizens.

The Schoolhouse Awaits

While the road to world citizenship should begin at home, children
then take the long path through elementary, junior, and senior high
school, and, if fortunate, a university or college. But what are the
prospects for a successful journey? What obstacles exist in the educational system?

National Purpose

Otto von Bismarck is considered to be the founder of the modern German state. As Germany's first chancellor, he developed a common currency, created a central bank, and instituted a system of state-supported

retirement payments as well as social security that insured workers against illness or accident.

More than a hundred years ago, he also created perhaps the first comprehensive public school system. The Volksschule—"people training"—evolved from the goal of national unity. Bismarck saw compulsory public education as a way to develop children into soldiers and loyal citizens. The mantra was education to the state, education for the state, education by the state.

Other nations adopted a similar attitude and approach. Jim Dator, a professor of political science, notes that modern educational systems only date back about one hundred to one hundred fifty years, and they were not established to produce world citizens. "They were originally created specifically to meet the needs of the early industrial states. Formal education was expected in part to indoctrinate youth into the myths and fables of national tradition" (Dator 2000, 70).

Above all, publicly funded education was designed to

> change ordinary people from being peasants and lords into the laborers and bosses needed in the factories of the new industrial states, each jostling for dominance over the other emerging industrial states of the world. (Dator 2000, 70)

Many prominent educators believed that schools should first and foremost develop loyal citizens with a strong sense of national identity. One of the founding fathers of American education, Noah Webster, promoted a common language to overcome regional distinctions and enhance a sense of cultural nationalism. Horace Mann, well known as the father of the American common school, believed public schools would help eliminate differences among classes and further the nation's unity and progress (Ravitch 2001, 16–17).

It has long been about the nation, not the world. It has been about building national values, a national identity, and a national workforce. From the time students first enter the doors of elementary school, they are treated to a parade of patriotic lessons designed to foster a distinctive sense of national pride. Growing up in Illinois in the 1960s, for example, children had to pass a rigorous civics test on national history and the US Constitution before advancing through the eighth grade.

This is not just an American phenomenon. It is common to almost all national systems of education. There is nothing wrong with cultivating pride in one's heritage, but there must be a balance between celebrating one's heritage or uniqueness and sharing stories from other nations.

That balance is often lacking. The national story dominates, with national symbols and heroic tales of national triumphs seemingly everywhere. As Edwin Reischauer wrote,

> Formal schooling centers on the American way of life, blatantly proclaimed or at least tacitly assumed to be superior to all others. Repeatedly, the school child is led through the story of American history, often as a tale of ever-victorious conflict between our country and other national groupings. The rest of the human race gets short historical shrift, except as the setting for our national story . . . (Reischauer 1973, 176)

Schools should help further national goals and interests, but they also must enable us to understand the whole world and our role in it.

Curricular Challenges

The challenge is similar at the university level. As Donald McCloud observes, American universities, with all their talent, resources, and scholarly activities, "continue to graduate significant numbers of students who are less than well-informed about the world outside the United States" and who "have difficulty with even the most elementary issues of international business and intercultural functionality" (McCloud 2004).

Part of the problem is overcoming institutional inertia and breaking free from original aims. McCloud writes, "American institutions of higher learning were created as products of and in response to needs of a very localized environment, and they remain true to that heritage with respect to most institutional contexts."

He adds that "curriculum design was and continues to be shaped largely by domestic social demand and the national organizations supporting the academic disciplines" (McCloud 2004).

Educational institutions are slow to adapt to new realities as noted in Chapter 6. It is astonishing that despite conspicuous change resulting from globalization, schools and colleges remain essentially the same. There are exceptions, but in general, schools will have to be dragged into the global age.

In her study of internationalization on campuses, Sheila Biddle points to several obstacles, including "the innate conservatism of academic culture." She explains, "University communities tend to regard with suspicion new structures and programs, because they threaten existing entitlements and traditional lines of authority" (Biddle 2002, 15).

International programs are widely dispersed across campuses and not well coordinated or organized. Faculty members generally focus on their disciplinary pursuits rather than on efforts that span borders. Interdisciplinary work, adds Biddle, "tends to be suspect in the eyes of disciplinary promotion and tenure committees" (Biddle 2002, 102).

Faculty face little incentive and great risk in pursuing international endeavors. Departmental turfs are zealously guarded to make sure that interdisciplinary initiatives do not interfere with the purity of specialized interests. Those remaining within the confines of the disciplinary walls are often better rewarded with promotions and increased academic reputations. These barriers in academia are real, and should not be underestimated.

Also, when funds are scarce, resistance to new offerings is bound to occur, because it could lead to cuts in existing programs. International elements are commonly viewed as extra components to be supported when money is available. One dean told Biddle that international programs were "icing on the cake" (Biddle 2002, 35). So when budget battles begin, international programs often lose out.

But the problem goes beyond funding. One of the biggest reasons why greater internationalization is more rhetoric than reality, says Biddle, is that there is no clear consensus or uniform vision about how a curriculum can be internationalized. But seeking a consensus is unnecessary. There are many paths to internationalization, and creative institutions and committed individuals can adapt their approaches to their specific environments.

Textbooks and Tools
Textbook publishing is a commercial enterprise. In *The Language Police: How Pressure Groups Restrict What Students Learn,* Diane Ravitch writes about how the pressures of the marketplace influence educational publishers. In a politicized environment, controversy is bad for business. She describes how pressure groups on both the right and the left have effectively lobbied textbook publishers to eliminate material that could be considered even remotely objectionable.

Major publishers have developed exhaustive bias guidelines and language codes, resulting in overly sanitized and maddeningly bland texts, particularly in history and literature. Bias and sensitivity review panels screen all texts and tests for potential problems that could upset students. Some examples are plainly absurd: Dinosaurs, for instance, are frowned upon because they raise the subject of evolution.

Texas and California have a major influence on textbook adoption nationwide. Both states have a formal process for review and approval of instructional materials, with detailed guidelines. Texas state law requires the Board of Education "to approve textbooks that promote democracy, patriotism, and the free-enterprise system" (Gillespie 2003).

Because California and Texas are so critical to a textbook's success, most other states usually end up with texts approved by them. If a text is rejected by either state, its chances for success are very slim.

The result is that a select few textbook publishers—with information tailored to the requirements of two states—increasingly define the curriculum. The product is massive uniformity of language and thought. And the end result is a bored student lacking in global awareness.

Ravitch and others, such as James Loewen, write about how American history textbooks have presented limited, narrow, and bland depictions of our country's people, heritage, and development. It should be no surprise, then, to see gaps between what Americans think of themselves and their history, and how others around the world see us.

As Loewen notes,

> Textbooks are often muddled by the conflicting desires to promote inquiry and to indoctrinate blind patriotism. "Take a look at your history book, and you'll see why we should be proud," goes an anthem often sung by high school glee clubs. But we need not even look inside. The titles themselves tell the story: *The Great Republic, The American Way, Land of Promise, Rise of the American Nation.* (Loewen 1995, 14)

Change the assumptions of textbook writers, curriculum planners, and teachers, and the message is dramatically altered. The national experience and the national culture still need to be emphasized. But as Reischauer noted,

> . . . these materials would not be presented in terms of a unique
> story of a presumably "chosen" people, who always demonstrated
> their spiritual superiority, if not necessarily their military domi-
> nance, over the "unchosen" multitudes. (Reischauer 1973, 182)

We need to find that balance and blend our national enthusiasm
with international lessons and impressions. In our globalized era, it
should be important, for example, to be knowledgeable about the
United Nations.

The United Nations Association of the United States (UNA-USA)
is an important, citizen-supported organization that encourages civic
participation in global issues, running programs such as the Model
United Nations. In 2002, the UNA-USA reported, "few widely used
high-school history and government textbooks in the United States
are adequate to teach fundamental concepts about the United Nations
and international cooperation" (UNA-USA 2002).

Ambassador William Luers, chairman and president of UNA-
USA, cited a 1999 Zogby survey finding that most students were not
aware of any UN activity other than peacekeeping. "The United
Nations plays an increasingly important role in American lives and is
a wellspring of information about how the world works, but few students know that" (UNA-USA 2002). When the dominant international organization of our time is not well understood, we have a
long way to go.

Textbooks that fuel nationalism and avoid controversy are not
limited to the United States. In 2005, anti-Japan protests were held in
China and South Korea because of Japanese history textbooks that
rationalized colonialism and glossed over Japanese atrocities. Of
course, the textbooks in China and South Korea have also been guilty
of glorifying the nation while ignoring negative acts.

Following the invasion of Iraq and the ouster of Saddam Hussein
in 2003, educational texts in Iraq were revised by a team of US-
appointed Iraqi educators. All images of Hussein and material deemed
anti-American were removed, but so were other subjects considered
controversial, such as the 1991 Gulf War, the Iran-Iraq war, and all ref-
erences to Israelis, Americans, or Kurds. Critics complained that Iraqi
education was altered from "one-sided" to "no-sided" (Asquith 2003).

Textbooks need to be upgraded and educational resources need
to be expanded. And teachers must shape their curricula to reflect our
global era, while students and parents demand they do exactly that.

In many respects, the burden upon schools is a very unfair one. Historically, humans have feared what is different and clung tightly to familiar faces. But while education cannot take the blame entirely, it must bear responsibility for cultivating a sense of world citizenship. As Reischauer put it,

> This clearly is the biggest educational task of all, for millenniums of history have conditioned men to think in terms of smaller and more exclusive units, while suspicion and hostility toward other groups lie deep in their patterns of thought. (Reischauer 1973, 138)

So again, we are left face to face with the challenge of overcoming our tribal tendencies. There is a growing sense that educational leaders are beginning to understand the importance of providing a global education. A year after the tragedy of September 11, 2001, then-US Secretary of Education Rod Paige said,

> We are ever mindful of the lessons of September 11—one of which is that all future measures of a rigorous K-12 education must include a solid grounding in other cultures, other languages and other histories. In other words, we need to put the "world" back into "world-class" education. (US Department of Education 2002)

Paige outlined new priorities for international education that included increasing US knowledge about the world and strengthening relationships with other countries.

> Our new focus will help us build on an already strong foundation of relationships with other countries and cultures and equip our children with the skills and knowledge they'll need to be responsible members of the world community. (US Department of Education 2002)

This rhetoric must translate into action, through substantive investment at all levels of education.

All the News that Fits Within the Border

Schools and families are tremendously important, but it can be argued that our view of the world is most influenced by the images and messages we receive from the mass media. Many children spend more time in front of a television than with a teacher or even a parent. And long after we are grown and diplomas are earned, we rely on the media to inform and educate us.

Unfortunately, unless we are at war with another country, or there is a horrible disaster abroad, it is hard to find coverage of other nations in most American media. According to the Center for Media and Public Affairs, at the start of the 1990s, international news represented one-third of network evening news programming. By 1999, it was down to 21 percent. According to the *Tyndall Report,* which monitors network newscasts, foreign and diplomatic news coverage fell by more than half between 1990 and 2000 (Ginsberg 2002, 50).

In 1971, about 10 percent of newspaper print inches were devoted to foreign news. That number, says the American Society of Newspaper Editors, dropped to 2 percent by the late 1990s (Ginsberg 2002, 50).

To lower costs, news organizations have cut staff and reduced or eliminated their foreign news bureaus. ABC News closed ten of its seventeen bureaus between the mid-1980s and 2002 (Ginsberg 2002, 50). The noted media scholar Ben Bagdikian reports that the United States "has fewer correspondents permanently stationed in foreign capitals than any other major Western nation" (Bagdikian 2004, 94).

While globalization was picking up steam and businesses and NGOs expanded their international activities, we were watching and reading less and less about the world. Certainly the Internet allows us to find international news, but television and newspapers remain our primary information sources.

According to a 2002 study by the Pew International Journalism Program, most US newspaper editors believe that the media are not doing a good job of covering international news. In fact, nearly two-thirds of the more than two hundred editors polled rated the media's performance in this area as fair or poor. Among those surveyed, 63 percent said that their publications usually dedicate 10 percent or less of their daily news space to international news. Writing in *American Journalism Review,* Thomas Ginsberg summarized,

> By the end of the '90s, with cable TV and the Internet splintering audiences, and media conglomerates demanding news divisions make more money, broadcasters and some publications gradually changed formats to cover more scandal, lifestyle, personalities. There simply were fewer shows and pages where hard news, much less foreign news, could find a home. (Ginsberg 2002, 50)

Study after study notes the increase of space and time devoted to crime and entertainment. These stories have effectively pushed international news to the fringes of the mass media spectrum. "When you don't cover the rest of the world, it's hard to know what they think," notes S. Robert Lichter, president of the Center for Media and Public Affairs (Tugend 2001, 27).

Many contend that the media are only catering to public demands. "I'd love to blame the media, but it's the public—foreign news is a tough sell," adds Lichter. "There's not much of a popular market out there for it" (Tugend 2001, 27).

It is true that American interest in foreign affairs is normally not high. But perhaps that is because we have few opportunities to become interested.

Even if Americans have not been longing for more international coverage, that may be changing. Particularly after September 11, many Americans have expressed greater interest in learning about the world, and the media need to respond. David Anable, former president of the International Center for Journalists, says that if there were any plusses from the tragedy, one is that the media should be compelled to pay greater attention to foreign affairs. But Anable says there is much work to do. "We paid very little attention to the rest of the world for a long time. We have to catch up and study like mad what we have ignored for decades" (Tugend 2001, 27).

As Ginsberg writes about September 11,

> For media executives who think all news is local, it should force them once and for all to broaden their definition of local. For journalists who believe in foreign coverage, it proves the need for compelling and relevant coverage that spells out why Americans should care. (Ginsberg 2002, 53)

Not that September 11 is the only motivator. The interconnections of globalization and the need for world citizenship demand our increased awareness and knowledge of other people and nations.

Most television networks and newspapers are for-profit institutions. Unlike other commercial enterprises, however, the media have a constitutional role and a clear public service mission. Newspapers often acknowledge this important public function. Broadcasters receive government licenses to use the publicly owned airwaves, and therefore must accept some responsibility to serve the public, even when the cost is high. As former ABC News president Roone Arledge once stated, "If you have access to the airwaves, there is some responsibility beyond just to stockholders" (Auletta 1992, 195).

This conflict between profits and public service is nowhere more evident than in producing international news coverage, which can be expensive and requires large staffs. According to the 2002 Pew study,

> Fifty-three percent of the editors surveyed said the high cost of providing foreign news—more than a lack of interest by readers or senior editors or the availability of foreign news on the Internet—was the main reason their newspaper doesn't provide more international news. (Pew International Journalism Program 2002)

With the decline of international news bureaus comes increasing reliance on American sources to interpret and explain international events. News beats collect information from American centers of power—whether the White House or US officials—and relay in most cases a distinctly American view. When there is not an obvious American angle to the story, the prospect of an international story receiving depth or significant coverage is very poor. No wonder we often see the world through red, white, and blue-colored glasses.

The point of all this is to convey the inadequacy of the major news organizations to tell us what we need to know about the world. What should we do?

The answer is fourfold.

1. Become an active consumer of both local and international news. Regularly read and watch the major sources in your area.
2. Question what you read and see. The Center for Media Literacy suggests that we learn to ask basic questions, such as who created the message and why. Also, "How might different people understand the message differently than me?" and "What values, lifestyles and points of view are represented in, or omitted from, this message?" (Center for Media Literacy 2005)
3. Find alternatives. Use the power of the Internet to seek out the news that our major media do not provide. Check out international newspapers online.

4. Use the power of your own voice to influence the media. Communicate your interest in international affairs.

Living in a global age means finding global sources of news and information.

The Planetary Context

So, there are major roadblocks that could interfere with or delay hopes to develop world citizenship in the United States. We must understand that human nature is compatible with peaceful cooperation. And we must learn early and often about the importance of acting as world citizens. Our schools and the mass media must better incorporate stories from around the world, and we need to actively search for global views and news. What we fail to learn in school, and what the media fail to tell us, can blur the road map to finding solutions to the world's problems. We need global awareness to form global connections.

There are other obstacles, of course. Certainly, economics plays a role in the acceptance of world citizenship. When people are poor and starving, world citizenship is not high in their order of priorities. While such troubles have international dimensions and require international solutions, those immediately facing them are not in the position to expand the levels of planetary cooperation.

Economics can also deprive people of the valuable tools that they need to foster connections. The number of people with access to new communications technologies, such as the Internet or mobile phones, is rapidly rising, but there remains a significant digital divide.

According to a 2003 report on the global diffusion of information and communication technologies, in countries such as the United States, South Korea, and Sweden, more than 50 percent of the population has Internet access. Compare this to Yemen, where the ratio of Internet users to the population is 1 out of 485. Or Ethiopia, where the ratio is 1 out of 1,347. In Myanmar, there is one Internet user for every 4,899 people (Paua 2003).

While Internet users represent 53 percent of the population in Canada and the United States, and 19 percent of the people in Europe, they constitute just 9 percent in Asia and the Pacific, 7 percent in Latin America and the Caribbean, 4 percent in North Africa and the Middle East, and just 1 percent in South Asia and sub-Saharan Africa.

Overall, just 10 percent of the global population used the Internet in 2002 (Paua 2003).

Those of us among the 53 percent take such access and privilege for granted. But that is associated with our historic "city on a hill" complex. Many of us believe that we are the center of the world and deserve special consideration. We often become embroiled in individual, local, and national concerns. But to become a world citizen requires some sense of proportion. Look at the whole, as Bucky Fuller would recommend.

On a universal level, it is sobering to realize that we are not much of a presence, no matter what nation we hail from. The best illustration of our lack of stature is Carl Sagan's "cosmic calendar," in which he condenses the roughly fifteen billion-year lifetime of the universe into a single year. That means every billion years would be equivalent to about twenty-four days of his cosmic year, and one second of that year would equal about 475 actual years.

Going by this calendar, the Big Bang occurs on January 1, with our Milky Way Galaxy forming on May 1. This is a very humbling exercise, Sagan notes.

> It is disconcerting to find that in such a cosmic year the Earth does not condense out of interstellar matter until early September; dinosaurs emerge on Christmas Eve; flowers arise on December 28th; and men and women originate at 10:30 p.m. on New Year's Eve. (Sagan 1977, 17)

He adds that all of our recorded history occurs in the last ten seconds of December 31. At 11:59 p.m. and 20 seconds, agriculture is invented, and at 11:59 p.m. and 59 seconds, Europe welcomes the Renaissance (Sagan 1977, 15–17). We have not been here long. And there is no assurance that we will be around much longer.

When our planet is viewed from an intergalactic perspective, it is humbling to realize that rather than occupying the center of the stellar kingdom, we barely rest inside the circle, relegated perhaps to an outer borough of the cosmic community.

Moving to our modern global village, it is worth taking another look at the big picture. More than a decade ago, Donella Meadows wrote a provocative report entitled *State of the Global Village,* with a compelling snapshot of the distribution and basic characteristics of humanity. Taking Meadows' lead, if we shrink Earth's population to a village of precisely one hundred people, with all of the existing human ratios remaining the same, it looks something like this:

57 Asians
21 Europeans
14 from the Western Hemisphere, both north and south
8 Africans

| 52 would be female | 70 would be non-white |
| 48 would be male | 30 would be white |

70 would be non-Christian
30 would be Christian
80 would live in substandard housing
70 would be unable to read
50 would suffer from malnutrition
One would own a computer
Only one would have a college education
And six people would possess 59% of the entire world's wealth
    and all six would be from the United States

Those in the United States, and indeed everyone in the Western hemisphere, are just a small group aboard this planetary vessel. Yet our small group possesses great power and tremendous wealth. At times, that has led to expressions of arrogance that stirred hostility and resentment around the world. Perhaps some believe that having such power means that we do not need to learn about others or concern ourselves with the rest of the world. That is foolhardy. Power is even more fleeting than our existence.

As our lives are mere blips on the cosmic radar, we have an important choice about how we spend our fleeting moments. Why not focus selfishly on our small group and relegate the interests of others to the background? Why not enjoy ourselves? Why not succumb to our tribal impulses and work to enrich our select few?

Such a mindset might work for some in the short term, but it could also perpetuate rivalries and resentments. Such a mindset will not propel humanity long into the next year of the cosmic calendar.

There is another choice. We can extend our connections to others and collectively work to overcome the obstacles that hinder world citizenship. We can learn more about others, how they see us as Americans, and how they view the global challenges before us. We can establish legacies of cooperation and understanding that inspire future generations. We can take pride in what is local, but also look beyond it and ensure the survival of what is global.

Building New Doorways

Maybe the obstacles to world citizenship are too daunting. Maybe we cannot hope to overcome human tribal impulses, or improve schools or the mass media. Maybe we cannot inspire the next generation. Or maybe some from the next generation will themselves provide the inspiration.

In 2003, just a few days before his fourteenth birthday, Gregory Robert Smith graduated with honors from Randolph-Macon College. But even at that age, Smith was not merely renowned for his exceptional academic accomplishments. He had already been nominated for the Nobel Peace Prize twice, for extraordinary work on behalf of International Youth Advocates, a group he founded to support children's rights throughout the world. Its primary purpose is to promote nonviolence, education, and improved welfare for the "neglected, abused and disenfranchised" (International Youth Advocates 2003).

Among the group's efforts have included assisting in constructing Rwanda's first public library and organizing humanitarian relief efforts for orphans in East Timor and youth in Sao Paulo, Brazil. Smith also is helping to build Peace Schools in Kenya and other conflict-torn regions. In 2004 and 2005, he was nominated again for a Nobel Peace Prize.

Smith, who in 2005 was a Ph.D. candidate in mathematics at the University of Virginia, says he is proud to be an American, but his goals and his efforts are directed on behalf of people everywhere. When doubting the possibility of cultivating global citizens, when questioning the ability to improve the future, carefully weigh the wisdom of this young activist's words.

> I try my best to be the best world citizen I can be and help others through my words and work to believe that they can achieve their dreams, too. . . . We need to look at the big picture . . . the

GLOBAL picture . . . if we ever hope to live in a world without
fear. (International Youth Advocates 2003)

Gregory Smith understands the importance of overcoming
obstacles. At the age of ten, he discussed his recommendations when
faced with a door that is locked or has been slammed in his face. He
said you could try to knock the door down, or bang on it, or beg for
someone to help, or sit and wait for the door to open. He selects a
fifth option. "I choose to build another door so all may enter!" (International Youth Advocates 2003).

World citizens, young and old alike, will overcome the obstacles that keep them apart, open closed doors, and look to build new
doors for all to enter.

References

Asquith, Christina. 2003. Rewriting History: New Textbooks Offer Iraqi
Children a U.S.-Approved Version of Their History. *Hackensack (NJ)
Record,* November 9.

Auletta, Ken. 1992. *Three Blind Mice: How the TV Networks Lost Their
Way.* New York: Vintage Books.

Bagdikian, Ben H. 2004. *The New Media Monopoly.* Boston: Beacon Press.

Barabási, Albert-László. 2003. *Linked: How Everything Is Connected to
Everything Else and What It Means for Business, Science, and Everyday Life.* New York: Plume.

Barber, Benjamin R. 2002. The Educated Student: Global Citizen or Global
Consumer? *Liberal Education* 88, no. 2 (Spring): 22–28.

Biddle, Sheila. 2002. Internationalization: Rhetoric or Reality? American
Council of Learned Societies. ACLS Occasional Paper, No. 56.

Brown, Donald E. 1991. *Human Universals.* New York: McGraw Hill.

Center for Media Literacy. 2005. Five Key Questions of Media Literacy.
http://www.medialit.org (accessed September 15, 2005).

Cetto, Ana Maria. 1997. Introduction of Courses on World Citizenship into
the Curricula of Schools and Universities. In *World Citizenship: Allegiance to Humanity,* edited by J. Rotblat, 145–154. New York: St.
Martin's Press.

Dator, Jim. 2000. The Futures for Higher Education: From Bricks to Bytes
to Fare Thee Well! In *The University in Transformation: Global Perspectives on the Futures of the University,* edited by S. Inayatullah and
J. Gidley, 69–78. Westport, CT: Bergin & Garvey.

Guare, John. 1990. *Six Degrees of Separation.* New York: Random House.

Gillespie, Spike. 2003. A Battle over Books in Texas. *Hackensack (NJ) Record,* November 9.

Ginsberg, Thomas. 2002. Rediscovering the World: September 11 Showed All Too Clearly What a Terrible Mistake It Was for America's News Media to Largely Ignore Foreign News. *American Journalism Review* (January–February): 48–53.

Inayatullah, Sohail, and Jennifer Gidley, eds. 2000. *The University in Transformation: Global Perspectives on the Futures of the University.* Westport, CT: Bergin and Garvey.

International Youth Advocates. 2003 and 2005. http://www.gregoryrsmith.com (accessed June 4, 2003 and September 14, 2005).

Kidder, Rushworth M. 1994. *Shared Values for a Troubled World: Conversations with Men and Women of Conscience.* San Francisco: Jossey-Bass Publishers.

Loewen, James W. 1995. *Lies My Teacher Told Me: Everything Your American History Textbook Got Wrong.* New York: Touchstone.

McCloud, Donald G. 2004. Globalization in Higher Education: An American Perspective. *Malaysian Business,* January 16.

Meadows, Donella. 1990. State of the Global Village. http://www.tidepool.org/gc/gc5.31.90.cfm (accessed September 15, 2005).

Myers-Walls, Judith A., and Péter Somlai, eds. 2001. *Families as Educators for Global Citizenship.* Burlington, VT: Ashgate Publishing Company.

Myers-Walls, Judith A. 2001. How Families Teach Their Children About the World. In *Families as Educators for Global Citizenship,* edited by J.A. Myers-Walls and P. Somlai, 3–12. Burlington, VT: Ashgate Publishing Company.

Paua, Fiona. 2003. Global Diffusion of ICT: A Progress Report. In *Global Information Technology Report, 2003–2004.* Boston: Harvard Center for International Development.

Pew International Journalism Program. 2002. *America and the World: The Impact of September 11 on U.S. Coverage of International News.* Centreville, VA: Dwight L. Morris & Associates.

Pinker, Steven. 2002. *The Blank Slate: The Modern Denial of Human Nature.* New York: Viking.

Ravitch, Diane. 2001. Education and Democracy. In *Making Good Citizens: Education and Civil Society,* edited by D. Ravitch and J.P. Viteritti, 15–29. New Haven, CT: Yale University Press.

Ravitch, Diane, and Joseph P. Viteritti, eds. 2001. *Making Good Citizens: Education and Civil Society.* New Haven, CT: Yale University Press.

Ravitch, Diane. 2003. *The Language Police: How Pressure Groups Restrict What Students Learn.* New York: Alfred A. Knopf.

Reischauer, Edwin O. 1973. *Toward the 21st Century: Education for a Changing World.* New York: Alfred A. Knopf.

Ridley, Matt. 1996. *The Origins of Virtue: Human Instincts and the Evolution of Cooperation*. New York: Penguin Books.

Ridley, Matt. 2003. *Nature via Nurture: Genes, Experience, & What Makes Us Human*. New York: HarperCollins Publishers.

Rotblat, Joseph, ed. 1977. *World Citizenship: Allegiance to Humanity*. New York: St. Martin's Press.

Sagan, Carl. 1977. *The Dragons of Eden: Speculations on the Evolution of Human Intelligence*. New York: Ballantine Books.

Tugend, Alina. 2001. Explaining the Rage: How Well Have the American Media Done in Analyzing Why Much of the Muslim World Seems So Resentful of the United States? *American Journalism Review* (December): 24–27.

United Nations Association of the United States of America (UNA-USA). 2002. UNA-USA Study Finds High-School, Jr. High-School Textbooks Inadequate for Teaching Future Leaders about the U.N., International Affairs. News release, January 31.

US Department of Education Office of Public Affairs. 2002. Paige Outlines New International Education Priorities: Announces Plans to Bolster Education Partnerships, Honor Teachers Who Contribute to International Education Efforts. News release, November 20.

Zinn, Howard. 1990. *Declarations of Independence: Cross-Examining American Ideology*. New York: HarperPerennial.

8

FLYING TOWARD THE FUTURE

What an immense mass of evil must result . . . from allowing
men to assume the right of anticipating what may happen.

—Leo Tolstoy
The Kingdom of God Is Within You, 1894

Whatever else I may repent of, therefore, let it be reckoned neither among my sins nor follies that I once had faith and force
enough to form generous hopes of the world's destiny . . .

—Nathaniel Hawthorne
The Blithedale Romance, 1852

A Planetary View

We are literally flying toward the future. Just a short time ago, no
human being had ever gazed at the world in its entirety. The technology that propelled humanity into space offered perhaps the most
magnificent view imaginable: a view of one planet divided by nothing. In spectacular photographs of this space-traveling planet, our
sphere appears remarkably small, but unmistakably majestic.

These images give us a glimpse of our home's beauty, but cannot substitute for the first-hand impressions of those who actually
witnessed the breathtaking beauty of Earth from outer space. Those
pioneers often observed that, when seen from above, the borders and
lines drawn on globes and maps dividing nations and peoples magi-
cally disappear.

In the words of Marc Garneau, the first Canadian to journey
into space,

> I was almost expecting to see these boundary lines, and they are
> not there. They're not there when you go through all of South
> America and through all of the Asian continent, and after a

while you realize it's a very artificial thing to put boundaries between us. In that sense you become more of a global citizen . . . (White 1987, 252)

Apollo 11 astronaut Michael Collins says this viewpoint could make a powerful difference:

I really believe that if the political leaders of the world could see their planet from a distance of . . . 100,000 miles, their outlook would be fundamentally changed. That all-important border would be invisible, that noisy argument suddenly silenced. The tiny globe would continue to turn, serenely ignoring its subdivisions, presenting a united façade that would cry out for unified treatment . . . I think the view from 100,000 miles could be invaluable in getting people together to work out joint solutions, by causing them to realize that the planet we share unites us in a way far more basic and far more important than differences in skin color or religion or economic system. (White 1987, 202)

We cannot all travel to outer space, but our imaginations must be capable of understanding this viewpoint. It is exactly this outlook that all citizens need to appreciate and understand. It is exactly this outlook that the next generation must possess.

Betting on the Future

In Greek mythology, the gods gave Pandora a box into which each had placed something harmful and told her never to open it. But her curiosity got the better of her; she opened the box, and out flew the evils of the world to plague humanity.

Most of us are familiar with that part of the tale, but fewer know the rest of the story. Pandora, in terror, managed to shut the lid before the one good thing in the box could escape: hope. It remains our source of comfort and strength, and it is with great hope for the future that we embark on this final chapter.

We all think and wonder about tomorrow. Thousands of people spend a good deal of time thinking about the probability of the Giants winning Sunday's football game. We are fascinated with predicting— and betting—on sports events. In fact, we like calculating the odds on nearly everything. There is an entire industry in the United States that will gladly take your money as you guess an outcome. There is even a Web site in which you can bet on long-range scenarios, such as when signs of alien life will be discovered, or whether computers can be created that think like humans. The gambling industry survives and flourishes because the odds are on its side, and because you will usually be wrong.

Venturing a look ahead is anything but a safe gamble. There are far too many variables to predict for certain what awaits us. Our record in the realm of prediction is dismal. In 1895, Auguste Lumière, who co-invented the motion picture camera, said his invention "has no commercial value whatsoever" and Charlie Chaplin later called the cinema "little more than a fad" (Cerf and Navasky 1998, 190).

In 1897, Lord Kelvin, a British mathematician and physicist, proclaimed, "Radio has no future" (Cerf and Navasky 1998, 227). In 1899, Maurice Levy, the president of the Paris Academie des Sciences, declared that heavier-than-air flight would never succeed (Barabási 2003, 230–231). On October 17, 1929, just twelve days before the stock market crashed, a distinguished economics professor said that stocks had reached a "permanently high plateau" (Cerf and Navasky 1998, 54).

In 1962, a record executive turned down the Beatles, saying that "groups of guitars are on the way out" (Cerf and Navasky 1998, 201). West German Chancellor Helmut Kohl said in 1988 that Germany would not be reunited in his lifetime; the Berlin Wall fell the next year (Yergin and Stanislaw 2002, 321).

The point is not to mock Lord Kelvin or Helmut Kohl, but merely to warn us from assuming that we can accurately predict the future. It is fun to hypothesize about tomorrow, but despite our best efforts, we are pathetically inept prognosticators. But we have hope. And we all dream.

When we ask college seniors what they hope for in their lives, the answers are typically concrete and very personal.

- A great job
- Someone to love
- A nice home in a safe neighborhood
- Wealth and fame

When we ask the same group what they hope does not happen, the responses are still personal, but connected to global issues.

- Economic crisis—in which they will be unable to find a job
- Terror and conflict—in which they fear for their safety

- Environmental catastrophe—in which droughts, famine, and rising temperatures threaten our way of life
- Spread of major diseases—particularly AIDS

Despite such concerns, most graduating seniors are filled with great hope for the future. Will their hopes be fulfilled? What will the world be like?

Clearly, we cannot accurately predict what the state of the globe will be ten years from now. We can, however, observe major trends. Forces and events are in motion that will affect our individual and collective futures.

Over the next decade, our world will be influenced and characterized by at least seven clear trends:

1. Changing demographic forces and increasing diversity
2. Conflicts of interest between developing and developed nations
3. Seemingly isolated, local events triggering global consequences
4. Persistent terrorism and violent conflict
5. Economic and environmental crises leading to, among other things, increased migration
6. The spread of new and existing illnesses to endemic proportions
7. A widening gap between those who have and do not have access to new technologies

In facing these trends, we must reconcile our individual hopes with the understanding that our personal futures are linked tightly to the world condition. Personal aspirations are directly connected to global health and welfare.

Individual and collective success are increasingly associated with world citizenship. It is critically important to pay attention to both the local and the distant—to connect the dots of a complex, interrelated world.

The Expanding Human Network

On a warm August afternoon in 2003, a few failed transmission lines in Ohio started a chain reaction that, in a matter of minutes, shut down power for more than fifty million people in eight Midwestern and Northeastern states and Canada, some for as long as two days.

The massive blackout knocked out a hundred power plants, closed twelve airports, and cost at least $6 billion (Iwata 2003).

Like our electrical grid, our human network has grown closer, and the potential for similarly dangerous chain reactions exists in nearly every sphere of life.

But these connections can also be positive. They can help us advance global causes, and thereby advance our personal hopes. These connections carry with them the promise of a better world.

We agree with educator Bill Bigelow, who writes,

> There is a hopeful dimension to the world's growing interconnectedness: We have more opportunities to recognize the far-flung social and ecological webs that we are a part of, and simultaneously more points of leverage to make a global difference. (Bigelow 2002, 330)

Cynics will point to the history of humanity and cite one vile event after another, climaxing in a twentieth century filled with terror and killing on a scale never before documented. They will further observe that with September 11, the twenty-first century is not off to a promising start.

The cynics would be correct, but incomplete. When viewed across the landscape of even the past two hundred years, humanity has made significant progress. Democracy, once the exception around the world, is increasingly the norm. Despite the continuing occurrence of violence and destruction, many practices once considered normal are now seen as intolerable.

> Customs that were common throughout history and prehistory—slavery, punishment by mutilation, execution by torture, genocide for convenience, endless blood feuds, the summary killing of strangers, rape as the spoils of war, infanticide as a form of birth control, and the legal ownership of women—have vanished from large parts of the world. (Pinker 2002, 166)

Much work remains, but the near extermination of such ills represents a giant step forward. The increasing acceptance and acknowledgement of our collective humanity and equality is no minor accomplishment, considering the rampant hostility and bigotry that have marked our past. As professor and author Robert Wright puts it, "The modern idea that people of all races and religions are morally equal is often taken for granted, but viewed against the human past, it is almost bizarre" (Wright 2003).

This is sometimes a difficult message to absorb, especially when we see turmoil all around us. But the script of human history presents the story of growing improvement. The prospects for world citizenship seem greater today than ever before. Through the centuries, the circle of humanity (see page 101) has expanded from the family and village, to the city and state, to the nation. It is now poised to include the entire planet.

In economic circles, a similar expansion has taken place. Lester Thurow describes how people in the mid-nineteenth century considered themselves part of local or regional economies. They did not view themselves as working in the American economy. Instead, they believed they were part of the Boston or Chicago economy (Thurow 2003, 15). Today, that local identification is gone, and we say we are part of the American economy. But even that identification is now slipping away. Many have taken the next step and consider themselves part of the global economy. Thurow predicts that fifty years from now, few will say they are part of a national economy.

It is this ever-widening circle of compassion and concern that makes us optimistic about the potential for world citizenship and the promise of the future. New technologies favor the hope for improvement. Before the printing press, a small intellectual elite controlled information, and they alone had access to knowledge. Printing and mass publishing created wonderful new possibilities for learning, which in turn inspired positive change.

Through the Internet and other communication tools, globalization has given us the opportunity to learn more about others than ever before. As Thurow pointedly declares, "If the charge is that globalization forces you to accept change . . . then globalization is guilty as charged" (Thurow 2003, 145).

We can now put a face on those who are distant and hear the voices of those from afar. This familiarity allows us to break down barriers that have divided us and further extend our circle of humanity.

Universal Goals

In *The Outline of History* (1920), H.G. Wells forcefully identified the choice staring at us. "Human history becomes more and more a race between education and catastrophe." To win the race, education must be complemented by action, in union with and on behalf of people everywhere.

Choosing to make a difference at any level is a deeply personal decision. Educated world citizens should take interest in specific causes that motivate them to action. The efforts need not be all-consuming. Activism can be accomplished quietly. But it should be part of our ordinary lives.

How do you decide on a specific problem or effort? One way is to review some specific priorities for the twenty-first century.

In the largest gathering of international leaders up to that point in history, nearly 150 world leaders met in 2000 for the Millennium Summit of the United Nations. Those leaders endorsed a set of goals that were built upon a belief in "certain fundamental values," including freedom, equality, solidarity, tolerance, respect for nature, and shared responsibility. The document they approved is called the United Nations Millennium Declaration. The declaration was clear in its purpose:

> We believe that the central challenge we face today is to ensure that globalization becomes a positive force for all the world's people. For while globalization offers great opportunities, at present its benefits are very unevenly shared, while its costs are unevenly distributed. (United Nations Millennium Declaration 2000)

It adds that "only through broad and sustained efforts to create a shared future, based upon our common humanity in all its diversity, can globalization be made fully inclusive and equitable."

All United Nations members—basically, all the countries of the world—pledged to address and reach eight essential Millennium Development Goals.

Eradicate extreme poverty and hunger
Target: Between 1990 and 2015, to halve the proportion of the world's people who suffer from hunger and those whose income is less than $1 a day.

Achieve universal primary education
Target: To ensure by 2015 that all children everywhere will complete primary school.

Promote gender equality and empower women
Targets: To eliminate gender disparities in primary and secondary education, preferably by 2005, and in all levels of education by 2015.

Reduce child mortality
Target: Between 1990 and 2015, to reduce by two-thirds the mortality rate among children under five.

Improve maternal health
Target: Between 1990 and 2015, to reduce by three-quarters the ratio of women dying in childbirth.

Combat HIV/AIDS, malaria, and other diseases
Target: By 2015, to halt and begin to reverse the spread of HIV/AIDS, malaria, and other major diseases.

Ensure environmental sustainability
Targets: To reverse the loss of environmental resources; by 2015, to halve the proportion of people without access to safe drinking water; and by 2020, to achieve significant improvement in the lives of at least one hundred million slum dwellers.

Develop a global partnership for development
Targets: To address the special needs of the least-developed countries and further develop an open trading and financial system that includes a commitment to good governance, development, and poverty reduction.

The declaration adds,

> We will spare no effort to make the United Nations a more effective instrument for pursuing all of these priorities: the fight for development for all the peoples of the world, the fight against poverty, ignorance and disease; the fight against injustice; the fight against violence, terror and crime; and the fight against the degradation and destruction of our common home. (United Nations Millennium Declaration 2000)

There is consensus. The world has agreed that universal values exist and specific goals need to be accomplished.

Like the Universal Declaration of Human Rights more than a half-century earlier, the Millennium Declaration emphasizes all the right things, and its pronouncements speak to our most noble ideals.

And yet, as with the human rights document, the commitment to action lags behind ambition.

There has been some progress toward the goals but not enough. If current trends continue, the goals will be missed by a wide margin in many countries. UN Secretary-General Kofi Annan early on warned, "Progress must be made on a much broader front. Otherwise, the ringing words of the Declaration will serve only as grim reminders of the human needs neglected and promises unmet" (United Nations 2002).

Five years after the Millennium Summit, an even larger group of international leaders met at the UN headquarters for the World Summit 2005 and reaffirmed their commitment and determination to reaching the Millennium Development Goals. Among other efforts, greater aid was pledged to help developing nations, progress was forged on debt relief, and commitments were made to develop national strategies to reach the objectives (United Nations World Summit Outcome 2005). These pledges and commitments must be fulfilled.

The immensity of the challenges facing the Millennium Development Goals should not paralyze us. Even if not completely met, the goals represent important targets and priorities that can and will signficantly help many people. And many other needs beckon us to respond with passion and commitment. What action can you take to improve some aspect of our world? What small element might you as an individual contribute? There are opportunities near and far.

Chapter 3 emphasized the potential of a computer and the Internet as tools of involvement and change. The greatest tool, though, remains the human will. Anyone can get involved in local or global projects that deliver meals to the elderly in the neighborhood, expand township recycling programs, clear landmines in Cambodia and Mozambique, bring life-saving vaccines and medicines to children and the sick in Indonesia and India, or provide educational opportunities for girls and women in Jordan and Bolivia. The possibilities are limited only by your imagination.

Those of us in the world's richer democracies have greater opportunity and responsibility to foster progress. Not only can we reach out to assist others, but we can also lobby and influence our government to adopt policies that benefit people down the block and around the globe.

In 1985, musician Bob Geldof organized the massive and hugely successful Live Aid concerts for famine relief in Ethiopia. Twenty years later, on July 2, 2005, he helped stage an unprecedented global call to action: the Live 8 concerts to help fight poverty in Africa. Performances were held nearly simultaneously in South Africa and each of the eight countries whose leaders were about to gather at a Group of Eight (G8) leading industrial nations summit meeting. The performers and fans called upon the rich nations to forgive debt, make trade concessions, and provide billions in aid.

The concerts featured legendary artists such as Paul McCartney, the Who, Pink Floyd, Stevie Wonder, U2, Elton John, and Madonna, along with newer sensations such as Green Day, Destiny's Child, Black Eyed Peas, and Coldplay.

Beyond the more than one million fans in attendance, five million people sampled live video streams on the Internet, and over twenty-six million people sent text messages supporting the cause.

World leaders seemed to pay attention. Less than a week later, at the summit meeting, they agreed to double aid to Africa to $50 billion, cancel the debt of many very poor nations, reduce trade barriers, and do more to fight diseases like AIDS and malaria. These agreements were not perfect, and they of course need to be fulfilled before we can celebrate, but the commitments represent real progress that directly stems from citizens speaking out and making their voices heard.

During the Live 8 segment in Philadelphia, not far from where our nation's founders formally declared their independence, actor and singer Will Smith said that the time had come to issue a declaration of "interdependence." He stated, "Today we hold this truth to be self-evident: We are all in this together!"

Increasingly, it is up to citizens, networks of civil society, and our emerging global civil society to work across boundaries and seize the opportunities afforded by globalization to answer the challenges of interdependence. It is up to you.

Tom Brokaw is a well-known television anchor and author. His book, *The Greatest Generation,* tells the stories of individual men and women during World War II and the building of the modern United States. It is an epic of shared values, courage, service, and perseverance. It is a tale of ordinary people who made a difference and changed the world. Brokaw believes that this was the greatest generation ever produced by any society.

We will not diminish the incredible sacrifice and accomplishment of that great generation. They faced daunting odds and gambled their lives in a global war with the hope of a better future for their children. But each generation contains the courage, heart, and wisdom to overcome obstacles in its path. We have the greatest confidence the next generation will answer history's call.

The Tides of History

A consistent theme throughout this book is that globalization has brought us closer together, in particular through new technologies. Robert Wright notes that the tide of events often flows with the forces of new technology. "This is history's drift: technology correlating the fortunes of ever-more-distant people, enmeshing humanity in a web of shared fate" (Wright 2003).

One of the greatest leaders of the abolitionist movement was Frederick Douglass, who fought to end slavery in the decades prior to the Civil War. In his powerful 1852 address, "What to the Slave is the Fourth of July," Douglass vividly described a great divide between American rhetoric and reality. But he expressed great hope for the future:

> . . . my spirit is also cheered by the obvious tendencies of the age. Nations do not now stand in the same relation to each other that they did ages ago. No nation can now shut itself up from the surrounding world, and trot round in the same old path of its fathers without interference. The time was when such could be done. Long established customs of hurtful character could formerly fence themselves in, and do their evil work with social impunity. Knowledge was then confined and enjoyed by the privileged few, and the multitude walked on in mental darkness. But a change has now come over the affairs of mankind. Walled cities and empires have become unfashionable. The arm of commerce has borne away the gates of the strong city. Intelligence is penetrating the darkest corners of the globe. . . . Oceans no longer divide, but link nations together. From Boston to London is now a holiday excursion. Space is comparatively annihilated. Thoughts expressed on one side of the Atlantic are, distinctly heard on the other. . . . No abuse, no outrage . . . can now hide itself from the all-pervading light.

Douglass described the same process of globalization that we see today. He could not possibly, however, imagine the degree and speed of the changes yet to come. We share Douglass's optimism and believe that globalization can shed further light on our common concerns. But while change is inevitable, it will take time for our attitudes to catch up with these realities. Our history is dominated by thinking in terms of national identities and "us" and "them." Overcoming that mindset is difficult. The real problem with an optimistic outlook is that we may not have the luxury of time to slowly develop our enormous potential.

But the bottom line is that there is no alternative. Because our destinies are linked, action must be taken, if only for self-interest. Such action will ultimately benefit our country and us as individuals.

As Wright observes,

> Assuming we like our liberty, we have little choice but to take an earnest interest in the situation of distant and seemingly strange people, working to elevate their welfare, exploring their discontent as a step toward expanding their moral horizons— and in the process expanding ours. . . . All along, technological evolution has been moving our species toward this nonzero-sum moment, when our welfare is crucially correlated with the welfare of the other, and our freedom depends on the sympathetic comprehension of the other. That history has driven us toward moral enlightenment—and then left the final choice to us, with momentous stakes—is scary but inspiring. (Wright 2003)

As weapons proliferate and intensify in destructive capacity, as our impact on the environment increases, the danger to our entire species and planet escalates. Considering the threat, can we afford to slowly expand our circle of humanity and gradually develop into world citizens?

The next generation will need a much stronger sense of global citizenship to deliver the promise of the future. They will need to know more about others and about issues that link and divide us. They will have to appreciate and help develop the fledgling world community, and learn how to work within its parameters.

We had centuries to create and connect to nation-states. We may, however, only have decades or years to embrace the entire world as a single construct. The task is not easy, but the stakes are enormous. The realities of the twenty-first century require that the world community act together to address global problems. Nation-states acting solely to advance their interests will not further our collective and individual security and welfare. In a world so dangerous, we will survive together or we will not survive at all. This universal desire for survival now stands at the top of the list of common interests and needs.

"One of the great liabilities of history," wrote Martin Luther King, Jr., "is that all too many people fail to remain awake through great periods of social change" (King 1967, 171). We are in the midst of one of these periods, and we must do more than recognize the changes occurring; we must adapt to and help shape our globalized world. As King added,

> . . . our very survival depends on our ability to stay awake, to adjust to new ideas, to remain vigilant and to face the challenge of change. The large house in which we live demands that we transform this world-wide neighborhood into a world-wide brotherhood. Together we must learn to live as brothers or together we will be forced to perish as fools. (King 1967, 171)

We cannot shrink from the realities of interdependence and strike out at all that is different and new. We cannot allow blind nationalism to arbitrarily divide people. We must continue to cherish our unique cultural identities as patriots, but we cannot use them to escape from common responsibilities as world citizens.

Such a change in view is possible, particularly for those not settled in the conventions of the past. Reconciling global and regional integration alongside national distinctions can be challenging. But it may be easier for those not conditioned to think solely in national terms, those well-accustomed to bridging global and regional divides. Tereza Spencerova, a Czech journalist, said, "My son is 15, and his way of thinking and seeing the world is very different from my point of view. This new generation won't have a problem with definitions, with the difference between being Czech or German, or something else" (Lyall 2004).

The next generation is rapidly gaining experience in assimilating their local traditions with global movements and forging transcultural identities. This transformation is a key step toward world citizenship.

Allied in Peace

If the next generation is one of world citizens, there will be no limits to the heights of human progress. The Millennium Development

Goals can be achieved and, perhaps above all, we can deliver the promise of peace. By peace, we mean not just the absence of violence, but also the presence of justice and the fulfillment of people's basic needs. But why should we believe that the prospect for peace is any greater than it has been at previous points in history?

The global economy has created the first and most conspicuous wave of globalization. A number of authors suggest that the increase in global trade and rise of interdependent markets may be the most powerful route to conflict prevention and resolution on a global scale.

There is evidence that increased economic links have helped reduce conflicts—at least conflicts between nations. Financial interests dictate compromise and conciliation. War disrupts those interests and the ties that accompany those financial interests. War interferes with profits.

One wonders if conflicts on the scale of World War I and World War II would have occurred if there were more significant economic bridges between European countries. The European Union, with its common currency, lack of trade barriers, and similar rules and regulations, is a prime example of a stable economic bridge. Economic bridges promote the transfer of goods and services, not tanks or military troops.

Despite increasingly connected financial interests, however, our world is far from a peaceful place, certainly not when measured by the number of violent conflicts. In many respects, the world is more dangerous today than it was during periods of much less financial interdependence.

So what is wrong? If interconnected financial interests drastically reduce the threat of violence, why is the path to peace so elusive?

It is true that significant violence continues, but the conflicts are mostly in the form of civil wars, ethnic and religious strife, and terrorism. Since World War II, many more deaths have occurred from internal conflicts and civil wars than wars between nation-states. There are far fewer instances of nations fighting other nations, and even fewer instances of an advanced economy going to war against another advanced economy. Complex financial ties among developed nations have made a big impact in preventing violence, at least at the level of nation-states.

But trade and economic links cannot eliminate war by themselves. The interconnected global economy alone will not ensure peace. The difference today, though, is the many levels of connections.

Globalization has built more than economic bridges. We know that with the Internet, we can instantly connect to someone in nearly every part of the globe. We know that we are vulnerable to diseases that start from another continent. We know that networks for both positive change and destructive purposes are coordinated across oceans. In sum, we know that beyond the economic realm, we are tied together as never before. Because we are all neighbors, cooperation becomes imperative. That is the motive and the need for world citizenship.

While economic interests alone will not ensure peace, imagine combining trade and economic links with global awareness and world citizenship. Then add a greater emphasis on global education in schools and more international coverage in the news. Figure on that accelerating the number of citizen activists who forge alliances across borders and connect with others from different cultures. Then we may be on to something.

This same sense of interdependence can also generate fierce resistance among those who feel that their traditional values are under attack. Some lash out at new forces that stimulate change. Resorting to fundamentalism and tribalism, many fight back with righteous fury. Seeking the comfort of isolation and nationalism, they oppose globalization, sometimes violently.

These forces cannot be discounted. We have hope, though, that through the power of education, growing networks of cooperation, and increasing consideration for the diversity of cultures, we can reduce this backlash.

Wars are energized by dehumanizing the "other" and exaggerating the differences between "us" and "them." This is much harder to do when we have learned about our neighbors and appreciate and understand their viewpoint and common humanity. Gaining that appreciation and understanding has never been easier, or more necessary, than it is today.

Having a global view and being a world citizen is a key element for peaceful solutions. Being able to look at problems through the eyes of others reduces the fears and misunderstandings that breed conflict and terror. Learning to work together across geographic and cultural frontiers counters the insidious forces that threaten all of humanity.

World citizens have a vested interest in prosperity and peace. Many will be propelled by humanitarian and unselfish desires to improve the lives of others. But beyond that, personal material goals and dreams dictate that individuals fight for peace. Acknowledging common threats and the danger from diseases and other crises that do not stop at borders requires that they win that fight. The threat to our own self-interest has become more obvious as the ties of globalization stretch further. This is what is new today. This is what makes it imperative that we fulfill our vision for a peaceful world.

So without a crystal ball and without making any predictions, we have great hope that a great generation of world citizens—the next generation—will forge the path to peace.

The Ultimate Choice

Václav Havel knew something about hope. Crusading for human rights in Czechoslovakia, the prize-winning playwright was jailed for nearly five years because of his activism. But even under the oppressive regimes that ruled Eastern Europe, he remained hopeful. He was once asked if he saw a grain of hope anywhere in the 1980s. He replied,

> The kind of hope I often think about I understand above all as a state of mind . . . Hope is not prognostication. It is an orientation of the spirit, an orientation of the heart; it transcends the world that is immediately experienced, and is anchored somewhere beyond its horizons. (Havel 1986, 82)

It does not matter that success in our quest appears elusive because, as Havel added, hope ultimately is "an ability to work for something because it is good, not just because it stands a chance to succeed. The more unpropitious the situation in which we demonstrate hope, the deeper the hope is" (Havel 1986, 82).

We know the rest of that story: the Communist regimes in Eastern Europe fell without bloodshed, and Havel became his country's president. Hope is a powerful thing.

But hope is also a very difficult thing because it requires action. On the other hand, can we afford to give in to despair? Catholic activist Dorothy Day once said, "No one has the right to sit down and feel hopeless. There's too much work to do."

Do we conclude that while admirable, the challenges are too daunting for us to make a difference? Do we succumb to hopelessness and give up the gift Pandora managed to save?

There are so few individuals whose actions have dramatically changed the world. Who is on your list? Gandhi, Churchill, Mandela, Kennedy, King? If only a few heroes can make a profound difference, why bother? Do we believe that our small contribution cannot possibly make a difference? Do we walk away from our responsibility to each other?

Even if we cannot all have the presence or the commitment of a Gandhi or a King, we can make a difference. History shows that great change is accomplished in gradual stages, through small measures taken by countless passionate citizens.

Change does require powerful leaders, but it also depends upon the momentum of many people working together. Oscar Arias, a Nobel Peace Prize winner and the former president of Costa Rica, wrote, "World leaders may see their effect in headlines, but the ultimate course of the globe will be determined by the efforts of innumerable individuals acting on their consciences" (Kidder 1994, 269).

How moved are we by the powerful and compelling need for world citizenship? Are we inspired to act to make real the natural connections that exist among people, to erect new bridges, and to build a peaceful world?

As Herman Melville wrote, "We cannot live for ourselves alone. Our lives are connected by a thousand invisible threads and along these sympathetic fibers, our actions run as causes and return to us as results."

We cannot predict the future, but we can create it. We can hope for and expect a better world. Individuals and their actions will make all the difference. The next generation has the magnificent opportunity to powerfully influence the twenty-first century and perhaps all of humanity's future. What will you make of the opportunity?

The choice is yours.

References

Barabási, Albert-László. 2003. *Linked: How Everything Is Connected to Everything Else and What It Means for Business, Science, and Everyday Life*. New York: Plume.

Bigelow, Bill. 2002. Defeating Despair. In *Rethinking Globalization: Teaching for Justice in an Unjust World,* edited by B. Bigelow and B. Peterson, 329–334. Milwaukee: Rethinking Schools Press.

Bigelow, Bill, and Bob Peterson, eds. 2002. *Rethinking Globalization: Teaching for Justice in an Unjust World*. Milwaukee: Rethinking Schools Press.

Cerf, Christopher, and Victor Navasky. 1998. *The Experts Speak: The Definitive Compendium of Authoritative Misinformation.* New York: Villard.

Douglass, Frederick. 1852. What To the Slave is the Fourth of July? http://douglassarchives.org/doug_a10.htm (accessed September 15, 2005).

Havel, Václav. 2004. An Orientation of the Heart (adapted from *Disturbing the Peace,* 1990, Alfred A. Knopf) (original Czech publication 1986). In *The Impossible Will Take a Little While: A Citizen's Guide to Hope in a Time of Fear,* edited by P. R. Loeb, 82–89. New York: Basic Books.

Iwata, Edward. 2003. Blackout Report Faults Ohio Utility. *USA Today,* November 20. http://www.usatoday.com/money/industries/energy/2003-11-19-blackout_x.htm (accessed September 15, 2005).

Kidder, Rushworth M. 1994. *Shared Values for a Troubled World: Conversations with Men and Women of Conscience.* San Francisco: Jossey-Bass Publishers.

King, Jr., Martin Luther. 1967. *Where Do We Go From Here: Chaos or Community?* New York: Harper & Row.

Loeb, Paul Rogat, ed. 2004. *The Impossible Will Take a Little While: A Citizen's Guide to Hope in a Time of Fear.* New York: Basic Books.

Lyall, Sarah. 2004. Newest 'Europeans' Struggle to Define That Label. *New York Times,* May 1.

Pinker, Steven. 2002. *The Blank Slate: The Modern Denial of Human Nature.* New York: Viking.

Thurow, Lester. 2003. *Fortune Favors the Bold: What We Must Do to Build a New and Lasting Global Prosperity.* New York: HarperCollins Publishers.

United Nations. 2000. Millennium Declaration. http://www.un.org/millennium/declaration/ARES552E.htm (accessed October 13, 2005).

United Nations. 2002. Secretary-General Warns World Falling Short of Millennium Summit Commitments; Outlines Steps to Accelerate Progress. News release, October 1.

United Nations. 2005. World Summit Outcome. http://www.un.org/summit2005/documents.html (accessed October 13, 2005).

White, Frank. 1987. *The Overview Effect: Space Exploration and Human Evolution.* Boston: Houghton Mifflin Company.

Wright. Robert. 2003. Two Years Later, a Thousand Years Ago. *New York Times,* September 11.

Yergin, Daniel, and Joseph Stanislaw. 2002. *The Commanding Heights: The Battle for the World Economy.* New York: Touchstone.

INDEX

239

About the Authors

A widely respected leader in higher education, **Dr. J. Michael Adams** became Fairleigh Dickinson University's sixth president on July 1, 1999, following 15 years as an academic dean at Drexel University in Philadelphia. At Fairleigh Dickinson, he has led the development of a new University vision and mission: creating global citizens who are comfortable in environments of diversity, increasingly sophisticated technology and rapid change. Dr. Adams is the author of nine books. His publications and research cover a wide variety of topics including print, publishing, communication and career development, as well as topics specific to the field of higher education. Prior to assuming the FDU presidency, Dr. Adams worked with many corporations providing expertise in management. A former professor at the State University of New York (SUNY) at Oswego, Dr. Adams was awarded the SUNY Chancellor's Award for Teaching Excellence. He also was named to the Soderstrom Society of Fellows for lifetime achievement and contributions to the printing and publishing industries. Dr. Adams is active on national and international education panels and commissions, including the United Nations/International Association of University Presidents (IAUP) Commission on Disarmament Education, Conflict Resolution and Peace; he served on the Commission on Effective Leadership of the American Council on Education; and is a National Council member of the United Nations Association of the United States of America. He also serves on the Executive Committee of the IAUP and is an IAUP representative to the United Nations. Dr. Adams holds a B.S. from Illinois State University, Normal; an M.S. from University of Illinois, Urbana; and a Ph.D. from Southern Illinois University, Carbondale.

Award-winning writer, editor, communications consultant and international affairs and media studies scholar, **Angelo Carfagna** has worked on behalf of higher education for 13 years. As the Director of Communications and Special Projects for Fairleigh Dickinson University, he has collaborated with Michael Adams to promote and garner attention for the University's global mission. They are frequent partners on various projects focusing on global education and world citizenship. These have included articles, op-ed pieces in newspapers, and major speeches and presentations. Since 1996, Carfagna has been executive editor of the university's award-winning flagship publication, *FDU Magazine*. A well-respected communications professional and higher education advocate, he also has written for the Jackie Robinson Scholarship Foundation and the Independent College Fund of New Jersey, as well as other universities in the New York/New Jersey Metropolitan Area. Angelo Carfagna holds a B.A. from Montclair State University and an M.A. in political science from Fairleigh Dickinson University.

Also from Kumarian Press...

International Public Administration, Globalization

Better Governance and Public Policy
Dele Olowu, and Soumana Sako

Globalization and Social Exclusion: A Transformationalist Perspective
Ronaldo Munck

Ethics and Global Politics: The Active Learning Sourcebook
April Morgan, Lucinda Joy Peach, and Colette Mazzucelli

Global Civil Society, Volume One
Lester M. Salamon, S. Wojciech Sokolowski, and Associates

Working for Change: Making a Career in International Public Service
Derick W. Brinkerhoff and Jennifer M. Brinkerhoff

Newer Kumarian Press Titles

Women and the Politics of Place
Wendy Harcourt and Arturo Escobar

The Economic Life of Refugees
Karen Jacobsen

Reducing Poverty, Building Peace
Coralie Bryant and Christina Kappaz

Sustainable Capitalism: A Matter of Common Sense
John Ikerd

Visit Kumarian Press at **www.kpbooks.com** or
call **toll-free 800.289.2664** for a complete catalog.

Kumarian Press, located in Bloomfield, Connecticut, is a forward-looking, scholarly press that promotes active international engagement and an awareness of global connectedness.